LAZARUS

ONLY DONE IT ONCE

LAZARUS
ONLY DONE IT ONCE

The Story of My Lives

Pat Lally
with Neil Baxter

HarperCollins*Publishers*

HarperCollins*Publishers*
77–85 Fulham Palace Road,
Hammersmith, London W6 8JB

www.**fireandwater**.com

Published by HarperCollins*Publishers* 2000
1 3 5 7 9 8 6 4 2

A catalogue record for this book
is available from the British Library

ISBN 0 00 257140 4

Set in Sabon by
Rowland Phototypesetting Ltd,
Bury St Edmunds, Suffolk

Printed and bound in Great Britain by
Clays Ltd, St Ives plc

Dedicated to Peggy, Robert and Derek
and my RAF colleague Derek Taylor

Acknowledgements

I would like to express my deep gratitude to all those who stood by me during the lengthy and difficult period of my 'trial' at the hands of the Labour Party, particularly the excellent individuals who staff the Lord Provost's Office, and the representatives of Glasgow's business community who continued to lend me their support, even in the face of continuous and extraordinarily negative press coverage.

I would also like to thank a number of individuals by name. Jim Clark, in his role as a special advisor within the Lord Provost's Office, saw the defence of the Lord Provost as a fundamental part of his responsibility. The witnesses who spoke in my defence at the various hearings and inquiries – Susan Baird, Jim Clark, Kenny Gibson, Steve Hamilton, Bill Harley and John Young – also merit particular praise. Great praise and my eternal gratitude go to Peter McCann, whose passion, intelligence and enthusiasm, allied to a sharp perception of the nuances of the legal system, made him a brilliant ally. I would also like to mention his assistant, Mr Jain, and David McVicar, the Lord Dean of Guild, who served with me for two years and was exceptionally supportive.

I am eternally grateful to their Lordships, the senior representatives of the Scottish legal system, for administering justice so effectively in the various cases that resulted from the Labour Party's assault upon my reputation. I know that Neil Baxter would like to extend his own thanks to Pat Marshall, for her assistance with the early drafts and particularly to Jon Jardine, for his substantial and continuous work, advice and support in the production of this book. Neil also wishes to thank Josh McGuire and Jean McArdle for putting up with him during the time- and labour-intensive gestation and production of the book.

List of Illustrations

Ma, Pa and the wean (1927) (Personal collection); Me and Robert (1932) (Personal collection); Mum, me and Robert (*c.* 1935) (Personal collection); Just after joining up (1944) (Personal collection); Just married – Peggy and me (1968) (Personal collection); Ma, Pa and the weans (1976) (Personal collection); The district team (1986) (Personal collection); Visions of things to come – looking over the Concert Hall site (1988) (Scottish Media Newspapers Ltd [SMN]); Launching the marketing campaign for 1990 (1989) (SMN); Finishing touches with Cameron McNicol (1990) (Personal collection); Richard Luce, me and M. Chirac (1990) (Personal collection); At the heart of the City of Culture (1990) (SMN); The district election count – Jean McFadden and me (1992) (SMN); The Biderlally (1993) (SMN); A glorious return – Mr Happy's comeback (1994) (SMN); Me and the Wets (glasses courtesy Mr Pellow (1994)) (Personal collection); A grand day out one – Edinburgh (1994) (SMN); A grand day out two – London (1994) (Stefan Rousseau/PA News); The concert hall murals – joining in with the Adrian Wiszniewski Quartet (1995) (SMN); A moment for reflection – the opening of the restored Tobacco Merchants House (1995) (SMN); Celebrating the great council victory – Tony Blair, George Robertson and me (1995) (Personal collection); With Julian Spalding at the launch of the Gallery of Modern Art in front of 'Punjab' by Bridget Riley (1996) (SMN); Press interview (1996) (SMN); Arriving at the Labour HQ for the NEC inquiry (1997) (SMN); Light relief – me and Sir Jimmy Savile (February 1998) (SMN); Close-up (1998) (SMN); The Party drops its case (1998) (SMN); Celebrating with the Toon Council – opening of the MGM Store, Buchanan Street (1998) (SMN); Glasgow, a real City of Culture. The poet Edwin Morgan, jazz saxophonist Tommy Smith and me launching the new Glasgow song in the Glasgow Royal Concert Hall (November 1998) (SMN); The launch of 'Winning – the Design of Sport' – the first major exhibition of Glasgow's reign as UK City of Architecture and Design 1999 (SMN); Presenting the Glasgow Loving Cup to the Princess Royal (1999) (Personal collection); Receiving the Order of St Lazarus (1999) (Paul Clements); Peggy, Carol Smillie, Nick Nairn and me at the Lady Provost's Fashion Show (1999) (Personal collection).

Preface

This book is based on material that I wrote and dictated, along with documents and correspondence that I gathered, in order to defend myself from attacks by the Labour Party which I served as an active member for forty-nine years. These, along with my twelve-year collection of press cuttings, assisted my colleague, collaborator and friend Neil Baxter, who undertook substantial research and brought this material together in a way that tells the story of my life, from my childhood in the Gorbals to being first citizen of the great City of Glasgow.

Others, over time, had offered to work with me to tell my story but I had always resisted, for a variety of reasons. I was not sure that it was something that I wanted to do, although I suppose that collecting press cuttings over a number of years must mean that somewhere at the back of my mind I had the intent to do so. I always felt that whoever I worked with, there would have to be a certain empathy of spirit, and that they would have to see things the way I do. The time would also have to be right.

When Neil Baxter suggested that we co-operate to tell my story I was surprised at how readily I agreed and just how short a time I took to consider the project. I had known Neil for a number of years through his work on civic projects in which I was interested – our activities on civic events seem to run in parallel, with him involved as consultant and organiser while I work on the civic political side to make things happen. I always admired his energy, enthusiasm and integrity; that he had a sense of humour not dissimilar to my own helped make up my mind.

The timing was certainly right, considering the ordeal I had been put through by the Labour Party. It was important that the record be set straight and the truth be told. I believed that collaborating with Neil would help me do that, and I was right.

He was a joy to work with. Everything has gone unbelievably

smoothly, and his energy and enthusiasm remain undiminished. I will always be grateful to him for enabling me to tell the story of my life.

Foreword

It is a bright, cold, sunny day in the West End of Glasgow. It is Friday 30 January 1998 but, given the circumstances, it might just as easily be the April of George Orwell's 1984.

I'm in Keir Hardie House, headquarters of the Scottish Labour Party. On the doorstep, the massed ranks of the media – press, radio and television – stand huddled against the cold, blowing into their hands to keep warm and stamping their feet to keep the circulation going.

It is hard to believe that I am here, after forty-eight years of service to the Labour Party. I am the Lord Provost of the City of Glasgow and Lord Lieutenant to Her Majesty the Queen, yet I'm appearing before the Party's National Constitutional Committee charged with breaching Party rule 2A.8. In the morning the Chairman of the NCC panel told my solicitor Peter McCann and me that the panel had decided that there was no question of corruption on my part, nor any reason for my expulsion from the Party. But now the hearing continues.

I listen to Councillor Jean McFadden giving evidence against me. She insists that she has never been a member of any group or faction within Glasgow City Council.

Like the other witnesses she has no hard evidence to offer to substantiate anything alleged against me. I recall that it was only after some initial hesitation that she finally decided to give evidence against me.

As I listen, I have a strange feeling of *déjà vu*. First, I had to endure the Scottish Labour Party inquiry, then the scrutiny of the Party's investigator, Mrs Murfin. After that, there was my appeal to the Party's National Executive Committee. With detailed documentation I exposed the various allegations as completely groundless, yet here we go again, as if in some kind of time warp. I feel like the character in *Groundhog Day*.

Why is no one listening? Why is no one seriously considering the facts? I did not expect a disinterested hearing from the Scottish Party officers who cobbled the whole case together in the first place, but why did people like Tom, now Lord, Sawyer, not listen to my rebuttal of the allegations? What happened to the ideals with which they joined the Party – of fighting injustice and defending the rights of the individual? Were they too busy fighting injustice in other parts of the world to notice it in their own back yard?

Why am I being abused by a Labour Party I have served loyally for so many years? The outcome of this hearing may ruin my reputation and cast a shadow over three decades of dedicated service to my native city. My mind strays a bit and I can't help wonder if such things ever happened in the Labour Party in 1926, the year of the General Strike . . .

CHAPTER ONE

I was born on 24 February 1926 in a room-and-kitchen tenement flat, three up at 241 Thistle Street, Gorbals, Glasgow. The building had four storeys with four homes on each landing, all room-and-kitchen flats with a shared toilet for each landing, half a flight down. Both my father, Patrick James Lally, and my mother Sarah, whose maiden name was Joyce, came from County Mayo in the north-west of Ireland. I think he came over in the early twenties for the tattie howkin'. She was working in a small hotel. I remember little about my father, who died when I was only ten. I do know that his own father was married twice, his first wife having died. My dad was one of four sons from the second marriage. Of his brothers, Michael went off to seek his fortune in America, Philip lived in Fife, and his stepbrother, my Uncle Martin, lived in Florence Street, Gorbals. His brother John also lived in Glasgow.

Dad was an avid reader. Virtually as soon as I could read he introduced me to Gorbals Library. Predictably for an Irish Catholic immigrant, he was also a keen fan of Glasgow Celtic. He took me to the Cup Final at Hampden in 1931 when I was far too young to understand what was going on. We were right up at the back of the ground, and I couldn't see very much. I remember being quite upset at the end of the game because I was convinced that Motherwell had beaten Celtic. In reality of course Celtic were the victors by four goals to two.

My mother was thirty when I was born. Her father, Michael, worked on the Southern Irish Railway. I remember visiting my grandparents during school holidays at their smallholding in Mulraney, a little town on the coast with beautiful sandy beaches and a rather grand railway hotel. Although the railway died long since, the hotel still stands. My mother's brothers, Uncle Michael and Uncle Patrick (the number of Patricks in the family sometimes caused confusion!) lived with us for a time in Thistle Street. Even after they were married, they still lived in the Gorbals, close by.

1

My mother was intensely religious and regularly attended Mass at St Francis Church in Cumberland Street. Conveniently located, right next door, was the Paragon Cinema, which had itself once been a church. Here and at Green's Picturedome and the BB Cinerama (known as the 'B's') in Commercial Road, my mother would twice-weekly indulge her veneration for the more earthly charms of Messrs Flynn, Gable and their ilk.

My mother and father actually met and married in Doune, Perthshire. When they first arrived in Glasgow, they naturally joined the large Irish emigré population in the Gorbals. Originally they lived in Florence Street, two streets away from Thistle Street where I was born. At one stage, there were six of us crowded into two rooms: my mother and father, my uncles Michael and Patrick, my younger brother Robert and myself. What would now be considered gross overcrowding didn't seem so bad, and was certainly much more civilised than the conditions some folk were forced to endure. The sleeping arrangements were straightforward, with the marital bed in the kitchen recess and two beds in the room, one shared by myself and my brother, the other by my uncles.

My father earned his living as a casual labourer, helping to build the new housing estates at Mosspark, Kings Park and Croftfoot. He also worked as a gravedigger at Lambhill Cemetery and, like most folk in the area, couldn't afford public transport. The few pennies that he would have spent on tram fares were always saved for his family, so he would walk the four miles from the Gorbals to Lambhill.

Two days after I was born I was baptised in St Francis Church. I suppose the unseemly haste was a tradition borne out of the high level of infant mortality. It was a sort of Christian insurance policy which I came perilously close to cashing in. When I was still a tiny baby, just a few months old, I became gravely ill. Fortunately, then as now, Glasgow had some of the finest doctors in the world. I was taken to the Western Infirmary and underwent a hernia operation. My parents feared for my life and the doctors did not rate my chances too highly. 'But you were a wee fighter!' my mother would later tell me. This was long before the introduction of the National Health Service, but somehow my parents had managed to keep up their insurance stamps. While I was in the Western, my mother walked there every day from Thistle Street, a round trip of about six miles.

My own earliest memories are of playing in the Gorbals streets. We were in the second close down from Caledonia Road. The block next door had been declared unsafe and was demolished. To secure the site, high walls were built on the building line to the front and back up to first-storey height. There was an entrance from Thistle Street, but this was securely boarded up. The backcourt area also had a small wall at the far side. These two mysterious enclosures became known as the 'buggie lawn'. The high walled bit where the tenement had stood was the 'big buggie' and the backcourt area the 'wee buggie'. It wasn't quite Frances Hodgson Burnett's Secret Garden, but to the local weans it was mysterious enough, and we would climb over the wall and spend hours playing there.

My best friends throughout my childhood were Duncan Smith who we knew as 'Doc', James Farrell and Frank McElhone. Doc became a book-binder with Collins. James, who was great at football, particularly heidies, would emigrate to Hamilton, Ontario. When we weren't playing on the buggie lawn, we played in the streets. There wasn't much traffic, although I do remember being interrupted by horse-drawn coal carts. We played football, kick the can, and cricket, using the stanks as a wicket.

As a child, I wasn't really aware of the city beyond the Gorbals. The local population was massive, living in small houses, hugely over-crowded dwellings. There were single apartments with ten of a family in them. One nearby, just up the road at 217 Thistle Street I think, was full of big families. In fourteen houses there were over 100 people. The Gorbals had the highest density of population anywhere in Scotland and probably in the United Kingdom.

Most of the Gorbals tenements at that time were black and grimy and bleak. People rarely painted doors or window frames, not because they didn't take pride in their houses but because that was the factor's job. Nobody liked the factors, but, looking back, we were wrong to blame them. There just wasn't enough money about. Everyone was paying low rents, although it was all most folk could afford. Rents couldn't be raised because of the Rent Act which had been introduced after the women's rent riots during the First World War, when the factors had introduced unreasonable and unmanageable rent increases. So the rents were very low, but the standard of service was very low as well.

The area was demonised in Alexander McArthur's novel *No Mean City*, published in 1935. The hard-pressed population had to bear the added burden imposed on them by that work of fiction. Some people, a very small minority, felt they had to live down to the image of its protagonist, the thug Johnnie Stark. We had problems enough. Given the density of population, disease was rife, and the Gorbals was ravaged by tuberculosis right up to the immunisation and anti-TB campaigns of the 1950s.

Thistle Street was fairly typical. Long dark rows of four-storey blocks lined streets which were laid out in a grid pattern, like much of the centre of Glasgow. The blocks themselves varied in shade across the whole range from dark grey to black. Their colour was a continuing legacy of the industrial revolution that had brought the city so much of its wealth. It had also brought the Gorbals its huddled masses, crowding into buildings designed for only a fraction of the numbers. Most blocks were four storeys high with four homes on each level. The ground floor was described as the bottom flat, while the others were one up, two up and three up.

On each half-landing there was a window and a toilet which served the four homes on the floor above. The homes consisted of two apartments in the style that was described as a 'room-and-kitchen'. The gas-lit closes which led into the homes were painted dark brown up to about shoulder height, and whitewashed above that. While the blocks were not identical, the differences between them were minimal and the monotonous blocks capped with grey slates gave the whole area a depressing air.

Like the closes, the streets themselves were gas-lit. Their one relieving feature was their width, which prevented the place from feeling too oppressive. On the corner of each block there would be a shop or, more often, a pub. Where I lived in Thistle Street, there were nine pubs within something like 200 yards.

At the top of Thistle Street, about 150 yards from my house, at the junction with Crown Street and Cathcart Road, was the dominating industrial structure of Dixons Blazes, which at night spewed out flames and smoke. Although this was a familiar sight to the locals, to visitors it must have seemed like Dante's Inferno, creating the impression that the Gorbals was a sort of ante-room to hell. Yet this was the Gorbals I grew up in, a place to which I am still fiercely loyal, and which, like the vast majority of folk who were born there, I have always loved.

In my memory, everyone in that community was friendly. It was certainly very mixed, with a large Jewish community concentrated at the Cross, a number of Polish people and, of course, many first- and second-generation Irish immigrants. It wasn't until I got to school that I became aware of any tension between the various groups, and then it was the inevitable one of Catholics versus Protestants. It might seem like an old socialist cliché, but there was a tremendous warmth and friendliness in the Gorbals, a great community spirit, a feeling that people were all toiling together. The trust between folk was such that if you lost your house key you could always borrow next door's, because all the big locks were the same. In fact, most people tied their keys on a piece of string so that anyone who wanted could get in. You could buy 'big lock' keys from the local shops. There wasn't much in the way of burglary, but then there wasn't much to steal.

The main road in the Gorbals was Cumberland Street. Busy every day, and packed on Saturdays, it was a really lively shopping street. While there were a few double shops, they were the exception, most of the street was filled with single shops and small traders. To a small child, it all seemed extraordinary. I remember the Maypole Dairy. At its entrance it had one of those glass corners so that if you stood on exactly the right spot, the window cut you in half and your reflection completed the image. On our way to school we did that thing that Harry Worth made famous many years later, lifting up one arm and one leg so it looked as if you were in mid-air and we all thought it was hilarious.

All along Cumberland Street the shops had painted exteriors and hand-lettered signs. I don't suppose any of them could afford a lit sign. Yet it always seemed lively; a dynamic, energetic place where, for a special treat, we would get 'flies graveyards' – heavy, soggy, currant squares – from Telfords, the baker's, or *Hotspur* or the *Wizard* from one of the newsagents. These comics were often a let-down: the dramatic, colourful cover would persuade you to buy the comic, but inside you could never find the story which had cast up this intriguing image. I suppose this was my first introduction to marketing.

I went to St Francis primary school, which sat directly behind the church where I was baptised and where my parents worshipped. My most memorable primary school teacher was the writer Paul Vincent Carrol, known to us as 'Pongo'. His regime was extraordinarily strict. If you got up to any mischief he would administer a sharp flick to the side of the face. This was often done on the mere suspicion of mischief, or for no reason at all.

There was an annexe of St Francis School on the other side of Matheson Street, but sheer pressure on numbers resulted in some of us being shifted to the local non-denominational school, Hayfield. Of course, while the education authority used the description non-denominational, to us it was a Protestant school.

At Hayfield, there was no attempt at integration. The Roman Catholic incomers were taught in separate classes, almost a school within a school. Inevitably, there was conflict. A white line was painted down the centre of the playground, a sort of early Gorbals version of the Berlin Wall, but still the fights went on. Only total integration would have really worked, but that was impossible, so we stayed in our separate enclaves, ignorant and distrustful of each other.

Inevitably, with St Patrick's Day or the twelfth of July, the tension would boil over. Outside the school, you had to think carefully when greeted with the challenge 'Billy, Dan or Auld Tin Can?' If you were honest, you were either greeted as a soul mate or given a thorough doin'. Pretending to be a Billy wasn't smart tactics, and could result in all sorts of complications, usually just delaying the inevitable. Trying to be smart and declaring yourself an 'auld tin can' resulted in a doin' no matter who'd asked the question.

My dad and I were very close. I remember him tall, handsome and strong. He would break great sticks across his knee, a feat of strength which filled me with admiration, although my mother would later claim that this seemingly inconsequential act contributed to his early death. He would come home after what must have been back-breaking work and take my wee brother and me to Glasgow Green. His only entertainment seemed to be reading, and he rarely took a drink – my mother wouldn't let him!

With Dad's encouragement, I too became an avid reader. He introduced me very early to the likes of H. G. Wells, Jules Verne, Charles Dickens and Jack London. All this was possible because of the libraries and we went to both the Gorbals Library and McNeil Street Library. Dad always emphasised that we were very lucky that we could get all these books and they were free. Whenever I had some spare time, I would settle down to read, very often with half a loaf of bread. One of my favourites, Richmal Crompton's William, ate far more exotic stuff called blancmange. I had no idea what it was, but he was always getting stuck in. I felt that blancmange was eminently to be desired.

I was never actually clear about what Dad died of. He had a sore on his lip which looked like a wart, and he was convinced that it was irritated by his smoking. It didn't stop him smoking, though. He was being treated at the Beatson, Glasgow's specialist cancer clinic, and then he went into hospital. He wasn't there very long when he died. My mother would later claim that he died of blood poisoning due to a leg wound. She felt that his habitual demonstration of strength to his sons – the breaking of hefty sticks over his knee – caused the problem. All I know is that he just went into hospital and didn't come back out. He was forty-two and I was ten.

My mother was absolutely inconsolable in her grief when my father died. I was a very naïve ten-year-old, totally mystified by what was happening. My father had been totally committed to the family and his failure to obtain proper medical treatment was probably because he didn't want to be absent from work and not be able to provide for us.

However, my mother had always been the driving force. She was the manager who organised what happened at home. Although we only lived in a room and kitchen, she would never sit down and relax. She was always caring, cleaning and organising. If she did sit down, she knitted. She was not a great knitter, and she specialised in socks. For years we all wore hand-knitted socks. On my father's death, she went into mourning and wore nothing but black right up until the early 1950s.

After my father died, my mother got eighteen shillings a week for us to live on. Rents were very low and we got Parish clothes. The Parish was in Coburg Street. You got a line to go there, and they fitted you out with a suit. The natural order of the day was short trousers until you were around twelve, and then the traditional Parish suit would be a heavy tweed herringbone. It was, of course, obvious to all and sundry that you'd got your clothes from the Parish.

Because we were so poor, when we came in from school we always had to take off our school clothes so that Mum could wash and iron them to be ready for school the next day. She was always meticulous about cleanliness and, like most folk in the Gorbals, we had to bathe in the traditional zinc bath in front of the coal fire. After my father's death, I took on more and more responsibility, although somehow my mother ensured that while I took on the tasks and responsibilities of the head of the house, I didn't sacrifice my childhood. It was from this period that I developed my mastery of many skills which my mother considered the proper responsibility of the senior male of the household, like laying lino and hanging wallpaper. My uncles had married and moved away, which I know she resented, feeling that she was being abandoned.

Although my mother was not a tall woman, probably about five foot three inches, she managed to maintain authority, and was a strict disciplinarian, determined that her sons should know the difference between right and wrong. If we were told to be in at a certain time at night, that was it – no questions. If she was very angry we got smacked on the legs, but I think we did as we were told more from the threat of what might happen than from actual punishment.

I suppose I still feel bitter about my secondary education. Holyrood School had just opened, but filled up very rapidly. The summer intake from my year at Hayfield all went to Holyrood, but because I was in the winter intake I ended up in Calton Central School in Bridgeton. Once again it was an 'us and them' situation, and all of us who went to Calton felt we'd got by far the worse deal.

Although Holyrood was just up the road, to get to Calton I had to walk over the suspension bridge and through Glasgow Green. You could take a tram car up Abercrombie Street, but that meant money. The silver lining to this particular cloud I suppose was that on our way up McNeil Street we would pass the magnificent Scottish Co-operative Wholesale Society Bakery, the central Co-op bakery which baked for the whole city. Early in the morning the sweet, warm, yeasty smell was intoxicating, and if you smiled and pleaded at the open windows the good-hearted women inside would give you fresh-baked Abernethy biscuits.

About the same time as I started going to secondary school, I joined the Boy Scouts. I'd previously been a member of the St Francis Silver Band for a very short time. I remember I started with the largest instrument, which, powerful as my lungs were, was probably a bit ambitious – I suppose that must have been a euphonium. Very rapidly, I worked my way down to the smallest instrument in the band, the cornet, and I still couldn't play. The Scouts met in the Boys Guild Hall. Like all these things, being in the Scouts had its good and bad points. When I joined, somebody was selling a kilt for ten shillings, and my mother, who'd been carefully saving money, decided that I should have it. We must have gone without quite a lot so she could pay for it.

Kilts were not exactly de rigueur in the Gorbals. I didn't have the nerve to walk through the streets in my new regalia. To avoid getting a shiricking from my pals, I took an alternative route to the Boys Guild Hall, so on the evenings of Scout meetings a furtive, kilted figure could be seen climbing over the dykes which separated the backcourts and scurrying along behind the tenements.

It was 1938, the year of the Empire Exhibition. Two boys from each scout troop in the city were to act as stewards for the groups of schoolchildren at Ibrox on the opening day. I was tall for my age, and was one of the boys chosen. It was a great honour to see the King and Queen so close. There were rumours that because of his speech impediment, the King might not be able to deliver the opening speech, but on the day he was brilliant. Then Harry Lauder sang. Everyone knew Harry Lauder. To us, he was a superstar and really the only choice to sing at the opening of the Exhibition.

For months beforehand the Exhibition was all that people talked about, so that when it opened, it was a magical event of which the whole city was proud. It's strange the things that stick in the mind: I remember the Mounties, and the technical marvels shown off in the industry and engineering pavilions, including, of all things, glass fibre.

Then, of course, there was Tait's Tower, which you could see from everywhere, including the Gorbals. It was the tallest structure in the city. Everybody had pictures of it. One of the most popular souvenirs was a picture of the tower in coloured silver paper on a mirrored background. It was like nothing we'd ever seen before, and for a twelve-year-old a revelation of just how great Glasgow could be.

By 1939 I was doing quite well at school, always managing to be in the top three in my class. Then we broke for summer, and the evacuations started. But my brother and I stayed at home. As the school didn't reopen, I had effectively, at the age of thirteen, left school. In the spring of 1940 my education officially ended, and at the age of fourteen I became available for work.

Over the next four years or so, my career, while never actually in the ascendant, didn't lack variety. My first job was in Candleriggs as an apprentice cutter for a tailoring firm. The building, which is still there, was in the southern half of the street, close to the corner of Wilson Street. Only part of the time was spent in learning the tailor's trade; otherwise I was mainly occupied with odd jobs. When the material arrived, in great bales, it had to be carried up endless flights of stairs to the factory.

It was a long day with no breaks, and all for ten shillings and sixpence a week. You were kept busy all the time, grabbing a moment if you could to eat whatever you'd managed to bring in for lunch. One morning I was discovered sitting on one of the bales which I'd just helped carry up half a dozen flights of stairs. My supervisor took a dim view of this behaviour, and fired me on the spot – for eating a roll!

There was no way I could go home and tell my mother I'd got my jotters, so I went round the corner into Albion Street to Todd, Cunningham and Petrie's warehouse. This was a big, beautiful, French-style building on the corner of Argyle Street; it too is still there, although the building next door, which belonged to the same company, has been demolished and is now the site of a multi-storey car park. In the transition, I took a drop of sixpence a week, down to ten shillings.

I worked in the fabrics and bedding department. It was my first experience of retail, but after a while there I went looking for a job that paid a little more, which I found a couple of streets further south at Teacher's Bond, King Street. The site has now become a car park.

I soon discovered that although I was earning more money, my new task was much more tedious. I was in the bottle-washing section. All I did was load bottles into a big machine. Bored, I took myself off to another department where they were bottling the spirits and worked there for a week. But when the management found out, they insisted that I go back to bottle washing. I decided to leave instead.

Again, in trepidation of my mother's reaction, I went and got a job in the slipper factory at Salkeld Street. All this job changing was quite straightforward in wartime when there were plenty of jobs and little competition. Even so, my attempt to get into the shipyards failed; they took my name and said they would let me know, but they still haven't got back in touch.

In the slipper factory, I did a variety of jobs, which included operating an impressive German machine which was used for air-pressure bonding the soles to the uppers of the slippers. As a rather odd reprise of my admiration of the glass wool at the Empire Exhibition, one of the strangest tasks in the slipper factory was to produce a one-off presentation pair of glass slippers for a Hollywood blonde who was visiting the city. Oddly, while I remember the slippers, I can't remember the blonde. It might well have been Betty Grable.

After I'd been in the slipper factory for about eighteen months, I got conscripted. I had my medical, as was the way, three months short of my eighteenth birthday, so in February 1944 I joined the Royal Air Force.

Getting into the RAF was no easy matter. By 1944 most recruitment was into the army, particularly the infantry where there was most demand. My pal 'Doc' Smith and I had anticipated this difficulty, and, because both of us were keen to become wireless operators, had joined the Air Training Corps a couple of years earlier.

Given her keenness to get me into a Boy Scout kilt, you'd have thought that my mother would be all for my donning the uniform of the Corps. Far from it. She stalwartly refused to discuss the matter, presumably seeing my willingness to volunteer as indicative of too much enthusiasm to join the real forces, who at that time were going into battle and getting killed. So for some months I would make appropriate excuses for going out in the evening and at weekends, and go round to my uncle's house in Caledonia Road to get changed into my ATC uniform. She found out, of course. She wasn't happy, but did accept the argument that my eventual call-up was inevitable, and if I was a qualified wireless operator the risk of my being in the front line was, perhaps, reduced.

I had joined 122 Squadron, Air Training Corps, and rapidly learned Morse Code and wireless operation. By the time I joined the RAF, I had quite good speed in Morse and was already a fairly skilled wireless operator. The other benefit of the ATC was that it helped to ensure you were fit. When we weren't training, we played football. Although the ATC helped me to get into the RAF, 'Doc' Smith was not so lucky. He ended up in the army.

First I was sent to Arbroath for six weeks' square bashing. Then I went to 17SFTS Signals Training School at RAF Cranwell in Lincolnshire. My Morse training stood me in good stead, but the demand for wireless operators was low as radar was beginning to take over. After a fairly rudimentary grounding in radar, which didn't really prepare me for operations, I was sent to Bamburgh in Northumberland, where I received a very thorough on-the-job training.

Late 1944 and the early months of 1945 saw fairly intensive activity by the RAF, which, for a radar operator, was fascinating. You would see all the blips assembling and gathering out over the North Sea, moving off towards Germany. There were two different types of radar stations, Chainhome stations with fixed aerials on concrete bases and Chainhome Low stations with revolving aerials which spotted low-flying aircraft coming in. We did spot the odd enemy plane, but most day-to-day activity just involved tracking weather planes. After Bamburgh, I was moved to Yeatsbury in Wiltshire for further training.

Here we were given a thorough grounding on how the equipment worked, as a basis for understanding its operation, and learned precision location techniques. For aircraft within thirty miles, a grid reference was easy to plot straight off the display unit. For further afield, the screen was a bit like a noise level chart. Information we provided was cross-referenced centrally to determine whether aircraft were friendly or enemy.

After a couple of months I was posted to St Cyrus, just north of Montrose. We were stationed in a big house and conditions were fairly rough. There was no electricity other than for operational requirements, and we lived, fairly miserably, in huts. My career as a peripatetic radar operator then took me to Durness in Sutherland and then, just when I thought they couldn't send me any further north, I was posted to one of the small islands in the Shetlands. When that base closed down, rather than waiting to be posted elsewhere, I volunteered to go to Germany. I think it was the only time during my RAF career that I'd ever volunteered for anything.

Germany, just after the end of the war, was a revelation. I remember being horrified by the poverty. To get to my radar station at Iburg, I had to pass through Hamburg. I can remember all the little children at the railway station begging for anything they could get from the troops. It was heart-breaking.

Iburg, which was on the road between Osnabruck and Münster, was one of three radar stations in Germany. There was another chain in France. Of course, radar operation required at least three stations to provide the necessary triangulation. It was my first posting in Germany. The radar station, which had been mobile, was now static. Soon I moved to another unit, and the next stop was Winterberg, which had an Olympic pool, part of, I think, the Hitler Games of 1936. Our next move was to Wasserkuppe, the place where I spent the longest part of my eighteen months in Germany. This was in the American zone. We lived on American rations, which were much more generous than those we'd been used to. I remember the cigarette allowance was two hundred a week, which cost about three shillings. Since we were on three shillings a day, you could smoke yourself silly. There was also the benefit that unlike the British, the Americans were allowed spirit rations, so things were looking up.

In Wasserkuppe, we lived in a large, modern building. It had been built as a glider school in this glorious location at the top of the Rhone mountains. We all had our own rooms, and there was even a swimming pool. When we arrived the pool was empty, but we managed to get it filled during the summer. Over the summer months the weather was fantastic, and when we weren't working we would swim or play football or cricket.

We regularly played football against the Germans, who regularly slaughtered us. As our matches took place at weekends, we decided that this was because there were dances or drinking sessions the night before. As the reputation of the RAF was at stake, we decided to give up drinking for two weeks before an important game. The discipline wasn't easy but after two weeks of early nights and sobriety, we ran out on to the field full of confidence and suffered our biggest ever defeat. So after that, we reverted to drinking and narrowed the margin of our defeats.

In the winter, the skiing at Wasserkuppe was superb. Already fit from football, I found learning to ski relatively easy. Of course, there was no ski lift, so we fishtailed up the slopes. I enjoyed skiing so much that when I came to the end of my service, I sent my skis home, intending to join the few people who at that time had begun to discover the joys of Scottish skiing. Sadly, the skis never arrived, presumably repatriated en route by some German post office. I haven't skied since.

My recollections of swimming, football, skiing and socialising may make my German sojourn sound like something of a holiday camp, but we were operating a radar station twenty-four hours a day. Our signals had to be kept on a specific frequency. When the apparatus broke down, you had two minutes to fix it, and if it wasn't working again within two minutes you were on a charge. There was a shortage of mechanics at that time, so I did a crash course to become a radar operator/mechanic and was elevated to the rank of corporal, in charge of operations.

Until I joined the RAF I had never done any intellectually taxing work. My technical training, both through the ATC and the RAF, required a high level of concentration. The mathematics were, at times, very complex and we were keenly aware that miscalculation could have dire consequences. In addition, the Air Force required regular, concise and coherent reporting, so altogether my Royal Air Force experience filled great gaps in my education.

After leaving the forces, the theory was that you would return to the job you had had before joining up, but somehow the slipper factory had lost its appeal. I had no idea what I really wanted to do, and as a sort of interim measure took up a job at the Renfrew Foundry at Hillington as a machine moulder.

The foundry made parts for Rolls Royce aero-engines. In the immediate post-war period, demand was greatly reduced and much of the foundry had been closed down, except for hot casting. I hadn't been working for long when I decided it really wasn't for me. I left to take up a job in a wholesale clothing warehouse in Bridgeton. I worked there from Monday to Friday, and then on Saturdays worked part-time in Connell & Sons shop in Trongate. They were doing well on the back of very successful marketing. They were among the first to get personalities to endorse their clothes. Charlie Tully, who played for Celtic, was one of a number of footballers wearing their gear at the time. After about eighteen months, they asked me to work full time. Here was a business on its way up, with real prospects. For the first time ever, I saw the possibility of a career, so I took the job.

CHAPTER TWO

I can't really remember when political awareness dawned. My parents had always voted Labour, like many folk around them in the Gorbals, but they weren't politically involved. The struggle to survive was always the thing that preoccupied them.

My first experience of political debate was in the RAF. In a small unit with folk from a whole variety of backgrounds and places, politics was often the subject of our discussions. In all of these conversations a socialist stance seemed the natural one to adopt. A kindred spirit in many of these discussions was Derek Taylor, who became a close friend and with whom I still correspond. Years later I was to name my younger son in his honour. Of course, some people among my RAF colleagues vigorously opposed my viewpoint on a whole range of issues. Just as I give the RAF credit for much of my education, this was a good grounding in the issues which preoccupy politicians and in how to argue my side.

The post-war election in 1945 which brought Labour to power gave many ordinary folk new hope. After my return to Glasgow, I would frequently attend the Labour meetings at the corner of Dunmore Street, near Gorbals Cross. John Mains, who became Lord Provost many years later, was among the persuasive orators who spoke at these gatherings. I started to read up on socialism, although I have to confess that I found *Das Kapital* pretty heavy going.

In the late 1940s, Glasgow was still a million-plus conurbation. Consequently, the parliamentary constituencies were very populous. My local Labour Party branch, Gorbals and Hutchesontown, had a relatively small but highly influential membership. John Mains had aspirations to Parliament; his fellow councillor in the branch was Alice Cullen. The constituency treasurer was Willie McGuinness, a bookie who ultimately transferred his allegiance to the Scottish National Party. Our Member of Parliament up to the 1950 election was George Buchanan. Just prior to the election, George decided to stand down, as he'd been offered the post of Chairman of the then equivalent of the Department of Health and Social Security.

The selection of the new parliamentary candidate was, I understand, a fairly heated affair. John Mains was very keen, but ultimately he threw his weight behind Alice's campaign. As she was no spring chicken, he probably thought that she wouldn't last too long! She ended up competing for the nomination against Willie McGuinness who, when he lost, stood against Labour as an Irish anti-Partition candidate. It made for an exciting campaign. Of course, Labour won and Alice Cullen became our MP, a position she would hold for many years to come, much to John Mains' chagrin.

This then was the local Labour branch that I joined in 1950. After two months, I was Vice-Chairman of the branch. It wasn't long before I was delegated to the constituency, and then elected Constituency Chairman.

This was a period when Council elections were an annual affair. Councillors served for three years before standing down or going forward for re-election. As election agent I ran the constituency elections, and it seemed that no sooner had one election concluded than the process of selection and campaigning for the next would start. The whole system was thoroughly inefficient, and resulted in a constant lack of cohesion within the City Council, much against the interests of the electorate.

Strangely, New Labour seems keen to revert to this system. I remember attending a conference in Birmingham at which this return to the bad old days was advocated. It was argued that such a system was good for democracy. I countered that if it was good for democracy at local level, then presumably it would be equally beneficial at Westminster. This proposal was greeted with less enthusiasm.

When I first joined the Party, I had no ambitions to join the Council or enter Parliament. I sincerely believed that I was doing my bit to change society simply by working within the branch and the constituency. I'm not usually slow on the uptake, but after something like fifteen years I'd worked out it was going to take a wee bit longer than I'd anticipated. Throughout this period, I was still living in the family home in Thistle Street. My brother, who had also been in the Air Force, was also back at home. In the sixties, the city began to clear properties in the comprehensive redevelopment areas, and folk from the Gorbals were moved out to Pollok, Castlemilk, Toryglen and Drumchapel. The majority of those who were moved from the Gorbals were rehoused on the south side of the city. There was an odd but understandable logic that people stuck to the side of the river they came from.

I had managed, over this period, to stay in the same job or, rather, make progress within the same company. By the mid-sixties, I was in a position to contemplate joining the Council. Working in the city centre made it relatively straightforward. At that time, most meetings were around lunchtime, and I agreed with my employers that if I worked a six-day week they would give me time off to attend the Council.

Alice Cullen was coming to the end of her parliamentary career, so the thought of going forward for election to Parliament did cross my mind. My childhood pal, Frank McElhone, had joined the Labour Party some time after me but was also keen to go forward for election. His was also an influential voice in the local party. At one stage Frank and I came to an agreement that when a Council vacancy came up, I would support him, and he would lend his support to my bid for Parliament. Things didn't quite work out this way. I'd been active in the constituency and the City Labour Party, where I'd been a member of the Executive for twelve years. As a well-kent face on the Executive and in the Party, I thought I was in with a good shout.

Bill Harley and I were the left-wing voices on the Glasgow Executive at that time. Bill was elected to the Corporation representing Cowcaddens. Years later, he moved on to Strathclyde Region, where he became Chairman of Education and Chairman of the Police Committee. Our collaboration was to resume in 1996 when we were both elected to the new Glasgow City Council. Bill has always been one of my closest friends and I was best man when he married his delightful wife, Rose.

The City Party was fairly right wing and reactionary, which, I suppose, made Bill Harley and myself seem even further to the left. We were the local Bevanites. Nye Bevan was one of my Labour heroes – I felt a great affinity with the political views he had espoused and the stance he had taken on numerous issues. At one point I resigned in frustration at the Glasgow Executive's consistently reactionary position, but my resignation made not one jot of difference, so after I'd been elected back on I decided that resignation did nothing other than leave the battlefield to the enemy. This was an object lesson, and I determined at this early stage in my political career never to resign from anything again – a personal dictum which has stood me in good stead ever since.

My first election to Glasgow Corporation was on Tuesday 3 May 1966. I was one of the three councillors representing the Kingston ward. My predecessor, Dame Jean Roberts, was one of the longest-standing and most distinguished of Glasgow's councillors. First elected in 1929, she became the first female Lord Provost of the city, a position she held from 1960 to 1963. I used to joke that being elected to her seat made it a dead cert that I too would be Lord Provost.

The main issue of my first term in office was the campaign against selective and fee-paying schools in Glasgow. Ironically, very shortly after I joined the Council, St Mungo's Former Pupils' Club in Great Western Road sent me an honorary membership. It seems this was their practice with all new Roman Catholic councillors, but I never attended St Mungo's Club, suspecting that it wouldn't be the kind of place I would feel at home in. Oddly, after Bill Harley and I started our campaigning against fee-paying and selective schools, my membership wasn't renewed.

Before I could really get into the thick of the education argument, however, I managed to get myself suspended from the Group over a housing issue. There was a proposal to transfer housing on Langside Road, facing Queens Park, to a housing ownership co-operative. Of course, at that time, I wasn't on the housing committee. In fact, the committee structure was largely determined by the amount of time you'd served on the Council: the longest-serving members had first choice of the committees they would sit on, while the most recent got what was left.

I learned about Langside Road from the papers going to Council. I considered the housing committee's decision to support this proposal to be against the public interest. Management by a co-operative, untried though it was, might have worked, but ownership was another matter. I felt that the measure would simply reduce our housing stock and transfer good-quality housing into private hands. So without consulting anybody, I moved against the proposition. I was seconded by Tom Fulton and about half a dozen others. We got slaughtered and the whip was duly taken away. After holding out for about six months, I decided that it was time to apologise and return to the fold.

The crux of the argument against the Corporation's funding of selective schools was that supporting such institutions reinforced divisions in society. Those who attended such schools tended to attract privilege and opportunity at the expense of their peers. Their parents were certainly a very articulate lobby and some of them were councillors. By backing this segregation in education, the Corporation was failing to address the fundamental issue of higher overall standards.

In the late fifties the shipyards apprentices' strike had generated a new political awareness among Glasgow's young people. Gus Mac-Donald, who would go on to great things in the media and Scottish politics, was one of the youthful leaders of the strike, a number of whom lived in my ward. They and the Reverend MacDonald of Glasgow University decided to create a support group in the interests of our educational campaign. Perhaps unwisely, and certainly provocatively, their Glasgow Education Reform Society paraded under the acronym GERS. I thought this was immensely funny and provocative, but some of my more right-wing Roman Catholic colleagues, the staunchest supporters of the St Mungo's Club, warned that any councillors who associated themselves with this calumny would be deprived of the whip.

While having the whip withdrawn twice in your first term of office might be some sort of record, I decided that discretion was the more appropriate course. Bill Harley, Dick Dynes and I formally disavowed any association with GERS. Gus and the rest of his team were understandably upset and their organisation collapsed shortly afterwards. Thinking back, it's the only time that I've ever accurately been described as a Gers supporter.

Another educational issue arose during the 1967 elections, when I was acting as election agent for Geoff Shaw. Geoff was one of a group of Church of Scotland ministers who'd settled in the Gorbals in the mid-fifties. He and Walter Fyfe had worked together in the New York slums. When they arrived in the Gorbals, they decided to live and work within the community, helping to improve the lives of local people and to counteract the increasing de-churching that was taking place.

By the mid-sixties, Geoff, Walter and John Harvey had decided that, in addition to their personal ministry and local campaigning, they should attempt to raise the status of the Gorbals on the political agenda. The most politically active of the three was actually Walter Fyfe, who had become a shop steward at Dixons Blazes and an officer of the union. But Walter never had any ambitions to be a political candidate; he preferred instead to work directly among the people to whom he'd dedicated his life. He later became active in race relations, where, as with everything else he did, his work was enormously influential and effective. John Harvey later pursued his vocation with the Iona Community and is now Moderator of the Church of Scotland's Glasgow presbytery.

Geoff's campaign in the Kingston ward seemed to be going well: people in the Gorbals were traditionally Labour supporters; he was also very likeable, articulate and honest. In the event it was, perhaps, this third quality which led to him losing this particular election.

I got a call from the *Glasgow Herald*'s municipal correspondent, Harry Dutch. He told me that he wanted to get in touch with Geoff because he'd heard that he had very strong views on the segregation of schools. Alarm bells started to ring, because I knew that if Geoff was as open on the issue as he would have been in ordinary conversation, the press coverage might well destroy his campaign. Non-segregated schooling is a laudable goal, but you don't persuade people on such a radical change overnight. So as soon as I put the phone down, I tried to get hold of Geoff. Unfortunately, I was too late. Harry's piece the next day quoted Geoff's view that educational segregation was a major factor in the bigotry and intolerance within our society.

After that, Geoff had no chance. The Roman Catholic population, by far the majority in the Gorbals, were up in arms. One of the local priests even delivered a sermon condemning Geoff's views on segregation and making it clear that good Catholics wouldn't want to vote for him. In the end, I think it was a testament to Geoff's goodness and the respect which so many people had for him that he lost by only a hundred votes or so.

During my first term in the Council, work continued much as before. The company, Connell's, had built the business up to around twelve shops all over Scotland, but the owners Isadore and Herbert Walton were gradually moving out of retail and into property under the new name, the Scottish Metropolitan Property Company. But their retail trade in Glasgow still held up well. I moved from sales to display work in the shops. A team of three of us travelled from branch to branch ensuring that the window displays were right up to the minute. I quite enjoyed this work. I had always been reasonably practical. From when I was fairly young, just after my father's death, I did the decorating in Thistle Street. Hanging wallpaper in those days was a particular skill, since the flour-based paste would stain the edges of the paper if you weren't very careful.

When the company acquired a menswear shop, McMurtries, in Trongate, just beside the Tron steeple, I was asked to manage it. Trongate was a busy and popular retail area, where there was a concentration of six or seven menswear shops. McMurtries had traditionally specialised in caps, and when I took over it had a window full of them. We knew that radical change wouldn't go down well, so we kept up this business in bunnets. However, Connell's long-established marketing ploy of dressing the local football stars quickly raised the profile of the shop. I was already friendly with lots of footballers.

Although nobody asked me to, I started buying for the shop, ordering small quantities of new styles. They sold, so I bought more, and soon I was buying all the gear for McMurtries and another shop we opened round the corner in King Street. McMurtries by this time had been modernised and was operating as an enormously successful and fashionable boutique.

We used a local knitwear company to create new styles, and had other local suppliers making fashion copies. Our association with celebrities expanded into pop music and although I don't think we ever created an outfit for Lulu, her band, the Luvvers, used to come in. Other local groups asked us to put their photographs on the front door of the shop and then gave us superb advertising by appearing in our clothes. I became very adept at spotting the coming thing, like Beatles jackets or, later, flares. We'd get a few made up and if they took off we were leading from the front.

One of my best decisions was to take on a young lady called Peggy McGuire. She'd been working as a machinist at Brook and Branders in the High Street. There was a tyre factory nearby and the fumes from burning tyres were making her ill. So her granddad pushed her into applying for a job elsewhere. We had advertised in the *Citizen* and Peggy's granddad saw the ad and, as she told me later, actually brought her along to McMurtries and waited outside while I was interviewing her.

So this bright, fresh-faced and attractive young lady with a ponytail appeared for interview. I didn't recognise her when she turned up to the interview, but she knew me. Many years before, during a party meeting in the Labour Party rooms in Rutherglen Road, I had been given the task of chasing off a group of noisy teenage girls who were carrying on outside. Peggy was one of those noisy teenagers. As I say, while I didn't know it at the time, this interview was my second meeting with Peggy McGuire. She immediately recognised me, but of course she didn't let on that we had met before and gave a very good interview. She was by far the best candidate and got the job.

A few days later, Herbert Walton came into the shop. I was out and, by chance, Herbert decided to speak to the only member of staff who wouldn't have a clue that he owned the company. There was a set of drawers in which we kept our stock of shirts. If you put too many in, they got crushed. 'How many shirts are in that drawer?' asked Herbert. Peggy, thinking this was a strange question for a customer to ask, replied, 'I've really no idea!' When this peculiar man's expression darkened, she decided to humour him: 'I'll count them – and who are you anyway?' Peggy and Herbert Walton were great friends from that minute on. Peggy was a fantastic sales person. She always got along with people and had that particular skill with the buying public, utterly disarming honesty.

After a time I got used to my chatty and humorous new assistant, but it wasn't until she'd worked with me for a number of years that I had the courage to invite her to a Labour Party dance. My next ploy was to invite her to the pictures. I remember we went to the Coliseum in Eglinton Street to see *Doctor Zhivago*. After that, we began to go steady. When we got married, the joke in the company was that it was the only way I could keep staff.

I can't quite remember how I proposed, but it was in the very romantic setting of the Trade Union Centre in Calton Place. Bill Harley had held his wedding reception there and a couple of years later Peggy and I followed suit. Our wedding, on 6 September 1968, was in Peggy's local church, St Martin's in Castlemilk. Castlemilk was a sprawling new housing area on the south side of the city, built largely in the fifties and consisting mainly of rows of three-, four- and five-apartment tenement houses, along with nine high-rise buildings of twenty-two storeys. It had a population of around 39,000, very poor shopping facilities and very little in the way of community facilities. St Martin's Church was a fairly new building which had been designed by Gillespie, Kidd and Coia and opened in 1961. Monsignor Lyne officiated at the wedding, and our reception in the Trade Union Centre's newly opened Tolpuddle Suite was attended by a number of councillors and trade-unionists, as well as my MP, Alice Cullen.

One of the telegrams was a request from Bill Gray, purporting to come from the Group Whip, that I immediately leave off what I was doing and attend for a vote in the Chambers. Given the venue and the proliferation of left-wingers in attendance, ours was quite opposite to the sort of affair that at that time would be photographed and displayed in *Country Life*. Peggy always described it with a touch of irony as 'the wedding of the season'.

Peggy and I didn't have enough money to get a place of our own, so we moved in with her mother at 63 Hoddam Avenue in Castlemilk. Peggy's mother, Winifred, is petite, a wee doll, and consequently always known by the nickname 'Dolly'. What she lacks in stature, she more than makes up for in character. She is a very determined, feisty lady. I got on remarkably well with her, but our living arrangements did not always make things easy.

Some five months after we were married, Peggy became ill. She had to stop work, and nobody could work out what was wrong. It wasn't long before her condition became so severe that she had to be taken into hospital. Happily, it was quickly discovered that she was suffering from a none too rare medical condition – pregnancy. But she remained unwell and was kept in the maternity hospital at Rottenrow for the rest of her term. It was lucky I was fit, because visiting hours would find me running up the steep hill to the hospital. Robert was born on 30 July 1969, an extremely healthy baby. Around that time mankind was making giant leaps on the moon. When Neil Armstrong made his immortal 'one small step for a man . . .' speech, I remember reflecting ruefully that he didn't have to face Rottenrow hill twice a day.

Just before Robert was born we managed to buy a flat in Pollokshields. The estate agents describe Pollokshields as a 'leafy suburb', but the area actually consists of two entirely different house types. In East Pollok-shields there are three-storey apartment blocks, in West Pollokshields large villas, many of them sub-divided. One part was much leafier than the other. We lived in the not quite so leafy part. Peggy, of course, had to read the estate agents' literature in her hospital bed.

By coincidence, John Mains, one of my Council colleagues rep-resenting the Hutchesontown ward, lived at number 28 Keir Street, and we moved into number 38. The flats were very big with enormously high ceilings and took a hell of a lot of decorating. When we bought the flat, the wiring was wall-mounted, so before I started on the never-ending painting and decorating I had to wraggle it in. It's remarkable how much energy you can muster when you're young and you have to. Somehow I managed to juggle my responsibilities at work with my Council duties, visits to the maternity hospital and painting endless high ceilings in Pollokshields.

By the time my turn to stand for election came round again, I was happily married, my new wife was expecting a baby and I was building our nest. Everything seemed to be going right, but in the election on 6 May 1969 I lost my seat. There was an ill omen: the weather on polling day was bad, and when I was out campaigning a little boy ran out in front of the car. Although I was crawling along, the car hit him. I was horrified. He seemed alright, but I decided that the best course was to take him and his mother to the Southern General, just to be sure. After waiting for a couple of hours, they confirmed that he was okay and no harm had been done. But when it was confirmed that I'd lost to the Tory candidate William Johnston, it seemed inevitable.

A few months later, my old Gorbals colleague Alice Cullen retired for health reasons. My childhood friend Frank McElhone, who rep-resented the Hutchesontown ward on the Council, was a popular figure in the Gorbals. He had a grocer's shop, which meant that local people had regular and easy access to their councillor. At the selection, Geoff Shaw and I stood against him, but Jimmy Wray, Frank's agent, made sure that the meetings were well stacked with Frank's supporters – in fact, I think there was a flurry of new memberships about that time. Frank was selected and won the by-election. When Frank gave up his Council seat, I secured the nomination. After a gap of nine months, I returned to the City Chambers on 20 January 1970. I was to defend this seat in May 1972 and held on to it until the abolition of the Corporation in May 1975.

Soon after my return to the Council, the Wilson government was defeated. The Conservatives' new housing legislation, the Housing (Scotland) Act, presented a major dilemma. The Act imposed regular increases in council house rents, over-riding the discretion of the Council. Rent levels were a major issue. Labour Party policy was that rents should be kept low, given the level of poverty and the need to avoid exploiting people at the bottom of the social scale – the kind of people who the Labour Party was there to defend.

The controversy over the Housing Act raged within the political parties and very strong views were expressed within the Council against the legislation. The Council's legal officers advised us that the imposition of the legislation was a matter of fiduciary responsibility. If we did not implement it, we would be personally liable. Michael Kelly had indicated that he would rather go to jail than implement the Act. His fellow councillor Gerry McGrath supported him. When it came to the vote in the Council, no Labour Group whip was imposed as this was a matter of individual legal responsibility. There was a general presumption that we would oppose the implementation of the legislation and the Tories would support it. However, Michael Kelly, seconded by Gerry McGrath, surprised us all by moving and seconding that the Council should allow this invidious legislation to be imposed on the people of Glasgow.

Despite these shenanigans, the motion against the Council implementing the new act was carried in a roll-call vote. We were, of course, putting ourselves in a very dangerous position. Several councillors transferred their assets to their wives in order to avoid the financial penalties which the Government was threatening to impose. I believe there was one instance where a member transferred his assets to his wife who subsequently decamped. Several people found that amusing; I suppose it wasn't so funny for him.

Eventually we were all surcharged for an extraordinary sum – about £18,000 each, I believe. Fortunately Labour won the 1974 General Election. But Willie Ross, the new Secretary of State for Scotland, did nothing to lift the financial penalties and it was only with the subsequent appointment of Bruce Millan that we were relieved of the liability. The basis of this decision was that we had acted in good faith which, indeed, we had.

My greatest success in this period was the pedestrianisation of Buchanan Street. I was Vice-Convenor of Highways. Steven Hamilton, who later became the Chief Executive, was a lowly town clerk at the time, and serviced the Highways Committee. Steven was one of those Council officials who would challenge elected members. Some of the longer-standing members of the Council didn't appreciate his attitude, particularly when he argued his case like an elected member, but I used to enjoy these intellectual tussles.

It was generally agreed that pedestrianisation of key city centre shopping streets would be good for the retailers. Sauchiehall Street and Buchanan Street were both considered. The priority was Sauchiehall Street, but our consultation with the traders was getting us nowhere. They held to the belief that unless people could drive past or park outside they wouldn't shop. But Buchanan Street, on the other hand, was much more achievable. So rather than wait for the Sauchiehall Street traders to decide that pedestrianisation might be a good thing, Steven Hamilton and I refocused our efforts on Buchanan Street. Of course, once this was pedestrianised, Sauchiehall Street soon followed.

I came to develop a great admiration for Steven Hamilton. He was an officer who would work very constructively with the members of the Council, although if he disagreed with you he would fiercely argue his corner. I was only too aware of the other type of council official who, rather than argue with elected representatives, went away and sabotaged good ideas. I suppose in this local government is no different from anywhere else. There are always those who, regardless of the potential benefits of change, try desperately to hold on to the status quo. These folk will give you a thousand reasons why you can't do something. Sadly there are far more of them than those who agree that something might be a good idea and help to achieve it. Once you make up your mind to do something, you can never be a hundred per cent sure that it's right. Do nothing, and you can be sure not to offend anybody. There's a lot of folk who don't like to cause offence.

In 1973 Peggy, who had continued to have nagging health problems, was taken into hospital to have a hysterectomy. She hadn't worked since Robert's birth. Between us I think we were doing quite a good job of bringing him up. Peggy always used to say that I was less nervous with Robert than she was. I think the reason was simply that home life was my relaxation. Spending time with Peggy and the baby was what I always wanted to do.

As I say, she went into hospital for a hysterectomy and they discovered once again that her health problem had been exacerbated by a small matter of being pregnant. Again, she was kept in throughout her pregnancy and for many weeks after Derek was born on 3 October 1973.

24

Peggy's Aunt Chris, who lived in London, came up to stay and, together with my mum and Dolly, helped to care for the children. Robert and Derek were probably the most pampered babies in Glasgow. After Peggy came out of hospital, her task was slightly easier as Robert had already started at primary school. I was out at a lot of meetings and I've always felt a bit guilty about giving too much time to politics and not enough to my family.

Like my own father, I tried to encourage the boys to read from an early age. Robert's first primary school was St Albert's in Pollokshields. I remember his teacher being greatly impressed when, after she had asked the class if anyone knew a story, Robert happily perched on the desk and retold my version of *Androcles and the Lion*.

When Derek was about a year old, we decided to move house. In Pollokshields we'd had the constant irritation, as owner-occupiers, of having to involve the factor whenever we needed repairs to the block. We found a new semi-detached house in Simshill, which would, we felt, give us more independence, more space for the boys and a little garden. We've stayed there ever since.

In 1975 local government was reorganised. A two-tier system was created which divided responsibility for services between districts and regions. It was an occasion of great political hiatus.

I thought deeply about standing for election to Strathclyde Region. I'd become increasingly preoccupied with housing. The campaign against the invidious Housing Act had reinforced my view that this was an area where ordinary people might all too easily be abused by government. We had to defend them.

The Wheatley Commission had concluded in 1969 that within the new two-tier system of seven regions and thirty-seven districts the regions would be responsible for housing, education and social work, in addition to the police, fire services and roads. The districts' remit would be cut to local planning, cleansing, parks, libraries and so forth. However, in 1971 the government transferred housing back to the districts. As housing was now to remain with the City, it was with great reservations that I competed for a Regional seat against Jim Wray. I was less than heartbroken when I lost as it meant that I could remain with the City.

In the previous year my old ally, Geoff Shaw, had become Leader of the administration. After his setback in 1967, he finally entered the Council in 1970. In 1972 after the sudden death of the then Lord Provost, John Mains, the then Leader, Bill Gray, decided to go for the Provostship. Geoff had become Senior Vice-Chairman of the Group, and a year later beat Dick Dynes for the leadership. It was an extraordinary and meteoric rise, but well deserved. Tom Fulton became Senior Vice-Chairman with myself as Junior Vice-Chairman. Or course, everything would change again with the advent of Strathclyde Region.

In the inaugural elections for Glasgow District Council in May 1974 I was elected to represent the Cathkin Ward, part of the Castlemilk area. I enjoyed a huge majority. The Labour Party had come out well ahead in both the regional and district elections, so we were jubilant.

One of my former colleagues in Hutchesontown, Cathy Cantley, kept the Hutchesontown seat in 1974. She had been an active member of the Constituency Labour Party for a number of years, and was an articulate and able member. She was also a personal friend. I had helped to get her a wee job as a cleaner in the shop. As it turned out, however, I was to discover that the trust I'd invested in Cathy was misplaced.

During that shadow year, there was one incident involving two of my councillor colleagues which was extensively reported in the press and, temporarily at least, took some of the shine off our recent success. On the evening of 6 January 1975 Dick Dynes and Gordon Kane had been dining together in the town, in the Vesuvio Restaurant. It was getting close to closing time and they didn't want to leave. Presumably, they were enjoying themselves too much and wanted to stay on for one or two further wee refreshments. It was alleged that Gordon Kane put his hand under the table, got dust on it, and then indicated that, if the restaurant was intent on them leaving, he would have no option as a senior member of the Council but to report them to the licensing board. It would have been a thinly veiled threat, and an abuse of his position. Both councillors denied the allegation.

The whole incident got substantial coverage in the press. I can't quite recall what the upshot was, but I do remember that their legal representative was Sir William Gray, Lord Provost at the time. It was resolved, and business continued as normal.

Given that Dick Dynes and I were rivals for the leadership, I might have made an issue of his conduct in the campaign. But my view was that, even if the story was true, these were two able individuals who had simply behaved with uncharacteristic arrogance, perhaps slightly the worse for having taken a drink or two. It would have been unfair to exploit such a minor incident for political gain.

In our elections within the new authority, Peter McCann became Lord Provost, Dick Dynes became Leader. Dick was a plumber by trade, compactly built and always dapper in appearance. However, in the role of Leader he became increasingly egotistical. Gordon Kane and I were voted Deputy Leaders. After the leadership election, I went off for a short holiday. I returned to find that the Labour Group had already determined the committee structure. I was to be Chairman of Housing, which suited me fine. In the Corporation, I'd been Vice-Chairman of Housing with Dick Dynes as the Convenor, so adjusting to my new role seemed fairly straightforward. I had no idea of just how challenging it would turn out to be.

CHAPTER THREE

In my new role as Chairman of Housing I felt that one of the key issues to be addressed was the feeling of isolation and lack of community within Glasgow's large housing estates. In places like Castlemilk, Pollok, Easterhouse and Drumchapel, it was clear that some people felt they didn't belong. These estates had been created with an extraordinary lack of imagination: far more effort seemed to have been given to meeting the government's quota for the numbers of houses than to creating genuine communities.

This lack of imagination revealed itself in the naming of the new developments. New estates in Easterhouse, for example, were not given new names. but simply numbers which corresponded to the phase of the overall development. So residents would live in Easterhouse Number One, or Number Two, and so on up to Easterhouse Number Six. It might as well have been called Stalag Luft 6 – the system was pretty dehumanising.

We did our best, we worked to create separate neighbourhoods within the large estates, where possible linking them with specific schools. We wanted to encourage people to identify more closely with their own locality. The hope was that if they felt a greater sense of ownership of their patch, they would be encouraged to work for the benefit of the area, and this in turn would create more of a sense of belonging.

A number of neighbourhood community organisations were developed, many of them meeting in the local school. We were able to help by publishing literature for distribution within each of these areas addressing local problems and issues, which again encouraged people to look after their own area. If people know the boundaries of their own neighbourhood and have some sense of how its problems might be solved, they have a common interest and tend to work together. The previous more remote 'big brother' organisation of these massive estates had been largely ineffective. People's problems, even within large new estates of similar housing types, were never identical. Local interest groups were needed to address the many unforeseen issues that would arise. By the time we became involved, there were entrenched problems within the estates. Many people had developed a defensive attitude to their own little patch, so building a new sense of community was going to be a long haul.

In the mid-seventies people didn't feel able to exercise enough control in the creation of their homes and environments. It was a time when the housing association movement was in its infancy. Raymond Young, whose influence on the development of community-based housing associations was immense, had written his architectural thesis on public participation in the planning process, and was working in Govan and changing things for the better. I think he had imported some of these new ideas from Canada.

As Chairman of Housing I was invited to open the first development by the Central Govan Housing Association at Luath Street. This was a very modest refurbishment of a tenement block, reorganising the internal configuration so that each house had its own facilities. The opening ceremony itself took place in the flat of a lady called Annie Gibbons. I didn't know it then, but the inauguration of Annie's bathroom was one of the defining moments for the housing association movement in the United Kingdom.

Although such refurbishment could lead to substantial improvement of individual flats, it struck me as a short-term fix, because many of the buildings in which the flats were situated could not be redeveloped to an acceptable standard. Compulsory purchase, demolition and rebuilding were often the only option in the case of tenement blocks that had been badly built to start with and were in an advanced stage of deterioration.

Glasgow Council owned 186,000 houses at that time. The management of such a huge stock was an incredibly demanding task and not one I felt that we were achieving in the best possible manner. Those who were employed within housing management rarely belonged to the communities they were dealing with, and didn't identify with the communities or their problems. I became extremely frustrated at the lack of a management system which gave people a stronger voice to deal with their own problems.

One night I was driving home listening to *Today in Parliament*. There was, of course, a Labour government at the time led by Harold Wilson, and the programme dealt with a new clause which had been introduced to the housing legislation, which concerned the establishment of housing co-operatives and the legal mechanisms for achieving them.

The next morning, I had a meeting with Jim Campbell, then the Clerk to the Housing Committee, and asked him to find out what the implications of this new legislation would be. He soon confirmed my view that we could now establish a meaningful co-operative enabling people to control both their own homes and their local environs. We agreed that an effective size for a housing co-operative would be about 250 homes. A smaller number would be unlikely to produce a meaningful co-operative – a recognisable community with which people could identify – which could exercise control over environmental standards, management and housing repairs. The next task was to identify a viable group of houses.

To convince an existing group of council tenants that they should rethink the basis of their housing tenure was unlikely to succeed. In the past, even relatively modest attempts to give people a degree of self-control had been viewed with extreme suspicion. I recalled an earlier initiative when I had tried to persuade the Housing Committee to allow people to paint their own doors and windows. Much of the Council's housing at that time was uniform and drab, and the fact that people were prevented from painting even their own front doors seemed absurd. The counter-argument from my colleagues was that giving people such freedom was potentially disastrous. They were preoccupied with the belief that you couldn't rely on people to have sufficient good taste to select colours which weren't garish. Someone even suggested that people might restyle their houses along sectarian lines, so we'd have orange colour schemes or attractive renderings in green, white and gold.

My attitude was that, given the freedom to decorate their houses, most people would endeavour to make them more attractive. It was thoroughly patronising to assume that people would make a mess.

Although the Housing Committee were not won over, they did agree to allow the measure in Castlemilk. What I hadn't anticipated was the level of resistance from the people there. The assumption was that a service which had previously been paid for by the Council was now being imposed on them, so my endeavour to give people a little bit of freedom led to a local furore. The measure was introduced in the end, but people were highly suspicious. Although some painted their doors, the majority seemed content to leave things as they were. It surprised me that people who believed in me enough to vote for me were unwilling to accept the offer at face value. It was the only time that I'd been accused of trying to sneak in privatisation by the front door!

In the light of this experience I knew that people would not necessarily look favourably upon the right to manage their homes. It was clear that we had to begin with new occupiers, and I asked the housing officers to identify a mixed group of 250 houses that would be completed in about a year's time. I felt we needed a year. Jim Campbell was a great officer and we worked on this together. It was proposed that this future co-operative would receive annual finance equivalent to the combined average management and repairs expenditure per house within our current stock. Those who elected to take a house within the co-operative would become jointly responsible for the management of their homes.

Once the officers had done their search for a suitable group of houses, they came back with a list of three options. One group at Darnley consisted of deck-access blocks which were not really suitable, while another at Berryknowes included a large number of flats for pensioners – not the mix that we were looking for. The group of houses we chose were part of a larger housing development at Summerston. Summerston was a new housing area in the north-west of the city with only a strip of greenbelt between it and the upmarket suburban areas of Bearsden and Milngavie. It consisted mainly of tenemental housing, but within this new development there was a grouping of 240 houses which formed a sort of separate enclave. Summerston was ideal because we were building identical housing in the same area, so we could offer people a choice, and this also gave us an opportunity to monitor the efficiency and effectiveness of our new management regime.

Those interviewed for the Summerston co-operative had risen through the Council's lists in the normal way. As we could offer them a choice of standard council tenure or participation in our co-operative experiment, nobody felt coerced. I invited the potential members of the co-operative to a meeting in the City Chambers. One of the group was Michael Buchanan, who went on to become chairman of the co-operative. He would later join the Labour Party and become a councillor for the Summerston area, and subsequently was to continue his work on housing co-operatives in Ayrshire.

What we were doing in Summerston was pioneering work. It was giving people the opportunity to show that they could manage their own homes and neighbourhood better than an inevitably more distant Council. The Council lacked sensitivity in the management of its homes. We hoped this bold experiment would enable people to create a housing service which answered their own needs. We also wanted to ensure it got a flying start before it was subjected to too much public exposure.

A press conference we held to publicise the initiative won substantial coverage. The Scottish Office was extremely interested. The legislation which had first prompted me to look into the formation of a co-operative in Glasgow had also caused co-operatives to be started up in two or three places in London. I discovered later that in London people on the housing lists were simply told that they were going into the co-operative. Our approach gave people the chance to say 'no'. I believe that if you want to empower people, you have to give them the choice. They have to opt in. Trying to coerce people into taking responsibility, even for something as important as their own homes, will never succeed.

I am pleased to say that Summerston was the first housing co-operative in the United Kingdom with central government approval. The Scottish Office studied the new style of housing management we had created and agreed that it should be recognised.

Of course, all this attention meant that my fellow councillors were taking note. But in my enthusiasm for the new concept, I'd neglected to outline our plans to the local councillor for Summerston, Dick Dynes, who was also the Leader of the Labour Group. In retrospect I suppose this omission was a little discourteous, and Dick made it quite clear that he wasn't at all pleased, but on reflection I don't think such substantial changes could have happened in my local area without my knowing about it, so perhaps he should have been paying attention.

The Summerston co-operative, once established, served as a good demonstration project. Instead of selling people an abstract idea, we could take them along to Summerston and introduce them to people who were living there and involved with the management of the co-operative.

Summerston spawned three other housing co-operatives in adjoining areas. We amended the procedure so that once the co-operatives were established, they were able to carry out interviews for vacancies themselves, selecting from the list of people qualified for a vacancy. Thus they applied their own experience to ensure that people who were coming to the co-operative understood and accepted the concept.

We also introduced a system whereby 25 per cent of the lets would be by the co-operative itself. In other words, the relatives of those who were already living within the co-operative could apply to go on to the co-operative's own housing list and, in turn, be interviewed for a place. One argument against this was that there was a risk that the co-operatives would gradually become ghettos divided on racial or religious grounds. But I pointed out we could redress the balance by retaining the right to approve the 75 per cent of applicants selected from the Council lists. Summerston never became a ghetto, and is still thriving.

Our success with this first co-operative led to a whole series of meetings with academics. Many of those we met had studied Danish housing co-operatives. It seemed that in Denmark housing co-operatives were such a frequent occurrence that many of those who lived in them didn't even know they were in a housing co-operative.

Some of the academics believed that to function effectively, co-operatives needed collective ownership. My view was that people wanted to ensure a high quality of environment, both within their homes and in the surrounding area, and to control the management and mainten-ance of the property. The ownership of bricks and mortar was quite irrelevant. But despite the evidence in Glasgow, many of the academics remained incredulous.

I was particularly proud of the Summerston co-operative. As a result of this achievement, a section in the housing department was established to promote co-operatives. Sometime later, Jim Campbell, the housing officer with whom I had worked so closely, praised me as the father of the Glasgow co-operative. 'Mind you,' he commented wryly, 'if you're the father, I suppose that makes me the mother – they're our baby.'

In 1976, some time before the 1977 Council elections, the housing manager Malcolm Smith approached me with a matter which, he indi-cated, was of great delicacy. One of the housing managers – whose name escapes me now – was being disciplined and was threatening to make some embarrassing revelations if the case went to a tribunal. This was, of course, the first indication I had of what was subsequently to be paraded in the press as the 'Cathy Cantley Affair'. My immediate response was that we had better investigate any possible irregularities in the housing department. If the aggrieved official was to raise anything in public, we should be fully armed with the facts.

As the 1977 elections approached, Dick Dynes became uneasy about the threat I posed to his leadership. My challenge was inevitable: my position in the Council was strong, and I had active support from a large number of my Council colleagues. So Dick ruled that members of the Executive should stand down from holding office and concentrate on the election. This process would, of course, exclude himself and he was to remain both Leader of the Council and Convenor of Planning. Dick would continue to have a public platform, while the rest of us focused on local matters in the crucial weeks before the elections. The only purpose of this 'smart ass' ploy – as the Americans would call it – was to take me out of the public eye. It was a clear indication that Dick was becoming increasingly worried about the level of support I was attracting within the Labour Group. The other, docile, members of the Executive who stood down from public office were never, to the best of my knowledge, asked to do anything in particular in relation to the election. Some, like pet poodles, did exactly what Dick told them.

I decided to resign from the Executive but carried on with my housing activities.

Soon afterwards the report I had asked for on alleged irregularities in the housing department was completed. Our officers identified *prima facie* cases which seemed to implicate several of my colleagues. Among these was my Vice-Chairman, Cathy Cantley. Her 'crime', typical of what was alleged, was that she had arranged a housing let for her son's girlfriend. The news was devastating.

The housing manager recommended that the investigation should be continued by the Chief Executive. I immediately agreed to this. He passed it to his Senior Depute, Charles Horsburgh. While it would have been expedient, given the impending elections, to have delayed the matter, I felt that as there were legal implications it had to be pursued.

Internal investigations within any large public body are, invariably, highly sensitive procedures. It is incumbent upon elected members and officers to ensure that the public interest is observed. In passing the investigation on to the Chief Executive's office, I was fully aware that in due course the Leader would be notified, but Dick Dynes' response surprised me, and, in my view, precipitated his downfall, and mine.

At the close of Council meetings, Dick was in the habit of inviting his closest Council colleagues and selected members of the press into the Lord Provost's office, which is rather grander than the Leader's room and has a bar. At the first such meeting after he had been notified of the investigation, rather than inform the press of the facts of the case, he alleged that I was involved in irregular activities.

John Lavelle, one of my Council colleagues, was in the Council corridor collecting material from his pigeonhole just by the door to the Lord Provost's office when John Enos of the *Daily Record* emerged, obviously agitated. He told John what Dick had said about me. John was horrified. He asked Enos if he had been given permission to publish this information. When Enos told him that there was no suggestion that it shouldn't be published, John asked him to go back into the Lord Provost's office to double-check. Dick Dynes' response was, it seems, unequivocal.

The next day the *Daily Record*'s headline story accused me of abusing my position as Chairman of Housing. The press furore had started – in those days, it wasn't called sleaze, as that particular catch-all had not yet been coined.

The irony of my having set up an inquiry to protect the Council and then myself being pilloried was, I suppose, an early lesson on the effect of a good story on the political process. It also taught me that engaging in an argument through the press and in full view of the public is rarely constructive. Dick Dynes had seen his political opportunity and gone for it. But he didn't spend enough time considering what the fall-out might be.

The mud-slinging between Dick Dynes and myself attracted massive headlines. The *Scottish Daily Express* came out and supported my position. Some time later, I asked their reporter, Charles Graham, why he had taken such a strong stand on my behalf. He told me that during one of the debates of the Labour Group on the issue, he had listened in from one of the adjoining committee rooms. He never revealed his source, but from then on the *Express* was unwavering in its support for my position.

The affair had escalated to an extraordinary degree and the accusations were flying, I felt that the only way to deal with the matter was to institute a public inquiry. This was approved by the Council just prior to the elections and Lord Mackay, then Dean of the Faculty of Advocates, took charge of the inquiry. The 1977 elections couldn't have arrived at a worse moment.

From the mid-seventies, the Scottish Nationalists had been making significant gains. Open warfare between two of the senior figures in the Labour administration could only help their cause. On 3 May 1977, the Nationalist Brenda Johnson defeated me in Cathkin by thirty-two votes. Dick Dynes, who had attempted to eliminate his competition for the leadership through vilification in the press, also lost his seat. Public slanging matches in the media are a poor way of scoring political points. The Labour Party won the election as the largest party but did not have an over-all majority.

Predictably, the Glasgow Labour Party suspended Dick Dynes and myself from the panel of candidates pending investigation. At my request my own constituency party set up a committee, and it reported in my favour. My next recourse was to appeal to the National Executive Committee, which established an inquiry. They also found in my favour. I was vindicated and the City Labour Party restored me to the panel of candidates.

The *Scottish Daily Express* reported under the heading 'A Welcome Comeback':

> Others in Glasgow who acted in haste only to live to repent are the Labour leaders who wrongly disciplined their former colleague Pat Lally, doubtless contributing to his defeat in last May's local elections. Now Party chiefs in London, as well as his local constitu-

ency party, fully exonerate him, and it will not be long before he makes his comeback in Glasgow, overcoming jealousies and personality clashes.

Citizens of all parties welcome his rehabilitation because Pat Lally has proved himself to be both an able and honest man, fit to be Party leader or, indeed, Lord Provost.

It was sad that his qualities won him more popularity among his political opponents and the public at large than within his own party. But for Mr Lally, integrity is the name of the game.

Those who jumped onto the then popular bandwagon and savaged him, had better mend their ways. It will be a new and better Labour Group when he returns to it.

But it was to be some time before I could make a comeback to the Council.

With Dick Dynes and myself off the scene, the very able Jean McFadden became Leader of the Council. She was obviously bright, and I had predicted that she would, in time, be one of the leading lights of the Council. However, her elevation was, perhaps, premature. Shortly after her election, she went into consultation with Geoff Shaw and his colleagues in the Regional Council, and with the Scottish Labour Party. For myself, I wouldn't have talked to this raft of outsiders – the only way to understand the mood of a council is to be within it. Having taken the wise counsel of her advisers, she decided to go into opposition.

In my view, this was a serious error. John Young, the Leader of the Tory Group, was certainly surprised to find himself leader of the administration.

Going voluntarily into opposition is madness. If you can hold the administration, even on a minority ticket, you have control of the Council's agenda. In such a situation implementing policies is certainly far from straightforward, but it is always easier to argue your case and to form alliances if you occupy the high ground.

During the period of the Tory administration, one incident occurred which would have a bearing upon my own future career. Because the Tories were a minority administration, there were occasions when crucial motions depended upon one or two votes. In one such case the Tories employed the dubious tactic of concealing the councillor for the Linn ward in the fireplace in the Chambers. Len Gourlay was a smallish chap, so it was possible for him to conceal himself beside the fireplace and behind the curved tiers of seating within the Council Chambers.

When the matter in hand came to the vote, Len Gourlay was spotted and rather naïvely posed for the press, earning himself the epithet the 'Tory up the lum'. All this would prove helpful when I later stood against him for the Linn ward.

During my 'sabbatical', I kept myself busy with constituency matters. I was, at one point, nominated for the Govan seat for the Regional Council, in competition with Iain Davidson, who won the selection and of course went on to become Govan's MP.

I had given up working in the shop in the mid-seventies, so, to pay the mortgage and support my wife and two young sons, I took a job at a Springburn social club. Helping to organise and supervise the club wasn't really my thing, so when it folded I decided to go back to what I knew best, and took a job in a menswear shop in Pollok Shopping Centre. It was much as I had been used to, selling jeans, t-shirts and casual gear, and, in addition, camping equipment. Even after I got back into the Council I carried on with the Pollok job, but in the early eighties the shop closed down. It has to be said that the demand for camping equipment in Pollok was not remarkably high.

My mother died on 10 January 1980. She passed away peacefully at home with my brother Robert and I at her bedside. She had long suffered from severe rheumatism and chronic anaemia, requiring weekly injections, but she never complained and had a great sense of humour.

I loved my mother and she set the standards by which I've tried to live my life. At first she didn't approve of my marriage to Peggy, I think largely because she felt insecure and threatened. She was, after all, losing one of her boys. But she came to love Peggy and they became very close. She also derived great joy from her grandchildren.

Just a couple of weeks before she died, she joined Peggy, the boys, my brother Robert and myself for Christmas dinner. She seemed happy and enjoyed herself despite being very fragile.

The night she died my brother and I sat by her bed all night. Her breathing, which had been very heavy, seemed to ease in the early hours of the morning. I thought she was settling into a more relaxed sleep when suddenly I realised she had gone. She was eighty-four years of age and had lived through hard times and a very difficult life. I sincerely hope that Robert and I had managed to make it up to her.

After my mother's funeral, I had to prepare for the 1980 Council elections. I knew I had a good chance of beating off my Tory opponent. In the 1977 election, Len Gourlay had enjoyed a majority of over a thousand. But after his antics in the City Chambers fireplace, his credibility was dented – or perhaps the word should be singed. The count was tight, but it seemed propitious that the election took place on May Day. I won by seventy-two votes.

When I arrived back in the Chambers, a number of my colleagues informed me that Michael Kelly had been seeking support for his election as Lord Provost. When in an aggrieved tone I said, 'You never contacted me', he replied: 'I didn't expect you to be here!' This doesn't say much for his political judgement, but many others on the Council shared his surprise.

Despite my past experience in the Council, after my return in 1980 the only committee role I was eventually given was the chairmanship of the South East Area Management Committee.

During the Labour Group's period in opposition, in order to achieve a consistent line in committee meetings, the Labour members had taken to having pre-group meetings to agree their strategy on key issues. When we were in control, these meetings should have been redundant. Instead, decisions were being made in advance of committee meetings, and without having recourse to the array of officers whose job it was to advise on agenda items. As we were in power with a substantial majority, this was simply daft.

I put forward a paper detailing these issues, and while my proposal was never formally adopted, in the course of time the pre-group meetings began to fall off. Of course, if there were disagreements in committee, I didn't see any problem with matters being referred up to the Labour Group, which gave people the opportunity to become better informed prior to the group meeting, and the group could make a decision on a more sensible and informed basis.

The area management committees were an innovation by Jean McFadden and a sensible one. The South East area covered Castlemilk, Rutherglen and Kings Park. Much of my time was spent encouraging the Scottish Development Agency to take stronger measures to attract investment to Cambuslang. The last vestiges of the ironworks were being cleared away, the SDA and the City were injecting money into the area to make it attractive for investment. I saw this as a key to providing employment for the South East area and also the East End of the city. Initially, the only proposals that came forward were for large-scale housing development, but my committee and I believed Cambuslang could be better used as industrial land, which the city was lacking.

In 1982 I was elected to the Executive of the Labour Group. In 1984, after the boundary changes which reflected the shifts in population within Glasgow and the reduction in the overall population, I stood for the first time for the new Castlemilk ward. I won by a huge margin of 1,664 votes. I became City Treasurer, a post which I was to hold for the next two years. By this time Margaret Thatcher had been in power for five years. After a honeymoon period of relatively moderate Conservative government, it was clear that she now regarded local authorities as the enemy. As we began to feel the squeeze on resources, the role of Treasurer became an increasingly influential but difficult one. It afforded me the opportunity to operate across the Council on the way policy developed.

Given the broad remit of local authorities and the restrictions imposed upon their funding, councils can work only at the financial margins. In order to introduce flexibility to make policy changes, I stipulated that the Council's officers should not only produce proposals which would reduce expenditure by up to 3 per cent, but also offer counter-proposals for increasing expenditure by up to 3 per cent. This gave officers and elected representatives flexibility in shifting resources from one area of activity to another. It also created a much less depressing scenario for officers, who were able to present arguments for spending more, however little, on special projects or deserving aspects of their activity.

One story from 1984 happened at the Sheraton Central Hotel in New York. I was sitting in this rather grand setting, a couple of hundred yards from Times Square, with the well-known Glasgow advertising executive John Struthers. We had just collected a Silver Medal for a 'Glasgow's Miles Better' audio-visual which John had created and entered in the 1984 New York Film and Television Festival.

I was deputising for Jean McFadden, who could not attend. It had been a last-minute invitation, and I had had to leave the day after receiving it. David Wiseman, who should have deputised, didn't have a dinner suit and couldn't go – fortunately, I had suitable attire and was selected.

John and I were sitting having a beer, celebrating our success. We were both quite elated, and John told me how the 'Miles Better' logo had been created. He and his young son Mark had been travelling on the London Underground when the idea for the logo came to him. He also told me of a friend who had sent him a tape of an interview with Michael Kelly on BBC London at the time of the Miles Better Campaign. When the interviewer asked where the idea arose, Michael claimed it was his. John was astonished. Shocked, I asked him what he'd done, and he said, 'Well, what could I do?'

John Struthers is a super guy who invested a lot of time and energy in the 'Miles Better' campaign. He certainly didn't get the credit he deserved for all he did for Glasgow. But I'm sure most people knew perfectly well who had created the logo of a lifetime.

By 1985, Jean McFadden had been Leader of the Labour Group for eight years. But the Group had changed. The redrawing of electoral boundaries had reduced the numbers in the chambers to 66, and while Labour held an impressive 59 of these seats, a goodly number of the new intake were rather to the left of Jean McFadden's particular style of socialism.

During the period of her leadership, the image of Glasgow had improved immensely. The city centre had been given a major face lift, particularly in the Merchant City; Glasgow now had its own major arts festival, Mayfest, which in time would come to rival the Edinburgh Festival in scale; and, of course, there was the opening of the Burrell Gallery, which, in its first year of operation, far outstripped Edinburgh Castle as Scotland's most popular tourist attraction. However, as Jean McFadden's then popular nickname 'the Duchess' implied, she had an autocratic style of leadership which concentrated decision-making within a narrow coterie of close confidants, who, like Mao's ruling clique, became affectionately known as the 'Gang of Four'.

I stood against her for the leadership on 29 May 1985. After eight years there was, I suppose, a 'better the devil you know' element in the voting, and she retained the leadership by four votes. This close call had been a warning shot, and I fully expected a change in the McFadden style, but as 1985 drew to a close it became clear that she meant to continue as she had before. References to Mrs McFadden's school-teacherly ways were frequent, although I'm sure the story about her asking a committee to raise their hands after they'd completed a particular task was apocryphal. Towards the end of the year, I circulated a discussion paper reviewing management issues, including the need to broaden the decision-making process within the Council and to redistribute responsibility to committees rather than the Executive or narrower groupings.

One frivolous distraction from the concerns of local policy and economics was the famous charity challenge football match between Glasgow District Council and Strathclyde Regional Council in early April 1986. I'm not quite sure who came up with the idea, although I have the impression that it was Hugh McRae, then the Glasgow Labour Group Whip – it seems consistent with his attitude. He and his colleagues set about arranging a suitable date.

A few of us decided to take the game seriously and we made arrangements to train at Firhill. Only four of us actually turned up, Bob

McKenzie, Bill Aitken and myself from the District Council and Pat Waters from the Region. If the truth is told, our major objective was not really to improve our proficiency, it was more an effort to become less unfit.

The game was played at the Crownpoint Sports Centre. I was in goal for the city. While it was a fun day, there were some very hefty tackles as both sides were very keen to win. There was one clash between Bill Perry of the Region and myself. Bill came racing towards my goal. He hit the ball a bit too far forward and I charged out to gather it. Bill's brakes were not too good and we clashed. I was all right, but Bill ended up in hospital with bruised ribs. Happily, it did not affect our friendship.

At the end of the match, the District Council won by four goals to nil. We were ecstatic. I was also delighted to be chosen as 'Man of the Match'. We never played another game as we were determined to retain our unbeaten record. The game was reported in the columns of the *Herald*, which pleased me. I don't often make the sports pages.

As the 1986 leadership election approached, I became increasingly confident that it presented me with a real opportunity to take control and to move Glasgow forward on a new agenda. But the day before the election, a number of senior representatives of the Scottish Labour Party, including the then Shadow Secretary of State for Scotland, Donald Dewar, made an unscheduled visit to the City Chambers to lobby in support of the Leader. They too had sensed that Jean McFadden's nine years of control over the Glasgow Labour Group was coming to an end.

It was, of course, quite outrageous that such a senior member of the Party should see fit to intervene in an election concerning an autonomous grouping within the Party structure. I don't know of any other local authorities where a candidate's friends in the upper echelons of the Party displayed such partisan and thoroughly inappropriate behaviour. He had from their university days onwards, been a friend of Jean McFadden. Some people unfairly attributed Donald's bias towards Jean as a pro-University educated snobbery against the ordinary working people who helped found the Labour Party and have traditionally been its strongest supporters. I disagree and have preferred to read it as loyal support for an old friend. After all, even great Ministers of State can be swayed by their fondness for their friends.

At the time, thankfully, Donald Dewar's interference had little or no bearing on the way members chose to vote. In fact, such an overtly partisan display from Big Brother Labour Party might well have worked in my favour. On 28 May 1986 I defeated Jean McFadden by thirty votes to twenty-seven and became Leader of the Glasgow Labour Group. Writing in the *Glasgow Herald*, Bill Robertson described my success as 'the greatest comeback since Lazarus'.

CHAPTER FOUR

It was vital, at the outset of my leadership, to set out my platform and to indicate through action that this was a genuine change in style and direction for the city.

My manifesto was straightforward. Glasgow was being blighted by a lack of capital investment, and I announced publicly that I had hopes for an early meeting with the Scottish Office in this regard. As the economic welfare of Glasgow was largely dependent on employment within the city, I was concerned that existing jobs should be retained and new jobs created for local people.

We'd already had substantial expert advice on Glasgow's housing problems. This was an area of particular concern, and an issue upon which I felt I could bring a lot of knowledge and experience to bear. I knew that people living in poor housing conditions didn't want platitudes. They wanted to see change.

I was also intent on changing the committee structure within the Chambers to create more direct and transparent lines of responsibility. Over the McFadden years, for example, the number of sub-committees of the Policy and Resources Committee had grown almost to the point of absurdity. While this gave councillors the illusion of an influential role, it was counter-productive and wasteful.

Many of my supporters at the time felt that neither Jean McFadden nor her supporters should be given any role within the new Council structure, but dismissing individuals with genuine talent seemed to me absurd. My view was that if people had a contribution to make, their talents should be exploited for the benefit of the city. In politics, opposition is healthy. Being in a position where everybody is in agreement all the time, apart from being very dull, removes a fundamental requirement of good government – healthy debate. Unless assumptions can be challenged, government is without rigour, which is contrary to the public interest. Shortly after my appointment, I offered Jean

McFadden the job of City Treasurer, a post which I was very happy she accepted.

In view of the city's financial situation and my stated aim of improving the city's finances, I quickly set up the Economic Development and Employment Committee. With this, along with the reduction in subcommittees and our new agenda, I had cleared the way for the endeavours to come. Malky McCormick celebrated my new management in a cartoon. A flattering caricature of me is depicted on the telephone. 'No it's not Bailie Jean, and cancel that state coach and send a taxi,' says the word bubble. To one side is the phrase: 'You'll now all get a Pat on your back.' Here I was launching a new era of consensual politics!

Something else of which I'd become aware during my time as City Treasurer was the need for Glasgow to broaden its outlook. We were operating within an increasingly influential structure of European government and, given the specialist nature of Glasgow's manufacturing by the 1980s, establishing favoured status trading connections internationally was becoming a priority.

While Glasgow's connection with the Chinese port of Dalian would not be formalised into a twinning agreement until the end of the following year, this connection, established by the then Lord Provost Bob Gray, fitted in neatly with my aspirations of creating strong international linkages.

Bob became Lord Provost at the same time as I was appointed City Treasurer in 1984. He'd met the Mayor of Dalian at a twinning conference in, I think, Sheffield. The Mayor subsequently visited Glasgow, and attended a Council meeting, at which he was introduced to the Council as a distinguished visitor, although he wasn't asked to speak.

While I could see the potential benefits of forming such international relationships, it was clear that Dalian was a long way off, and to establish a relationship would be expensive. I drew advice from a number of academics, including Bill Wallace and Henry Wong at Glasgow University, who had experience of China. I also attended a conference in London organised by the *Observer* newspaper in 1986 on trading with China, at which the speakers were Ted Heath and Jim Prior. The conference included contributions from major industrialists and retailers, and representatives of the Hong Kong Trade Development Office. I made a point of speaking to both Ted Heath and Jim Prior separately to seek their advice on whether formalising a relationship between Glasgow and Dalian was a good idea. Both considered China to be a potentially massive market for the UK, and felt that establishing contacts there could only benefit Glasgow.

Dalian is a city with a population of over 1½ million, directly responsible for a wider area of 6½ million people, with a degree of autonomy from the Chinese Government. If we were to consider a twinning arrangement with this potentially major ally, I was determined that it should be undertaken in a professional manner and we should be equipped to take advantage of the opportunities. Bill Wallace's aerial photographs of Dalian showed an impressive and diverse city, the breadth of whose economy extended from heavy industry to fish farming.

There were clearly opportunities for Glasgow's specialist equipment manufacturers. Howden Compressors were represented in Dalian, and Tom Gibson of the Gibson Group was in discussion with the city's representatives. Tom, who was personally friendly with Ted Heath, became involved in the design of coal-fired power stations and their implementation. Both of these Glasgow companies made further progress through the support of the Council. As far as more substantial exports were concerned, our subsequent representations on behalf of Tennent Caledonian seemed to prove highly beneficial to that extremely important Glasgow company.

Closer to home, we began to tackle the shortage of jobs in the city itself, and the serious shortfalls in our depleted coffers. The Economic Development and Employment Committee was chaired by David Wiseman, my Depute Leader. Its membership had some big hitters, including representatives of the Chamber of Commerce, the Scottish Development Agency and the trade unions.

The problems they had to address were substantial. Unemployment statistics published at the time made frightening reading – 40 per cent of the adult population in Calton was out of work. A number of the city's post-war housing initiatives had not been successful, and while the worst of them, including the notorious Hutchie-'E' blocks in the Gorbals, were scheduled for demolition, there was clearly a need for focused action within specific communities.

But there were bright spots. Soon after I became Leader, I was delighted to be able to celebrate the tenth anniversary of the housing management co-operative I'd established in Summerston. It seemed a fitting occasion for my first public address as the City's new leader. The co-operative's Chairman, Robert Tamburrini, confirmed that the Summerston community had consistently demonstrated its commitment to co-operative endeavour. My own comments, perhaps a little self-indulgently, described Summerston as 'a shining example of what can be achieved when a caring council and committed tenants combine to improve their quality of life'.

My early appeal to Malcolm Rifkind, then Secretary of State for Scotland within Mrs Thatcher's Government, seemed to fall on deaf ears. But the Economic Development and Employment Committee's endeavours started to show tangible results as early as September 1986. We were able to announce preliminary investment of nearly £2 million in housing improvements for Castlemilk and a broad range of initiatives intended to alleviate unemployment in the area of close to 40 per cent. We drew together numerous organisations in this scheme, winning the commitment of such bodies as Glasgow Opportunities, the Health Board and the Scottish Development Agency.

I was keenly aware that elected members of the Council have two clear areas of accountability – one to the city, the other to the people and area they represent. As a member assumes increased responsibility, it's easy for him to think only about the big, city-level picture and lose sight of grassroots issues.

The people of Castlemilk were a high priority. They elected me and trusted me to look after them. I tried never to let them down. I took the view that at the end of the day they would judge me on what had been done to raise standards and improve their quality of life. I believe that in the time I served Castlemilk the area has been transformed and everyone has benefited, although there is still work to be done.

While we created new jobs and better infrastructure and housing for individual communities, the bigger issue was how to use our limited powers to move the whole city forwards. One way of doing this was to continue to build upon our growing reputation as a centre for the arts.

During my period as City Treasurer, I had helped to consolidate the growing success of Mayfest, which had originally started as an extension of the traditional May Day Parade. Mayfest's grant had been fairly modest, I think £27,000, and the event ran for two weeks. I took the view that to create a wider impact it should run for three weeks. To encourage this and put the event on a stronger footing, we increased Mayfest's funding to £100,000, guaranteed for three years. This allowed the organisers to project activity into subsequent years and to attract performance on a much larger scale than before. The new funding was readily agreed to. They weren't very enthusiastic about extending the run to three weeks, but they did appreciate the hundred grand.

Then there was the Garden Festival. When the idea was originally mooted, it was scheduled to take place in 1989, but the fact that Glasgow's first great exhibition had taken place in 1888 made 1988 a much more sensible choice. Of course, this made the timing tight.

When the Garden Festival was offered by the Government, the City Council had at first wanted to hold the event on Glasgow Green, where some exhibits might remain to become a permanent feature of the city's life. However, this was turned down because the Government's policy was that the festival should contribute to the regeneration of derelict industrial land. The obvious site was the former docks stretching on the south side of the river westwards from the Kingston Bridge. It would be costly to clear and decontaminate the area, but its riverside location was highly visible, and offered tremendous potential for both the temporary delights of the festival and future redevelopment for housing or industry.

But before we could purchase the site, it was acquired for housing, by the developer, Laing, who then enjoyed the huge benefit of the public investment not only to clear and decontaminate the ground but to landscape it for the Garden Festival. When we were negotiating with Laing for the use of the site, they demanded off-set sites in the city, arguing that the Garden Festival would prevent them from developing their site for several years. My view was they had already had a very successful speculation and that we shouldn't contemplate giving them off-set sites. Time was against us, and as the Scottish Development Agency was keen on the site as the only truly viable location for the festival, we reluctantly acceded to Laing's demands, and the Agency put something like thirty-five million pounds into the development of the festival.

As the Leader of the Council, in order to see what we were letting ourselves in for, I visited the Stoke Garden Festival. The Stoke site was bigger than ours. There was a lot of green space between attractions, but it was drawing sizeable crowds. Yet although the Garden Festival itself was lively, little else seemed to be happening in the rest of Stoke, and there was no buzz in the city inspired by the Garden Festival. Their festival might have been on the moon for all it contributed to the vitality of Stoke itself. I happened to make a comment along those lines to Mark Fisher, not realising that he was MP for Stoke.

I worried about the same thing happening in Glasgow. To extract the greatest benefit from our Garden Festival we shouldn't simply see it as a sort of temporary up-market funfair, contributing only to the regeneration of its own site. What we had to do was run a parallel city festival alongside. If visitors who had enjoyed the Garden Festival also found that Glasgow was lively and interesting, then when the festival had gone they might still consider coming back to visit the city. The opportunity to achieve this goal was to present itself later in 1986, when the city received its next big prize.

We had Mayfest, and we were looking forward to the Garden Festival, when the head of the Greater Glasgow Tourist Board, Eddie Friel, came to me with another idea. Eddie felt that there was a substantial gap in Glasgow's music scene. We had a lively rock and pop scene. Country music and folk had their own venues, and we even had regular operatic performance, as the Scottish Opera was based at the Theatre Royal. But jazz was not at all well represented.

Eddie was keen that we should promote local musicians and attract international performers. His friend, Jim Waugh, whose alter ego was Radio Clyde's jazz DJ Nighthawk, and others had shown that there was a big potential audience for jazz. I myself had always liked Stan Kenton's progressive jazz, and the big band sounds of Count Basie, Duke Ellington and Harry James. I also enjoyed some of the great jazz vocalists, predictably Ol' Blue Eyes doing it his way, but also some of his female compatriots, including Billie Holiday and Bessie Smith. The idea of a jazz festival was a good one, as it would undoubtedly expand our cultural range.

In September 1986 we announced that Glasgow's first ten-day-long jazz festival would take place in 1987 with, we hoped, more than sixty events. The Lord Provost would be Patron of the Festival, and I would be Chairman of the Board.

The following month, I was able to enjoy the biggest coup of my first year as Leader when it was announced that Glasgow had beaten off stiff competition from eight other British cities, including Edinburgh, to take the title European Capital of Culture for 1990. Our bid had been written up by David Ferguson, a brilliant officer in the Town Clerk's office, who then moved on to the Confederation of Scottish Local Authorities. Sadly, he was later killed in a car accident – a great loss to Scotland. After we'd submitted our original documentation the adjudicators of the award sought further information, and we eventually submitted two fairly substantial documents.

Shortly before the announcement we got a phone call from Michael Kelly. Having served as Glasgow's Lord Provost, he had moved out of local politics and was working as a public relations consultant. In this role he was representing Edinburgh, the other front runner for the Capital of Culture crown. He suggested that we should announce that Glasgow and Edinburgh were amalgamating their bids. This simply served to confirm my view that we were winning. He'd contacted the Town Clerk's office, and I was asked to give my response, which was fairly succinct: 'Tell him to get lost.' I suspect that the officer concerned was a little more diplomatic when conveying the message.

Whatever the reason, I was fairly confident that Glasgow would beat off the opposition. Mind you, I'm confident about a lot of things that don't happen.

In winning the title, Glasgow joined a distinguished list of previous capitals of culture: Athens, Florence, Amsterdam, Berlin and Paris. But I had no doubts about our fitness to be part of this august company. The Arts minister, Richard Luce, came to Glasgow to announce our success. His comment was simply that Glasgow had put forward the best case. By contrast, the Lord Provost of Edinburgh, Dr John McKay, did not share his leader Lesley Hinds' aspiration for more harmonious relations between Edinburgh and Glasgow. He announced that the decision was 'political and vindictive'. For myself, I felt that Glasgow had achieved something of real world importance which, properly exploited, could change the perception of the city permanently. This was the funeral service for Glasgow's old image, I remarked, and I meant it.

The City of Culture award was, like the Garden Festival, another opportunity to create long-term benefits. Unlike larger centres of population, where shows and theatrical performances are put on year round, in Glasgow even in the late 1980s, the theatres went dark in the spring and didn't reopen until September. Tourists visiting Glasgow in the summer would find the place closed. The appointment of Bob Palmer as Director of Festivals in April 1987 was a major step towards ensuring that Glasgow's cultural scene would be lively twelve months a year. In addition to running the city festival during the Garden Festival and co-ordinating Glasgow's year as European Capital of Culture, our new Director would also be involved in encouraging existing organisations to operate during the summer.

While we were busy creating new cultural opportunities and enhancing the attractions of the city centre for local people and tourists alike, the day-to-day business of the City Council – matters of economy, employment and housing – continued. A major preoccupation was the Grieve Inquiry into the condition of Glasgow's housing, which had been commissioned by my predecessor.

Professor Sir Robert Grieve was a gentle and humane man with a very sharp mind and a pawky sense of humour. Like myself, he had been brought up in a Glasgow room-and-kitchen tenement flat, in his case in Maryhill. His career was highly distinguished, and he'd been both Chief Planner for Scotland and the first Chairman of the Highlands and Islands Development Board. He had impeccable credentials for reporting on Glasgow's housing and provided an independent voice respected by civil servants and politicians alike.

The inquiry had heard evidence from community organisations and from the Council. Grieve concluded that 40,000 of the city's houses were at risk, unless they could be improved within the next decade. He estimated that £3 billion was needed to bring Glasgow's housing stock up to standard, and he recommended that the city's capital debt be written off, which would raise £60 million per annum to reinvest in our housing stock.

The Conservative Government had recently written off London Underground's debt of over £700 million. This seemed a good precedent, but in spite of Sir Robert Grieve's considerable authority, the Government, with its obsessive preoccupation with owner occupation, totally ignored his report. In fact, they actually cut back their support for housing in Glasgow in 1987, a cynical and vengeful act which added to the city's problems and the misery of many of our council tenants.

Housing was far from the only area in which we were having financial difficulties. We were working hard to prepare for our 1990 celebrations, and top of our list of priorities was the building of a new concert hall in the city centre. It had been on the Council's agenda ever since Glasgow's superb concert hall, the St Andrew's Halls, had burned down in 1962. As City Treasurer, in the mid 1980s I had sat on a committee with the then Leader, Jean McFadden, Iain Dyer, then Leader of the Opposition, Tony Wheeler, representing the Royal Fine Arts Commission, and the architect Sir Leslie Martin.

Sir Leslie's design had been worked up over this period to the point that we were satisfied that it suited one of the most prominent sites in the city, at the head of Buchanan Street. The process of refining the design had not been easy. Despite the fact that Anthony Wheeler was an architect, was in the Royal Fine Arts Commission, subsequently became Chairman of the Royal Scottish Academy and was awarded a knighthood, his contribution, in terms of helping the lay members of the committee to understand Sir Leslie's design, was less helpful than I had hoped. However, it was important to have the Royal Fine Arts Commission at the table, and at least he wasn't raising major objections.

The two aspects of the design which we were uneasy about were the roof and the approach from Sauchiehall Street. The drawings suggested that the roof would be massive and form a prominent part of the view of the hall. But Sir Leslie was able to reassure us that this impression was misleading and that from most angles the roof would not be seen. Sir Leslie Martin was one of the most distinguished architects of his generation: he had been involved in numerous educational and cultural buildings, including his museum for the Gulbenkian Foundation in

Lisbon and, closer to home, the new headquarters of the Royal Scottish Academy of Music and Drama, which was opened in 1987.

He described his design for the concert hall as post-modernist, although in the view of the committee, his design for the approach from Sauchiehall Street was less post-modern than post-fascist. A ramp lined with columns led visitors up Sauchiehall Street to the hall. This aspect of the design was just a bit too Albert Speer for comfort, and was revised at an early date.

Although we had agreed the design by the time I took over as leader, the finance was still a huge problem. We had the insurance pay-out from St Andrew's Halls, which, as it had been gathering interest for a quarter of a century, was now quite a tidy sum. But we still had to finalise the sale of the adjoining site. There was a provisional agreement with the City of London Property Company that they would buy it for retail development, and to make any progress we had to assume that this money was as good as in the bank. The vision was a major complex which would bring together a shopping centre, the concert hall and associated bars and restaurants. Spilling out on to a pedestrianised streetscape, it would create new economic vitality in this key location.

But even with the developer's money and £6 million from the insurance payment, we were still well short of the target, as the estimated cost of building was well over £20 million. At that time, our capital allocation for non-housing activity was a miserly £2.3 million – in a good year we might get £3 million. As we needed to raise £10 million, we had a major problem. As I moved towards the end of my first year as leader, we were heading for a fight with the Government.

CHAPTER FIVE

People seem to think that every time there was a Glasgow leadership election there was a ding-dong battle between Jean McFadden and myself. In fact, from my success in 1986 until Mrs McFadden took the leadership in 1992, I was unopposed as Group Leader in four out of five leadership elections. In May 1987 I was the sole nominee, so it was business as usual.

Cultural matters were high on the agenda. As already mentioned we had appointed Bob Palmer to the post of Director of Festivals. His experience was invaluable. Canadian by birth, he had worked on arts festivals in Canada and with a number of festivals and cultural institutions in the UK. His move to Glasgow followed a period as Dance and Drama Director of the Scottish Arts Council. I had chaired the committee which appointed him, and felt that this was an individual who could create the city festival which we needed in 1988 and work up to what would be one of Glasgow's most momentous years in 1990.

While we planned our impending festivals and tried to secure the necessary finance for the new concert hall, our established programme of events was continuing. Mayfest that year was better than ever, although I had a bit of a set-to with the then Director of Museums, Alistair Auld, over the fact that his department had nothing special organised for what had become a significant annual attraction.

Our limited powers as a local authority and the constraints of government finance meant that improving the fortunes of the city was a slow process. As Leader I quickly realised that we needed to change the profile of the city, locally, nationally and internationally to achieve real and permanent improvement in the circumstances of local people. Our emphasis on culture created a more user-friendly city centre and generated new business start-ups and new investment.

The obvious objection to expenditure on the arts is: 'Why are you spending all this money on museums, festivals and concert halls when our houses still have leaky roofs?' But very often the local authority is not in a position simply to reallocate funds, much as it might like to, and the key point is that without attracting business to Glasgow money spent on repairing houses is a short-term solution. The vital goal is to ensure that people have jobs, so that they can pay their rent and the city can afford to improve its housing from its own resources.

At this time our major weapon against the Government on the housing issue was the Grieve Report. Malcolm Rifkind, then Secretary of State for Scotland, continued to refuse to meet councillors or tenants' representatives to discuss the issues which Sir Robert's report had raised. It was only when we threatened to lobby the Tory conference that he indicated that he was studying the Grieve Report and needed time to consider its findings. Later in the year, we saw Lord James Douglas Hamilton, the Scottish Office Minister with responsibility for housing, and had what the Government described as 'a useful meeting'. But privately Sir Robert Grieve and I felt this meeting had been a complete waste of time. I felt that the Government's offer to establish a joint working party on the issue was merely a ruse to prolong the debate and continue their policy of ignoring Glasgow's housing problems.

In 1987, a specific housing issue became the focus of considerable public debate and coverage in the press. Ever since 1981, the Hutcheson-town 'E' development, an unattractive estate of 800 concrete deck-access houses, had been lying empty. Their architectural style was described as Brutalist, which also summed up the experience of the people who had to live in them.

These houses were among the worst examples of developer system building. They dated from the early seventies, and had been opened by the Queen in 1972. From the word go they'd been cold and damp. As they were so new, several reports were written and various attempts made to refurbish them. People are always reluctant to demolish anything new, as it just doesn't seem to make sense, but the traditional methods of treating condensation with heating and ventilation would not work in these buildings. I remember suggesting that the amount of heating and ventilation required to keep these buildings dry would be like forcing people to live in a wind tunnel.

As I say, the Hutchie 'E' development, as it was known, had been lying empty and a deal was made with a development consortium to demolish the blocks and build new housing and retail on the site. But like all developers, the consortium was trying to squeeze as much return out of its proposals as possible. Originally they proposed 200,000 square feet of retail for a housing site which Strathclyde Region's Structure

Plan had designated as suitable for 20,000 square feet of retail. Planning permission was inevitably refused. The abandoned houses remained an eyesore and although fenced off were becoming dangerous. Local children were getting through the security fences, so the buildings were representing a genuine risk. The fact that thieves had pulled off wall panels to remove copper wiring created another danger, since the panels contained a high proportion of brown asbestos. The site had effectively been turned into a potential death trap. The Council had no option but to insist that the developers proceed with the demolition.

We had a legal agreement with the developers that they would demolish the blocks and redevelop the site, but as planning permission had been refused and planning terms couldn't be agreed, there was an impasse. We demanded that the developers start the demolition within twenty-eight days, or we'd do it ourselves. We also greatly increased the level of security on site. The *Evening Times* ran a vociferous campaign that helped to keep the matter in the public forum, and ensured that every mother in the Gorbals warned their weans within an inch of their lives not to go anywhere near the site.

Our demolition ultimatum was against the terms of our agreement with the developers, but I believed that circumstances had changed and that the public interest overrode any fine legal considerations. I made it quite clear that if we proceeded with the demolition and the developers wanted to sue us they would just have to go ahead. Our negotiations to find an acceptable legal solution continued and, as it took longer than our four-week deadline, demolition of Hutchie 'E' began on 22 June 1987.

Frank Lafferty's company had been one of the developers in the consortium, and went bust in August 1988, a little over a year after the whole Hutchie 'E' débâcle. He had been highly successful in Glasgow and had undertaken a huge amount of work over the previous decade. He had also been very generous to the city. His firm cleaned the front of the City Chambers during Michael Kelly's Lord Provostship and charged just one penny. When his company's insolvency was declared, they had around £9 million worth of Council contracts. It was a typical developer scenario: such companies grow during housing booms, become over-ambitious, over-stretch themselves and then collapse.

Hutchie 'E' was a salutary experience. The Gorbals of my youth had been swept away, but the solution to its overcrowding and inadequate housing conditions had simply not worked. The District Council could ill afford the additional debt that was being imposed by the mistakes of too recent history. Our income from domestic rates was far too low to support the services it was meant to fund. The Tory Government was aware of this, but their solution to the problem was both unworkable and unfair.

Marsden Pirrie, who headed up the Conservative Party think tank, had been promoting the introduction of a poll tax. The Scottish Conservative Party thought it was a marvellous idea, and sold it to Mrs Thatcher, who proceeded to impose it first on Scotland, bringing near disaster upon the Government and the local authorities. The tax was uncollectable and didn't deserve to work.

One of the most invidious aspects of the Poll Tax was the Government's insistence that the local authorities should act as collection and policing agencies. It was quite clear that Scotland was being used to test out the new tax – after all, the Tories had few further votes to lose in Scotland.

Treating people across the board as equals in terms of the amount of tax levied was grossly unfair. Those on the extreme left of the Labour Party advocated a 'can't pay, won't pay' stance. Although this might have had a moral justification, I felt that it would simply get people into trouble that they couldn't handle. Many of those who refused to pay might well have merited a rebate; instead, they would end up paying the full tax with penalties.

While the advocates of 'can't pay, won't pay' achieved a short-term popularity, the suffering they imposed upon many people who were already struggling was utterly unjustifiable. I felt that the fight should be between the local authorities and the Government, who were, after all, expecting us to act as their agents in imposing an unfair tax. We weren't prepared to tell people not to pay; instead, we were saying to the Government, 'It's your tax, so you collect it!'

In November 1987 Glasgow District Council voted that it was not prepared to collect the Poll Tax. On the same day Scotland's churches announced their own joint campaign against it. The momentum was building against what was arguably the most absurd measure in Margaret Thatcher's long career of creating absurd legislation. The issue would rattle on for quite some time, but the District Council, by refusing to bow to the Government's demands, was at least making nails for the Poll Tax's coffin.

My next minor skirmish with the Government was a rather odd literary diversion for a local authority leader. Peter Wright's book, *Spycatcher*, had been banned as a breach of the Official Secrets Act. But I believed that what the book had to say about the relationship between the Government and the people was so important that the people of

Glasgow were entitled to know and Peter Wright was entitled to speak out.

The fuss started because we tried to obtain copies of the book for the city's libraries. Then on a sunny Friday towards the end of August, I read extracts of *Spycatcher* in George Square, beneath the statue of Robert Burns, whose advocacy of free speech and scorn of petty government made this spot particularly appropriate.

It has to be said that the press didn't really get all these literary allusions, nor, sadly, did they echo our view that the banning of *Spycatcher* was a threat to democracy. My Tory colleague on the Council, Bill Aitken, did react to our gesture, but his comment in a television interview that there was something wrong with 'some odious little squirt making a few bob' (I assume he was referring to Mr Wright!) also seemed to miss the point. The press concentrated on the fact that the reading hadn't drawn a large crowd, but we did, I think, make the point that Glasgow was one place in the United Kingdom which was prepared to take a stand against oppressive government.

Towards the end of 1987 our biggest fight with the Tories was hotting up. Malcolm Rifkind declared that he did not see the need for the new Glasgow concert hall to be completed by 1990. No additional Government funding would be allocated, and, even worse, he refused borrowing consent, although we had a viable project with well over half its finance in place. The Government adamantly refused to grant the simple permission which would allow work to proceed. The clock was ticking, and time was already short for a project of this scale and ambition.

In normal circumstances, the Council would have realised some of its assets. Local authorities have substantial holdings of land and property. While some parts of this property bank have to be held within the Council's portfolio in order to be effectively managed to produce maximum public benefit, there are other properties, usually in more prosperous areas, which can be disposed of with the assurance that the jobs they house will be sustained. But Rifkind seemed immovable. On 19 October, *The Times* recorded that 'the 2,500 seat hall will almost certainly not be completed by 1990'.

Something had to be done to break the stalemate. I felt that the shortfall of about £10 million was too much of an obstacle for the Government to allow the additional borrowing. The financial argument would be strengthened immensely if we could reduce it to a much more modest amount so that instead of about fifty per cent of the required total, a much more modest figure was required.

Somehow, we had to find something over £5 million to create a situation in the press and in the public mind so that the Government would look very petty if they didn't allow us the little extra that we needed. Property disposals were the answer, but some of my Council colleagues were highly resistant. I remember Patricia Chalmers, who some years later was to become Secretary to the Labour Group, was vociferous in her objection to land sales. Pat Chalmers was a school teacher at Notre Dame, Glasgow's only all-girl comprehensive. An energetic redhead of Irish extraction, she has always been a lady of strong views. Pat has the infuriating habit of carrying her Council papers round in a polythene bag which she frequently leaves behind. She is a committed and dedicated councillor with a heart of gold. On land sales Pat had a point. One should always try, as far as possible, not to dispose of the family silver, but this was a necessity, the only way we were going to lever the much needed concert hall into being.

The Scottish Development Agency, our major partner in the Garden Festival, was very sympathetic. The executives there understood that the concert hall was required not merely as another jewel in Glasgow's cultural crown, but as a major component in our economic drive. To attract the new investment we needed, our programme of festivals and events had to continue, and for this we needed first-class conference and performance facilities. The Agency agreed to purchase a number of sites, primarily in the Merchant City, to help boost the process.

On 6 November 1987, the *Scotsman* announced 'Glasgow produces a £5 million miracle'. In fact, we had raised £5.2 million in land sales, reducing the concert hall deficit to £4.8 million. Now the Government had little option but to help fund this figure, which was about a fifth of the total cost of the concert hall. If Malcolm Rifkind said no to that, he was going to look very churlish indeed.

The developers had been searching, it seemed for years, for an anchor tenant to enable them to move ahead with the development. They were to pay, I think, £10 million in total, comprising £8 million for the site running east and south of the concert hall and £2 million for the shops under the hall. I became thoroughly exasperated and insisted that they pay the money forthwith or we would re-advertise the site. 'If they're speculative developers,' I declared, 'they bloody well ought to start speculating.'

The developers' response to my ultimatum was to offer us the cash on condition that we returned it if they were unable to get a tenant. This was unacceptable to us and we decided to put the site on the market in January 1988. I had a feeling that we hadn't seen the last of the City of London Property Company, and indeed soon after the new year, they came back with a solution which provided the money with no strings attached. Galvanised into action by our threatened disposal of the site, they found themselves a partner, Grosvenor Square Properties, which put up the money for the development, while they themselves moved into a consultancy role with which they were much more comfortable. Around the same time our Director of Finance, Bill English, finalised the details of a mechanism to help overcome our impasse with the Government.

Instead of the concert hall being a Council venture, a new company, Glasgow Cultural Enterprises Limited, would be established, funded by grant monies from the Council and borrowing against the security of the concert hall building itself. The Council grant would of course consist of the £10 million land lease from the developers, the £6 million insurance pay-out for St Andrew's Halls and £5.2 million from our land sales to the Scottish Development Agency.

By February 1988, the concert hall had the go-ahead. Surely building it in thirty months would be a lot less trouble than raising the money had been, even if completing such a big project so quickly had never been done before. It would turn out to be a huge challenge. It was to prove a great deal more challenging as the process developed.

A number of other notable incidents occurred through the latter part of 1987. In August we invited Margaret Thatcher to visit Glasgow. I felt that she had to see Glasgow for herself to understand its special problems, particularly those concerning housing.

Whether she took our invitation as a challenge I don't know, but on 4 September Margaret Thatcher did visit Glasgow. I felt that her attitude was very arrogant. She ignored the Council completely, seeming to have as little regard for my Tory colleagues as she had for the rest of us. She didn't even meet them.

She did go along to Howden, a specialist engineering company with a worldwide reputation which has long been a credit to the City of Glasgow. She announced to cheers an order for two boring machines for the Channel Tunnel worth £15 million. I imagine that after our invitation she probably asked her mandarins if there was anything good she could announce in Glasgow to generate a bit of positive publicity and put us in our place. I can't say her visit gained her much respect from yours truly.

Something which should have been a great deal more upbeat but went very wrong was our Christmas market in George Square. Glasgow was twinned with Nuremberg, and I'd been over a couple of times at

Christmas time. Nuremberg has a market in the main square in front of the cathedral every Christmas. It's an ancient tradition and the stalls sell only Christmas food, special gifts and decorations. People drink gluhwein, eat local delicacies like Nuremberg sausages and sauerkraut, and the event is of a very high quality, great fun and a tremendous boost to the local economy.

I'd observed that Nuremberg drew literally millions of visitors to its market. They come from all over Germany, the rest of Europe and the United States, and they all enjoy the market and spend money in the city. One little irony which I appreciated was the fact that Hitler's Nuremberg Rally ground is used as a car park, which seems a fitting downgrading.

Having studied the Nuremberg market, I became convinced we could establish a similar market, using stands of the same design, and as long as it was of the appropriate quality there was no reason why it wouldn't be a great success. When it was mooted, relatively early in 1987, there were immediate complaints from stallholders at the Barras, Glasgow's traditional East End weekend market, but I responded that this was very different. Even if there were only six specialist stalls in the first year, the market would bring people into the centre of Glasgow and bring new business to the city. The Nuremberg market filled up the department stores and I was sure that there would be extra benefits, even to those who were complaining.

When the market was being set up, I led a trade mission to China. We had just, at long last, signed our twinning agreement with Dalian. The city's status as a special economic zone reinforced our view that this link had significant potential benefits for Glasgow. As Ewan Marwick, the brilliant Secretary of the Glasgow Chamber of Commerce, who sadly was to die later in a tragic car accident in Moscow, argued at the time, the Chinese were mightily impressed by our civic delegation, as our agreement was among the few connections which had then been created with the West. They were immensely flattered and we translated this feeling into tangible economic connections with Glasgow. Just a few years earlier the notion of Glasgow being twinned with a port in the north-east of China would have seemed absurd, but now Dalian could join our other twin towns, Nuremberg in West Germany and Rostov-on-Don in Russia.

I came back from China on something of a high. We had been greeted with great celebrations and I'd even managed to give interviews to the *Hong Kong Standard* and live on local radio, giving Glasgow just a little bit more international promotion. When I saw what had been done in George Square I was horrified. The quality was no better than that of an average street market anywhere in the United Kingdom, which is pretty poor.

My aspiration to create something like Nuremberg's annual Christmas glory had been translated into something cheap and tawdry. The criticism started to build, and I could do nothing but agree. There was nobody more unhappy about the whole affair than myself, and I was very angry. We'd bought seventy-five stalls so they could be erected as required. Our idea was that, had the Christmas Market been the tremendous success that it should have been, they could have been reused, perhaps even brought out at other times of the year.

I realised that a tactical withdrawal was the only course of action, so I asked that the market be removed and that the stalls be donated to a suitable cause. In the end they went to Armenia, to provide shelter for earthquake victims. It was, I suppose, a worthwhile humanitarian contribution from the City of Glasgow, but the Christmas Market idea was killed off for good.

CHAPTER SIX

Our fight with the Government over the introduction of the Poll Tax rumbled on into 1988. In April the Council presented a united front at a press conference when we posed with a giant mock-up of the Poll Tax registration form stamped with 'return to sender'. We asked Glaswegians to follow our lead and send the form back requesting more information. We were concerned to protest as vigorously as we could but to remain on the right side of the law.

On the Poll Tax we were taking as hostile a position as we could, and one which was entirely in line with Labour Party policy. Later in the year, Donald Dewar, the Shadow Scottish Secretary, confirmed that the Labour Party in Scotland would not be leading a campaign of civil disobedience. His comments focused on the fact that if Labour had real aspirations to government, it could not repudiate its obligations under the law. He was quoted in the *Scotsman*: 'You can't argue for the rule of law when the right people are in charge, and have the luxury of picking and choosing when they are not. A party which takes this course forfeits respect.' I had to agree with him. Those protesters who advocated non-payment had failed to suggest any means of protecting people from the consequences of this action.

The Poll Tax was to continue as an issue for some time to come. Unquestionably it helped to improve the standing of Labour in local government. When in late April I called for Glasgow to be declared a Tory-free zone, it was not just propaganda. We felt that the Scots were thoroughly disillusioned with a government that seemed to pay scant attention to their problems. In the City of Glasgow, it had ignored our pleas on housing and on infrastructure; while it was happy for us to win cultural laurels. The Secretary of State's inflexibility over additional funding for the concert hall and our upcoming year as European Capital of Culture just added to the general sense of disillusionment.

There were two particular issues on which we were forced to take a stand. One was a fundamental matter of housing legislation, the other a minor skirmish on an important point of principle. The Tories, having passed the so-called 'Right to Buy' legislation, were pushing hard for the sale of council houses. The strong implication of their rhetoric was that until you owned your own home, you didn't really qualify as an achiever. It didn't bother them that this was forcing many people into mortgage debt and maintenance burdens that they could ill-afford.

Resistance to the legislation on our part had, of course, proven futile, and the Government had railroaded it through in its usual manner. However, council house sales represented a major problem as far as the City Council's own maintenance of its stock was concerned. We took the view that it was unfair for people to wait for their houses to be improved from the public purse and then to purchase them at discount prices. If council tenants wanted to own their own houses, then they should declare this up front. We suggested that if people did not make such a declaration prior to major housing improvements, they should be required to wait for ten years or pay a suitable proportion of the repair cost pro rata with the number of years left until the ten years were up. Tenants were, after all, benefiting from very substantial discounts, which already represented a major loss to local authorities.

The Secretary of State, Malcolm Rifkind, decided to order a public inquiry on the matter, and we moved for a judicial review to examine our position. It was simply absurd that people were buying their improved homes with a discount of, in some cases, up to 70 per cent, and there was no mechanism for adding the value of improvements to the purchase price. It amounted to a straightforward levy on our other tenants.

The other skirmish at that time was with the Department of Transport, over the riverbuses which were being established to take people from the city centre to the Garden Festival. For years people had complained about the way the city had turned its back on the Clyde. Now, when we were creating a magnificent visitor experience in the form of the Garden Festival, right beside the river, the Government was proposing to deny people the simple pleasure of travelling on it. A riverbus service was available in many other European cities and we were determined not to be thwarted by petty bureaucrats. Along with our partners Clydeport and the independent operators who were going to run the service, we'd invested half a million pounds in a valuable addition to the Garden Festival event. Given that only fifty boats a year used the section of the river in question, and there was always plenty of forewarning, the Department of Transport's argument that the riverbus would be a 'danger to shipping' was just nonsense. This was an extreme example of pen pushers exercising obscure powers.

As I had done a year earlier in the case of Hutchie 'E', I made it quite clear that the threat of legal action would not stand in the way of the Council doing what was best for local people. Yet again, this time in a situation which seemed absurd by comparison, we had to stand up and be counted, although I suppose our adversary on this occasion was far more powerful. My rejoinder to the Department of Transport's threats was a simple 'take us to court'. Happily, the matter was rapidly resolved. The Department of Transport backed down and the riverbuses ran throughout a long and glorious summer.

In the council elections that year we won sixty out of sixty-six seats, the highest majority in the City's history, nearly achieving my aspiration of a Tory-free zone. The official opposition consisted of four Tories and two Liberal Democrats. The Scottish National Party came a good second in many seats, but failed to win any. One notable newcomer was a fairly callow youth, Francis McAveety. Frank, a school teacher, was later to become one of the best-known players in Glasgow politics. Tall, slim and dark-haired, he would become Leader of Glasgow City Council and, latterly, a Member of the Scottish Parliament. He is also known for his interest in music – he plays the guitar and is known for his fabulous record collection.

On matters cultural, we were moving ahead. On a rainy day in mid-April I had the considerable pleasure of cutting the first sod on the site of the concert hall. The symbolic act was carried out with the assistance of a pile-drill. I was happy to use the occasion to report that funding at last looked assured, and George Ross, the director of Bovis responsible for the contract, confidently announced that the contract would be completed on schedule. There were problems to come but, after all our struggles, it really seemed as if we would have a concert hall for our year as European Capital of Culture. Negotiations for the rest of the concert hall site were on-going, but the reports were positive. The fact that work was underway on the first major part of the development must have given potential tenants a great deal of confidence, and in early July 1988 John Lewis announced, to our delight, that they would be the anchor tenants in the Buchanan Centre. We felt that their proposed opening date of 1992 was a little ambitious – after all, this was an even more substantial undertaking than the concert hall – and we knew that our own twenty-seven-month schedule was really pushing things.

The Garden Festival itself was a huge success. Varied, lively and attractive, it was crowded every day. The weather was on the whole good throughout the summer. Most of the pavilions were created by the various sponsoring organisations or around specific themes, but the landscape wove them all together and gave tremendous cohesion. Highlights included the High Street, an inspired and simple design by the architect David Leslie that reproduced a number of Glasgow landmarks on scaffolding skeletons, and the fondly remembered trams, which were very warmly welcomed by older Glaswegians. There was a lot of nostalgia but also a lot that was new. Nardini's Café in the Rotunda, which had been the southern entrance pavilion for the pedestrian tunnel under the Clyde, did a roaring trade throughout the summer.

I complained about the admission charges, which I felt were a little bit steep, but the organisers did arrange for special access for local folk, and many Glaswegians bought season tickets, which were the bargain of the decade.

In order to use Pacific Quay for the Garden Festival we had to grant Laings the offset sites elsewhere in the city which they required. However, these required grouting to stabilise the brownfield land for new house building. We sold the sites to the Scottish Development Agency at a good price and they carried out the work, which fitted in with their remit for urban brownfield sites. In the end, I suppose we really got the Garden Festival for nothing, and the only cost to ourselves was the City Festival, which maintained a good level of activity through the whole of Glasgow. Highlights included the Moscow State Circus and the only UK performances of the *Mahabharata*, Peter Brook's dramatisation of the five-thousand-year-old Sanskrit epic. Among the more local delights was the return of Jack Milroy and Rikki Fulton's timeless and superb double-act Francie and Josie at the Kings Theatre. The city's second jazz festival at the end of June, which featured well over a hundred events, included such major international artists as Oscar Peterson and Ray Charles. These festivals supplemented an established calendar, which included Mayfest and the World Pipe Band Championships, to create summer-long entertainment. There was no doubt that Bob Palmer and his team delivered the buzz that I felt was so important during that glorious Garden Festival year.

Peter Brook's visit to Glasgow led to a further development. When he came to the city, he insisted on using an industrial shed as the setting for the *Mahabharata*. South of the river, on Albert Drive, the former home of the Transport Museum had been lying empty ever since the city's impressive collection of trains, buses, trams and cars had been shifted to Kelvin Hall. The shed leaked, the wind whistled through the cracks, and the place was littered with debris. Peter Brook loved it.

When we were staging the *Mahabharata* we'd given the building a clean-up and the fairly unimaginative name, the 'Old Transport Museum'. I hadn't been very happy about the name, but nobody had come up with anything more inspired. As we had spent £50,000 on its conversion into a large-scale performance centre, I felt that we had to find a better name for the future, and I suggested to Bob Palmer's deputy, Neil Wallace, that as it had once been a tram shed, the name 'Tramway' had quite a nice ring to it. It referred to the history of the building and had the virtue of brevity. The Glasgow audience loved Peter Brook's epic, and the city acquired a new venue which was ideal for promenade theatre, avant-garde art and all sorts of other performance. Almost by chance the 1988 Festival had given the city another cultural asset.

The build-up to 1990 had begun in earnest. I was determined to show that Glasgow meant business. One of our boldest moves, in August 1988, was to mount a visit to the then holder of the Capital of Culture crown, Berlin. We didn't just go along with the usual delegation. Instead, we mounted a mini-festival of Glasgow-produced music, dance, literature, sculpture and design. We put on an open-air ceilidh, a pipe band performance, and an outdoor concert by the Scottish National Orchestra, and we mounted various workshops, performances and exhibitions. We also used our secret weapon, the sculptor George Wyllie, who created one of his characteristic spire sculptures, as well as a flight of storks ready to take off and fly over the Berlin Wall. Glasgow's most substantial ever international cultural exchange was a huge success. In August 1988 we were welcomed enthusiastically by the people of Berlin.

Glasgow also sponsored the Berlin Military Tattoo. The large military presence there made the Edinburgh Tattoo seem very small by comparison. When the city of Berlin, which had funded the event, decided to do so no longer, the British military approached the city of Edinburgh for sponsorship. But little progress was made and they came to us. We embraced the idea as a great opportunity to promote Glasgow as the next European Capital of Culture after Berlin. The event would receive widespread media coverage in Germany and elsewhere in Europe. As sponsors we would be represented at the high profile activities that took place on each of the six weekends of the Tattoo. The important guests who took the salute included the German President, the British Chancellor of the Exchequer (then Nigel Lawson) and His Royal Highness the Duke of Kent. The event was a very great success, and it meant that the Lord Provost Susan Baird and I had very busy weekends. We came to know something about the city which was still divided by the Wall at that time.

In late August, just after our return from Berlin, we announced a cash injection of £15 million for the 1990 programme. This sum had been achieved by careful management of the City's resources over the preceding three years. Effectively, we had managed to make savings on a number of budgets to produce an overall surplus of £36 million. It made it possible to fund the city's ambitious plans for 1990 from our own resources, which was only prudent given the Government's reluctance to invest in anything that Glasgow was undertaking.

The Government's announcement that they would contribute half a million pounds from the Department of Arts and Libraries only confirmed their negative attitude towards the city. My response, 'that's fine for starters', reflected sheer frustration that Glasgow was building a concert hall of international quality and had established a £15 million fund towards 1990 because it realised that the city's tenure as European Capital of Culture would radically alter the world's perception of it and provide Glasgow with a permanent economic boost. By comparison the Government's half a million pounds was truly miserly.

It had been a good year for Glasgow. The Garden Festival had achieved superb attendance figures, the city was being seen in a new light by local people and visitors, and we were making positive advances on the international stage. The year ended with the key appointment of Julian Spalding to replace Alastair Auld, who had retired at the age of fifty-eight. His announcement of his departure was fairly typical of his style. He invited his senior staff into his office on a Friday morning, gave them tea and strawberry tarts and announced he was going. As a way of bowing out, it had a certain low-key style.

The task of getting someone who was capable of maintaining the largest local authority museums department in the UK and managing its improvement was never going to be easy. By late November, we had a shortlist of six men and one woman. The favourite was Julian Spalding, who had been the successful and high-profile head of the Manchester City Art Gallery. The others included the former Depute Director of Glasgow Museums and Art Galleries and Roger Billcliffe, then Director of the Glasgow Fine Arts Society and a renowned expert on Charles Rennie Mackintosh. The woman on the list was Elspeth King, who had successfully steered the People's Palace for several years, in the process creating one of the most fascinating museums of social history in the United Kingdom. Elspeth reminded me of the poet Pam Ayres, although she lacked her jollity, being altogether more dark and sombre.

Spalding was the favourite as far as the press was concerned, but in these situations it is important to try to maintain objectivity. I sincerely hoped that the Scots would make a good showing. On the day, Elspeth did not perform well. She may have been nervous, but she lacked a vision. The former Depute Director would have been a steady hand on the tiller, but in the lead-up to 1990 that wasn't what we needed. Roger Bilcliffe was very impressive indeed, demonstrating a grasp of the issues, an understanding of the City of Glasgow and, as you might expect from our only private sector interviewee, a focus on the entrepreneurial opportunities. The latter had perhaps been underplayed in our museums and galleries in the past, and would certainly be a requirement for the future if the museum service was to continue and grow.

Spalding had vision, and his understanding of the current state of our museums service was profound. He argued that unless we changed our acquisitions policy, Glasgow's art galleries and museums would become moribund. The Victorians had collected widely and with zeal, indeed sometimes without too much discrimination. But they were prepared to gather the work of their contemporaries, even when this was not in the prevailing taste. Julian Spalding made it clear that unless we did likewise, the city's museums would remain a useful and engaging window on the past but play no part in the real vitality and future of the city.

After the interviews there was a lengthy debate. It was clear that some of my colleagues had been convinced by Julian Spalding's performance, but I still wanted to ensure that the other candidates were properly considered. In the end, however, we were persuaded and Julian got the job.

Early in the new year we made the controversial appointment of Saatchi and Saatchi to the £2-million job of promoting our Capital of Culture year. Their slogan 'There's a lot Glasgowing on in 1990' was not, in my view, up to the standard of Struthers Advertising's 'Get to the Art of Glasgow', in terms of its humour, but their experience and sense of overall strategy were exactly what we required. The City Labour Party objected to the appointment because of Saatchi's famous campaigns for the Conservative Party, but I took the view that it was a commercial commission and we should be engaging the firm who would do the best job, not making decisions based on our low opinion of certain of their previous clients.

In February we announced our £40-million programme for the City of Culture. The broad range of community-based projects included grants for local groups, a fund for amateur productions and a massive lantern procession. New dramatic works would include Bill Bryden's *The Ship* and Liz Lochhead's *Jock Tamson's Bairns*. There would also be public art commissions, spectacular music and major new theatrical productions. We pledged a year of truly European scope, which would attract as many visitors as possible to the city, and fulfil the key goal of enhancing the city's image and economic viability.

One major element of the 1990 programme which gave us problems in its early stages was the exhibition then known as *The Words and the Stones*, which was to take place in the arches below Central Station. Conceived by Doug Clelland, the exhibition would offer a comprehensive review of the life and history of Glasgow.

Below the platforms and the lines out of Central Station there was something like 100,000 square feet of covered, usable space. Much of this vast area had lain empty for several decades and only a small proportion was being used.

British Rail were initially enthusiastic, but questioned their potential return in terms of refurbished, lettable space at the exhibition's conclusion. By the end of March, we had agreement on the use of 60,000 square feet under Central Station and the exhibition was given the go-ahead.

Planned to run from April 1990 until the end of the year, *The Words and The Stones* would cover the development of Glasgow from the medieval period, the city's lengthy period of trade with the Americas, and would explore the world-class railway and shipbuilding industries of the Victorian era and the early part of the twentieth century, right up to the present day. A little bit of crystal-ball gazing would be employed to explore the Glasgow of the millennium.

The Scottish Development Agency agreed to put nearly a million pounds into preparing the space beneath Central Station and British Rail invested a quarter of a million. The balance of just over £3 million was to be funded by gate money. The City would, of course, underwrite the exhibition.

Some potential lenders of objects, particularly local authorities, were wary about making loans to an organisation which, although it had charitable status, was a private company. To give them the necessary reassurance, we agreed that a number of senior officials, including our Director of Finance, Bill English, and the new Director of Museums, would be co-opted onto the company's board.

Meanwhile Glasgow's growing international status was causing problems for other areas of Scotland. Edinburgh City Council made worried noises about our stealing the thunder of the Edinburgh Festival. This was ironic since the Festival organisers had complained for years about Edinburgh City Council's lack of support.

I met with the Leader of Edinburgh City Council, Mark Lazarowicz, and made it clear that we had no intention of competing with the Festival. Our plan was, after all, to create a year-long event. We talked about joint promotional activities and, for a short time at least, the relationship between Glasgow and Edinburgh, often described as 'friendly rivalry', was genuinely friendly.

Our relationship with Prestwick was destined to be less amicable. For many years, travellers from the Central Belt wishing to fly to the States had no option but to drive down the A77 to Prestwick. Flights were infrequent – we used to tell the story of a dangerous near miss at Prestwick when two aircraft landed on the same day. The travelling distance to Prestwick and the lack of regular services was immensely inconvenient and, given the far superior facilities and scale of Glasgow Airport, less than sensible. Early in 1989 we decided to ask the British Airports Authority to give Glasgow Airport Gateway status. Our reasoning was quite straightforward – this would be far more convenient and the potential economic benefits to Glasgow were huge. The Authority duly granted our request, which was a considerable boost for the city.

If we weren't making friends and influencing people on the Ayrshire coast, we were equally determined that, on the issue of the Poll Tax, the Government wasn't going to get everything its own way. In mid-January, six extreme left-wing councillors walked out of a meeting in protest at the Council's policy on the issue. They were adamant that not only should we refuse to have anything to do with the Poll Tax, but we should lead a campaign against it. All six were suspended for twelve months for failing to support a Labour Group decision. The administration was of course fighting against the Poll Tax, but within the law.

At a Labour Group meeting in February there was considerable argument over what attitude we should adopt to supplying information to the Poll Tax Registration Officer. I argued that we should carry out our obligations under the law, but could do so in a way that would continue to make the collection of the tax difficult. The fairly stormy meeting had reached an impasse and I indicated that if we didn't achieve a resolution I would have no option but to resign as Leader. When the meeting adjourned, there were heated exchanges in the Council corridor. The Conservative Leader, John Young, seeking to make as much political capital as possible from our internal disagreement, decided to occupy the Lord Provost's chair and preside over a non-existent Council meeting.

Of course, when the whole thing hit the press, the bold headline in the *Evening Times* was 'Lally Shock Over Poll Tax'. The disagreement in the corridor was exaggerated into a punch-up and John Young's mock Council meeting was given far more significance than it deserved. John Young naturally made the most of the moment. In the *Herald*, he described me as the 'Grand Duke of Lally', and he called the events the 'worst shambles I've seen in the Labour Group for many years'. He also suggested that Mary Poppins could emerge as Leader after our Group elections in May. From my recollection of the poem, it was the Grand *Old* Duke of York who led his ten thousand men to the top of the hill and back down again. I suppose I should be grateful for small mercies – at least Councillor Young hadn't described me as 'old'.

When the Council meeting proper convened, we agreed to continue the issue of the Poll Tax for a month, and we eventually decided to give our eighteen-inch-high pile of council tenant information to the Government, who could sort through it for themselves.

CHAPTER SEVEN

Whatever difficulties the Poll Tax may have caused, the Council's position on another piece of daft Tory legislation was quite clear. In response to our very sensible ruling that if council houses were improved their tenants should not be able to buy them within ten years, Mr Rifkind, the Scottish Secretary, issued an order stating that we were in default of our statutory duties. It was absurd and unfair to require the people of Glasgow to fund repairs on houses which might then shift, immediately, into the private sector. Tenants already received huge reductions in price which corresponded to their length of tenancy. Purchases were, of course, concentrated in areas of terraced or semi-detached housing.

At about this time a comedy sketch on television featured a snobbish working-class couple who were holding a drinks party in their house which they had recently bought from the Council. They waxed lyrical about the benefits of home ownership and expressed their surprise that their neighbours hadn't followed suit. The camera then pulled back to show that they had refurbished their dwelling in an absurd Spanish hacienda style with particularly naff cladding. It then pulled further back to reveal that this atrocious example of the 'Right to Buy' was located fifteen storeys up a tower block. The point the sketch made of course was that there were tenants in some kinds of property who were never realistically going to be able to buy their flats from the Council. The rent gathered from these people would give an unfair benefit to those tenants in more self-contained and easily mortgageable properties.

Meanwhile, work on the concert hall was falling behind schedule. There was a real danger that it might not be ready in time for the City's reign as European Capital of Culture.

We'd appointed an impressive director, Cameron McNicol, a Scot, who had been General Manager of the Royal Albert Hall. His CV was remarkable and made him the ideal candidate for the job. Originally from Alexandria on the Clyde coast, he studied at the Royal Scottish Academy of Music and Drama before becoming a music lecturer at Langside College. In twenty-two years of working in venue management he had risen steadily to achieve one of the most senior positions in the UK. In addition to managing the Albert Hall auditorium, he was also responsible for the retail and catering operations and much of the marketing. His return to Scotland was a major coup for Glasgow.

The appointment of a director should have been the last step in ensuring that the concert hall and its programme would happen on time and the first step towards ensuring that the City's new asset assumed its place among the great European concert halls.

Even while we were interviewing for the new Director, I was aware that progress on the hall had slowed. Discussions with the management contractor, Bovis Construction, indicated that there were problems with their major subcontractor, Whatlings Construction. As we were determined to open the new concert hall on the anniversary of the burning-down of the old St Andrew's Halls and to programme a number of major events during 1990, we needed all of those involved in the contract to be putting in maximum effort. The executive architects, RMJM, were producing the contract packages on time and Bovis were letting these expeditiously as required in their contract. However, Whatlings were building the main structural frame and they simply weren't putting in the manpower that was required to get the thing done on time. We were several weeks behind.

I was keenly aware that meddling with building contracts is a danger-ous activity. But Bovis shared my assessment of the situation and sup-ported the Council's decision to dismiss Whatlings. They were ordered to quit the site on 20 February 1989. They were required to pay us a substantial sum in recompense, and Bovis managed to get new contrac-tors on site very rapidly. We were once again on target.

The press made a huge fuss. It was about this time that Ewan Bain did one of his Angus Ogg cartoons in which the eponymous hero has been projected forward to 1990. He stands in front of a giant structural frame shrouded in scaffolding, upon which construction workers are still busying away. 'And this is Glasgow Concert Hall,' he says.

Early in March, Michael Tumelty, the *Glasgow Herald*'s music correspondent, wrote a lengthy piece complaining about the proposed name of the hall – Glasgow International Concert Hall. Mr Tumelty felt that neither the name nor the acronym, GICH, served us well. His complaint was two-fold. He felt that including the city in the name was 'shabby parochialism' and that 'international' was unnecessary, perhaps defensive. He also bet me a bottle of elderly malt that it wouldn't open on time and suggested that we should give ourselves a more generous schedule and open the hall in 1991.

My response, on the *Herald*'s letters page, was to point out that we'd taken our director's advice in including the word 'international', which was proving a positive advantage in securing major orchestras and international names. In conclusion I wrote that although I didn't like whisky, I was looking forward to accepting his offer on behalf of the Castlemilk Pensioners Action Group. I also promised him a personal ticket for the opening.

A short while later a suggestion from a Mr Gordon Kennedy of Partick appeared in Tom Shield's Diary in the *Glasgow Herald* that we call the building the Lally Palais. Many others since have used this name, but Mr Kennedy has rarely been given the credit for first thinking of it.

The story of McLellan Galleries is not unlike that of the concert hall. In the past, the Royal Glasgow Institute had held their exhibition there, and there was also a regular Salon des Refusées, where anybody in the city who painted was able to submit their works. The whole place had been fairly low key and not really exploited to the benefit of the city. Then disaster occurred in the mid-eighties when a dreadful fire gutted the famous Treron's Store which occupied the rest of the block. Although relatively undamaged, the gallery had remained empty since. We initiated a refurbishment of the galleries, to the designs of our Department of Architecture and Related Services, to create a gallery which would equal anything in the United Kingdom. They would be an impressive suite of large, airy, well-lit and well-ventilated exhibition rooms.

The cost of the conversion was expected to be about £3.5 million. As the shell of Treron's Store had been sold by the Council some time before for £1 million, our new Director of Museums, Julian Spalding, was shocked to find that the gallery's only connection with Sauchiehall Street was an entrance corridor. Buying the shops back on either side would have been prohibitively expensive. But it was quite clear that, in order to make the new gallery viable, we had to create some sort of marker on Sauchiehall Street to break up the long frontage of the old Treron building and to make it clear that the narrow entrance-way led to an important venue behind. The old gallery had had a canopy which opened out onto Sauchiehall Street but Historic Scotland were reluctant to allow this solution for the conversion.

Their architects proposed a pathetic little blister on the front of the building, which would never had done the job and would have been quite costly. I turned this down, but Historic Scotland made it quite clear that that was the limit of what we could do. The solution was straightforward. I indicated that if we were not allowed to 'attach a canopy to the building', we would simply 'detach a canopy from the building', creating a new entrance structure separated from the building by an inch. They agreed to the canopy and approved of the design. Finally finished in time, the McLellan Galleries played host in 1990 to a number of important and prestigious exhibitions. And happily, with its rather fine entrance canopy on Sauchiehall Street, visitors to the city have never had any problem finding it.

In our internal elections in 1989, I was once again elected unopposed to the leadership. Jean McFadden became my Depute. The press, of course, interpreted this as the first stage in her assault on the leadership. The *Daily Record* was slightly less than flattering to her with its headline, 'Lady Jean Claws Her Way Back to the Top', but I was in fact firmly in control. Councillor McFadden was focusing her energies on the Convention of Scottish Local Authorities, where she was due to take over as President – a notable achievement.

But pleased as I was with my victory, there was no time for complacency. There were problems at that important repository of Glasgow's identity, the People's Palace. Its curator, Elspeth King, had been one of the short-listed candidates to become Director of Museums and Galleries. Ever since she had failed to win the job, supporters of the People's Palace had been muttering that the East End museum was under-resourced, and that Ms King and her pale, lanky deputy, Michael Donnelly, were not receiving their due recognition.

There is no question that under Elspeth King's curatorship the People's Palace had grown in stature. Its collections and displays had improved and its role in the city had been reinforced. However, in June a group of Glasgow worthies, including the sculptor George Wyllie and the writers James Kelman and Liz Lochhead, demanded assurances over the future of the Palace, and supported Elspeth King. This coincided with the announcement that a new post of Keeper of Social History was being established within the museum service. The role would include the supervision of the People's Palace.

The intervention of this group of worthy and talented Glaswegians might have been construed as a number of high-profile references, before the event, in support of her bid for the post. However, I have always taken the view that it is up to senior officers to determine the structures and appointments within their own departments. It was inevitable that, after Alasdair Auld's departure and Julian Spalding's arrival in the city, the new director would want to reorganise the museums service, as, until his arrival, the service had been looking increasingly tired. With a few notable exceptions, which included the People's Palace, the museums service seemed to be focussing more on maintaining the status quo and less on making change or improvements.

It was quite clear to me that without change and development things would move backwards. It was undoubtedly a good thing that some of Glasgow's best-known and most talented creative individuals were passionate about the quality of our museums service, but whether it was appropriate for them to lobby for a particular museum employee is another matter.

Towards the end of the year the Contemporary Art Fund was established. As I have already mentioned, Julian Spalding had criticised the city's acquisition policy. This was very poor and underfunded, particularly with regard to contemporary artists. This criticism had dwelt on my mind. I became more and more convinced that a key part of our role as the City of Culture was to encourage living artists. But funds for acquisitions were really little more than petty cash – a few thousand pounds a year. I decided to put the notion of establishing a fund to Bill English, our Director of Finance, and I went to see him one afternoon.

As I left my room the figure in my mind was around £5 million. En route, I reflected that this would generate around £500,000 a year in interest, an extraordinary amount. By the time I got to the finance office, the conjectural Contemporary Art Fund had been cut to £3 million. This was the figure I put to Bill English. He liked the idea and felt that we could achieve it within our resources. We agreed that he would produce a report on this basis for the Committee. I then called in Julian Spalding and intimated that we were proposing to establish a £3 million fund which would not be expended directly, but would generate interest which then could be used to buy art on behalf of the City, the selection of which would be his responsibility. In due time, the Contemporary Art Fund came into being. Our policy, which I feel was a wise one, was to purchase only work by living artists, because in this way the Fund wasn't paying the inflated prices which the art market imposes on the work of artists who are no longer around to influence the pricing of their work.

In the years since my initial brainwave, the City has built up an impressive and valuable collection. The Contemporary Art Fund was I suppose a fairly straightforward idea which could only be achieved because we had been carefully marshalling funds towards 1990. It is a credit both to Julian Spalding's vision of a new collection of modern art for the city and to Bill English's prudent housekeeping.

While we were working towards 1990, I continued my day-to-day activities on behalf of my constituents. These local responsibilities remain a major element in any councillor's workload, regardless of his position. Indeed, one undoubted benefit of holding office within the Council is the opportunity it provides to put local interests on the agenda. Over my fifteen years of service as the representative of Castlemilk, I have constantly sought to speak out on its behalf. Fortunately, it has been a period in which the local infrastructure, environment and quality of housing in Glasgow's so-called peripheral communities, and particularly Castlemilk, has markedly improved.

On one occasion I had been invited to Castlemilk to participate in an event at which one of the main contributors was to be Jimmy Boyle. I don't recall the nature of the event or who was organising it, but after reflecting on the matter, I decided to decline the invitation. As a former resident of the Gorbals, I had known of Jimmy Boyle for a very long time. His criminal career in the Gorbals was unedifying and had caused many people a great deal of distress. Many of Castlemilk's residents had once lived in the Gorbals and I was sure they shared my view that, even if Mr Boyle had reformed, he was hardly someone who should be looked to as an example. And certainly it wasn't appropriate that the leader of the Council should share a platform with him. So after reflecting on the matter I decided to decline the invitation. I did not make a great issue of it, I simply indicated that I would be unable to attend.

Early one lovely sunny afternoon, I and two of my Council colleagues, Eddie and Christine Devine, arrived at one of my periodic meetings with representatives of the Castlemilk community. The meeting was held at the Birgidale Complex in West Castlemilk, a Council community facility, partly funded by Urban Aid, which had only just opened. In the years since it has become an important focal point for the area, and a venue for meetings and social events.

I parked my car a short distance from the complex and as I started to walk towards the entrance I was confronted by a figure in a leather jerkin and jeans. This was Jimmy Boyle. To say I was taken aback is an understatement. I was even more surprised when he began an impassioned denunciation of me. It seemed inappropriate and unnecessary in a public street. Such grandstanding really deserved an audience, but there was none to be seen. Yet Mr Boyle continued to rant. He blocked my path into the building and accused me of destroying his life. He regarded my refusal to join him on the platform of an obscure meeting in Castlemilk as in some way profoundly damaging to himself and his family. All I could do was vigorously deny his allegations.

I found his onslaught inexplicable. After all, he had been condemned on innumerable occasions in the past, and the fact that I couldn't attend a meeting with him was hardly the worst slight he had ever received. Things just weren't adding up. After his rant had subsided and he had stepped aside to let me into the place, I took a minute or two to look round. In the distance, across a patch of open ground, I spotted a BBC TV camera and crew. Standing beside me, I assume all wired up, was Jimmy Boyle. The whole thing had been a set up.

After the meeting I set off back to the City Chambers and mulled over what had happened. What could they have hoped to achieve? Did they want me to break out into a rant in response to his? Or perhaps they even expected physical violence? They must have been disappointed with the result.

Back in my office, I phoned Pat Chalmers, the Controller of BBC Scotland, an impressive and able individual. I told him what had happened. I made it clear that I felt some members of his staff had behaved in a completely unacceptable fashion. He assured me that he was wholly unaware of what the film crew had been up to and that it was quite contrary to the BBC's code of practice. I was to leave the matter with him.

A few days later, I received an apology from the producer, who gave me assurances that the material would not be used. It was a satisfactory outcome to an extraordinary episode, which left me convinced that, for all his renunciation of violence, Jimmy Boyle's reformation had some way to go. And I couldn't help take some pride in the thought that it's not easy to put one over on a guy from the Gorbals – something Mr Boyle should know.

While much of our effort at that time was focused on the year to come and ensuring that we achieved all we hoped to for the City, we were also considering Glasgow's well being in the long term. It was apparent, even as early as 1989, that no matter what system of local tax collection was adopted, the city's population had fallen to danger-ously low levels. The economic equation simply wasn't adding up.

In the autumn of 1989 we submitted proposals to the Scottish Labour Party on the future of Glasgow under a Scottish Assembly. In addition to a reallocation of powers from Strathclyde Region to the City, effec-tively the creation of a unitary authority, our proposals sought a new boundary dictated by geography, key communication routes or simply patterns of living, which would embrace a number of satellites of Glasgow. Effectively the people in most of these areas already considered themselves Glaswegian, but although most were working in the city and using it for leisure, they were not contributing directly either to its economy or to the decision-making process which affected their daily lives.

There was a huge furore. Stirred by the Tories, a number of people in Eastwood and Bearsden became vociferous opponents of the proposal before they even had time to consider all its implications. The Conservative MP for Eastwood, Allan Stewart, referred disparagingly to the 'Glasgow socialist takeover plans'. His local association fanned the flames with its predictably named 'Keep Out of Glasgow' campaign.

It was only when people began to appreciate that our proposals were merely proposals and that it would take a Government decision to implement them that the uproar subsided. The fact is that Glasgow's boundary was then, as it still is today, unfair. When the Tories subsequently redrew it, they merely reinforced existing anomalies in the belief that this would help sustain their vote. Sadly, the advent of New Labour did not change matters, and it remains to be seen whether the Scottish Parliament will see fit to reduce the undue burden on Glasgow's council tax payers.

As 1989 wore on, anticipation of the City's new mantle as European Capital of Culture inevitably grew. Innumerable community organisations, institutions and businesses became involved in planning events themselves or supporting the work of others. Saatchi's had done the groundwork for our major national and international promotional campaigns, but resources were stretched and, at Saatchi's suggestion, our own team took responsibility for the more local promotion. Jill Campbell-Mackay was appointed as overall PR manager and Jim Waugh took charge of press activity.

The first day of Glasgow's most important year of the twentieth century was welcomed with a number of notable international exchanges and an unedifying cock-up. I was thrilled to be invited, along with Margaret Thatcher and Neil Kinnock, to send greetings to the Soviet Union on the BBC's Russian Service. The invitation resulted from Glasgow's close links with Russia through its twin city, Rostov-on-Don. My message was simple and sincere: 'The present policies of your government have unlocked for us a wonderful treasure-house of friendship, of new cultural experiences and of opportunities for trade.' Thankfully, the BBC supplied a voice-over translation so I didn't have to learn Russian for the occasion. They also agreed to play my choice of music, the Scottish National Orchestra's recording of Prokofiev's 1st Symphony.

Another, more notable, international exchange was a New Year's greeting from the then Mayor of Paris, Jacques Chirac, who handed on the baton of the European Capital of Culture to Glasgow.

All this was thoroughly inspiring and reflected a genuine change in Glasgow's image, both in the UK and internationally. Happily, neither the Russians nor the good folk of Paris were witness to the fairly shambolic start to the concert which greeted the New Year in George Square. This was the event which spawned the new Glasgow expression 'Happy New three minutes past midnight'. Poor Robbie Coltrane, who was compering the evening, was left stranded in the middle of the stage with no one to tell him when the stroke of midnight was about to occur. But in fairness to the BBC, if the moment itself was missed the live concert that followed it in Glasgow's main public square was very successful and thoroughly enjoyed by the huge crowd who came along to welcome 1990. Elsewhere in the city, there were genuine fireworks, which went very well.

CHAPTER EIGHT

The formal opening of Glasgow's year as European City of Culture was scheduled for March 1990. In February, we learned that although the Queen, the Duke of Edinburgh, the Leader of the Opposition and the Mayor of Paris were all going to be there, Mrs Thatcher would not attend the launch. Given her previous disregard of Glasgow and her Government's extraordinary attitude to what should have been warmly welcomed as an accolade for Britain, this was hardly surprising. A total contribution from the UK Government of £500,000 was, frankly, laughable.

Our private sponsors, who would attend the launch, had between them contributed approximately £5 million. At no stage had we asked the Government for absurd sums, just a figure which acknowledged that a major European event was happening in the UK, which had the potential to improve the lives of a very large number of Glaswegians and others in Scotland by offering both temporary delights and permanent economic improvement through enhanced tourism and new business set-ups.

However, we had become quite inured to the Conservative Government's attitude to Glasgow. Within two weeks of our becoming Capital of Culture they managed to deliver their first, presumably celebratory, snub. The Secretary of State, Malcolm Rifkind, announced that the new Museum of Scotland was to be built next to the Royal Museum of Scotland in Edinburgh. To add insult to injury, the Arts Minister, Iain Lang, revealed that the alternative sites had been Perth and Stirling.

We immediately offered the superb building which, at that stage, housed Stirlings Library. I also pointed out that there were good precedents in Liverpool, Bradford and York, all cities which housed national collections. Sir Nicholas Fairbairn, a Trustee of the Royal Museums of Scotland, helped to put the Government's attitude into perspective when he commented that, while Glasgow might be artistic, it was no more

European City of Culture than the Garden Festival had anything to do with gardens. His comments confirmed that the decision had been solely rooted in Scottish Tory élitism and narrow-minded prejudice. Nicholas Fairbairn, who was one of the most notable drunks of the latter half of the twentieth century, never pretended to be anything other than an anti-Glasgow bigot.

Nobody seemed unduly put out that Margaret Thatcher wasn't at the Royal opening. It was an enormously exciting day. The formal launch was at the King's Theatre. The Queen and Prince Phillip seemed to enjoy themselves. As ever, they attracted enormous attention and were warmly greeted by the people of Glasgow.

There was one minor complaint after the event that a number of MPs, including Donald Dewar, hadn't been introduced to Her Majesty. They'd been waiting in expectation and then were invited in to lunch. This minor hiccup arose, I think, because of my insistence that the Queen should meet all those who were sponsoring 1990; lunch was called immediately afterwards and there was no time for further introductions on what was an extremely tight programme. Happily, Donald Dewar and his fellow MPs took the thing in good part.

After the success of our launch, I felt it was important to maintain the momentum of 1990 and build upon the expectation of what was to come. A number of key officers from the City had become involved in the exhibition *The Words and The Stones*, although its title was changed. Julian Spalding pointed out that the acronym of *The Words and The Stones*, TWATS, was hardly appropriate for an exhibition intended to be an enjoyable and educational experience for the whole family. So at Julian's suggestion, it was reborn as *Glasgow's Glasgow*. Doug Clelland, the originator of the exhibition, had previously been involved in *Berlin Berlin*, which had inspired the Glasgow event. The exhibition opened in the spring.

Towards the end of April, two spectacular events were announced – one very much about Glasgow, the other truly international. Bill Bryden's *The Ship*, a hugely ambitious promenade theatre event, was scheduled to take place in Harland & Wolff Engine shed in the autumn. Bill is an internationally renowned producer and director, who at one stage worked for the BBC. The Harland & Wolff shed, 120 yards long and 40 yards wide, was large enough to accommodate a huge moving stage in the form of a ship aboard which there would be over a thousand people a night during the two-month run. At the press conference announcing this project, Bill Bryden was in a cheerful and ironic mood. He revealed that the Harland & Wolff shed was his second choice. He had originally favoured Yarrow's giant shed but this was ruled out by the happy inconvenience that 'they got an order for a ship'! *The Ship*, through its sheer scale and the uniqueness of its venue, was arguably the most extraordinary and memorable theatrical performance ever seen in Glasgow. The immediacy of the performance itself made a lasting impression on many people, and introduced many others to theatre for the first time. It was a huge success.

The other event to be announced in April was the visit to the city of the world-famous Bolshoi Opera and Ballet companies. It was a unique first and a major logistical nightmare for its organisers. There were 450 artists and an audience of over 5,000 was expected every night. It was yet another undertaking of quite unprecedented scale for Glasgow. The *Scotsman* quoted the comment of our normally circumspect Director of Festivals, Bob Palmer, that it would be 'the biggest sonic event since Jericho!' Unfortunately my *sotto voce* rejoinder 'And we all know what happened there,' was also quoted!

Although the city was in festive mood, the business of the Council continued much as always. One matter which arose around the middle of the year has a minor bearing on much later events, even if only for its irony value. I had been persuaded to go along to a housing conference in Aviemore. It was an annual event. I knew we were regularly represented, but I was horrified by the number of our members and officers attending. It was like a local authority jamboree. The content of the conference was relevant only for those members and officers with specific responsibility for housing issues, perhaps even just for the Convenor and Vice-Convenors of the Housing Committee. It looked as if folk were simply there for a pleasant break. I wondered whether there was anyone left back at City Chambers. The whole situation was horrendous, and I was annoyed with myself for not checking in advance on the nature of the event and who from the Council was actually attending.

I said nothing at the time, but when I returned to Glasgow I made my views known to the Labour Group and intimated that we would have to tighten up on such matters. In future, travel would be restricted to the number necessary to give us proper representation. Such procedures were already in place with regards to overseas travel. International conferences were carefully checked to make sure they justified attendance, and the level of representation agreed beforehand. Now closer scrutiny would be applied to travel across the board, and would even form part of the agenda of the relevant committee. More than ever before, members of the Council would be required to take votes for, or against, trips.

From mid 1990 onwards a number of issues attracted the attention of the press, and we had a succession of *fêtes de scandal*. Two of these issues came to be the subject of a joint campaign. They were conflated by protesters, in the press and, as a consequence, in the public imagination. They were presented as a sort of grand Pat Lally conspiracy, although against whom it was never made clear. This was complete nonsense.

The events in question were the so-called Elspeth King Affair and the lengthy debate over the redevelopment of Flesher's Haugh. In truth, the only real connection between the two lay in accidents of time and location. Both came to a head in the summer of 1990 and had Glasgow Green as their locus. As far as the theory of a grand Lally plot is concerned, I had no involvement whatever in the Elspeth King affair at its outset, and I had worked hard towards achieving a positive development at Fleshers' Haugh. My motives for the East End, where the People's Palace was based, were much the same as for the rest of Glasgow. I was determined that throughout the city ordinary people should benefit from an improved economy, new jobs and a better environment. Happily all over the city the positive effects of Glasgow's tenure as European Capital of Culture had begun.

Elspeth King had reinvented the People's Palace. She had helped to build upon its collections and improved their presentation in such a way as to reinforce the Palace's position as an impressive and internationally renowned museum of social history. Her passion for Glasgow's past and the artefacts which told its story had, over her sixteen years' work there, significantly changed and strengthened the collection. Her Depute, Michael Donnelly, had an interest in stained glass and had rescued fine examples of the Glasgow glassmakers' art from destruction.

Elspeth's post was secure, but her many friends in Glasgow were troubled by the appointment of Julian Spalding and the changes which had been mooted to reorganise Glasgow Museums. Julian's task was to ensure that the City's museums service had a viable future. It was a task which was entrusted to him when he was appointed to the job of Director, and having appointed him, my view was that like any other employee of the City he should be allowed to do his job without interference.

There was much that clearly needed attention. The existing structures within the Museums Department did not recognise the enormous changes in emphasis in how museums should be presented to the public. The new post of Keeper of Social History was one of a number of appointments intended to update the service. By raising the status of social history, it was really responding to the agenda established by Elspeth King herself and a number of her colleagues. They had appreciated the importance of displaying and explaining objects in an accessible way so that ordinary Glaswegians had genuine contact with their own history.

Ever since Elspeth had failed to win the post of Director of Museums and Galleries, a number of her friends within the art, theatrical and literary establishments in the city and beyond had been campaigning to promote her within the service. It would have been wholly inappropriate for any department to decide an appointment on the basis of an external campaign, no matter how high profile or well positioned were the campaigners.

In the event the appointment was won by the relatively young Mark O'Neill, whom Elspeth King had some years previously chosen to run Springburn Museum. Mark O'Neill's subsequent career would vindicate Julian Spalding's decision, but at the time provoked enormous controversy. Elspeth King was quoted as saying that Spalding had told her 'there would be no automatic jobs for the girls'. But later he explained to me that they had had a meeting in which she seemed to believe that the new job was effectively hers before the interviews even took place. So what he had said was that there would be 'no jobs for the boys' and then, suddenly it occurred to him that this was politically incorrect, so he added, 'or the girls'. This, he explained, was subsequently misquoted.

In early June, Elspeth King lodged a sex discrimination appeal. The basis of her appeal was that, as the best candidate for the post, the only reason for not selecting her was that she was a woman. It may have had a certain logic as a legal position, but it was hardly objective. Unfortunately for Ms King we pointed out that, as was frequently the case, the District Council's Equal Opportunities Officer, Jess Fitzgerald, sat on the interview panel. It was scarcely credible that she would indulge in or support the sort of misogynist decision-making process alleged.

While all of this stushie was going on, I happened to be on a trade mission to one of Glasgow's twin cities, Rostov-on-Don. The 'Defend Elspeth King' campaign had got into its stride. Her high-profile supporters included Spike Milligan, Billy Connolly, Pat Kane and Liz Lochhead. There was leafleting and protests outside the City Chambers. Many of my younger colleagues actively took Elspeth King's side, some perhaps driven by the belief that there's nothing quite like a good row to help make a political mark. Councillor Martin Hilland reported that there was widespread anger in the Labour Group, indeed something like twenty-five Labour councillors had signed up in protest against the

Ma, Pa and the wean (1927).

Me and Robert (1932).

Mum, me and Robert (*c.* 1935).

Just after joining up (1944).

Just married – Peggy and me (1968).

Ma, Pa and the weans (1976).

The district team (1986). Back row: J. Mutter (second from left), Stuart Bates, Bob McKenzie, Lord Provost Bob Gray, Me, Bill Aitken, Hugh McCrae; front row: Larry Flanagan, Frank White, Alex Mosson (with son), Ron Davie, Danny Crawford.

Visions of things to come – looking over the Concert Hall site (1988).

Launching the marketing campaign for 1990 (1989).

Finishing touches with Cameron McNicol (1990).

Richard Luce, me and M. Chirac (1990).

At the heart of the City of Culture (1990).

The district election count
– Jean McFadden and me
(1992).

The Biderlally (1993).

A glorious return – Mr Happy's comeback (1994).

Me and the Wets
(glasses courtesy
Mr Pellow (1994).

A grand day out one –
Edinburgh (1994).

A grand day out two –
London (1994).

decision not to appoint Elspeth King. Frank McAveety spoke at a public meeting, I think at the Dolphin Arts Centre, and was vociferously condemning my position on the matter.

I held that the appointment had been made by the Director, following due process, and that was the end of the matter. If elected members of the Council got involved in deciding internal appointments at every level, the situation would be open to abuse and would diminish the accountability of senior officers. If they were not allowed to appoint their own team, they could hardly be held responsible if that team failed to perform. In my absence, my Depute, Jean McFadden, who had been recently confirmed as the new President of the Convention of Scottish Local Authorities, reaffirmed the Council's position: 'I have no personal feelings on the matter. It was a properly made appointment.'

An unfortunate twist in the Elspeth King Affair was the decision of her Depute Director, Michael Donnelly, to criticise the Council in public. As it emerged that he and Elspeth King had been living together for seventeen years, it was difficult not to question his objectivity, and certainly his scathing comments, which took on a very personal edge with attacks on Julian Spalding, Mark O'Neill and myself, lacked professional detachment. And his views were vitriolic.

In an 'Outsider' article in the *Glasgow Herald* he referred to what he took as evidence of the abandonment of socialism by the Labour Party:

> That process, combined with the wish locally to bury the facts of a past which had become inconvenient, and to superimpose a new, sanitised, marketable image of the city, required not a critical social history rooted in the verities of our existence, but a bland, self-congratulatory hype, which found its true apotheosis in the insultingly patronising 'Mr Happy' of 'Glasgow's Miles Better'.

His flow of invective continued:

> When a dream dies the tribe perishes, for instead of leading the people who have loyally voted for it towards greater democratic freedom and accountability, they have become a bureaucratic conspiracy against them. The Tammany Hall style of party pyramid, with its utterly undemocratic concepts of junior and senior councillors answerable to an all-powerful boss, is the very antithesis of the kind of democracy envisaged by Whitman, Morris or Keir Hardie.

In conclusion, he stormed that the title 'The Elspeth King Affair' was:

> Too bland for what is one of the dirtiest and most immoral witch-hunts since the days of McCarthy. The chief witch-finder is Lally and that is why he threatens me in classic Stalinist fashion, with removal for my 'own good'. It is inconceivable to him that I am expressing opposition to his behaviour out of principle, so he foully attributes my alleged 'clouded judgement' to my 'personal relationship' with Elspeth King.

Michael Donnelly's rhetoric was powerful and his passion unquestionable. He knew that the outcome of writing such a piece was inevitable. Such a forthright condemnation of his employer could have only one result. Sadly, after his many years of valuable service to the City, the Museums Department had no option but to dismiss him. When he made an unsuccessful appeal against his dismissal, the Depute Director of Personnel confirmed that he had been dismissed 'for breaking the mutual trust, confidence and loyalty necessary in the relationship between employer and employee'.

As Elspeth King eventually withdrew her appeal against the appointment of Mark O'Neill, I have to assume that, despite her campaign, she ultimately concluded that Mark O'Neill's appointment was a fair one.

Anyone who seeks a job without passionately believing that he or she is by far the best candidate should not be applying for the post, and failure after an interview should not subsequently diminish that self-belief. The sadness of the Elspeth King Affair was that her bad luck was shanghaied by a group who seemed to me to be as interested in scoring political points as in providing support for her. Their espousal of the other contemporary cause, the saving of Fleshers' Haugh, was further evidence of their political opportunism.

Glasgow Green is made up of a number of parcels of land purchased by the City between the mid-seventeenth century and the end of the eighteenth. In 1792 the twenty-four acres now known as Fleshers' Haugh were the last piece of this impressive landscape to be acquired. Until around the middle of the present century, Glasgow Green was hugely important as a recreational facility for the whole of the East End and the massive Gorbals community. My own boyhood recollections are of a busy, populous park. The Green is one of the few places in the city which brings back memories of my father and, as it is for very many Glaswegians, it is very special to me.

After the massive exodus of the sixties and seventies from the East

End, and particularly from the Gorbals, the character of Glasgow Green changed. It was no longer the place where thousands came to walk, play or watch the world go by; instead, it became a venue for one-off events, a running track for joggers and a play park for relatively few.

In 1988, the District Council's Parks and Recreational Committee reviewed the Green and considered its future. Their proposals were to improve the quality of the Green overall, to create a new, more civic entrance at its west end, to upgrade its paths and its southern edge on the banks of the Clyde. It was also proposed to replace trees which had been lost through old age or disease and generally to improve the attractions of the Green for local people and for visitors.

The most significant proposal was the introduction of new leisure facilities at the eastern extremity, Fleshers' Haugh. The Haugh had, for many years, been used as an industrial dump site, and was heavily contaminated with chemical waste. It had subsequently been safely used for red blaze football pitches, but a substantial amount of money needed to be spent on the decontamination of the site if building works were to proceed.

The ambitious plans for Glasgow Green would without question turn the Green into a leisure facility of the highest quality. They promised 400 new jobs and prosperity for an area of the city which was in dire need of both.

Three developers, Citygrove Leisure, Rank Leisure and Sport and Leisure Developments submitted detailed proposals. Of these, Rank Leisure's proposal seemed the most likely to succeed since it was being put forward by a particularly well-funded and successful national company. All the proposals were criticised in a report in July by the Council's South Area Co-ordinator: they paid insufficient attention to the river, and the Rank Leisure scheme would have entailed too much car-parking.

These objections were relatively easy to resolve, but now it became opportune for protesters to lump together the Glasgow Green proposals with the Elspeth King Affair as evidence of a conspiracy against the interests of local people. A motley group of whingers calling itself Workers City had canvassed the support of the literati and glitterati from Glasgow and further afield to campaign on three fronts: 'Defend Elspeth King – Save Glasgow Green – Support the People's Culture'. This unelected coterie was drawing substantial media coverage.

A survey by the District Council's Market Information Team revealed that about 75 per cent of those who lived in the area approved of the proposals, but this did not deter the campaigners.

In late October, a meeting of the Labour Group agreed that there should be a further consultation exercise. Local meetings would be organised to reassure people about the proposals and the benefits they would bring. The opponents of those proposals had just one line of argument: Glasgow Green was sacred. No matter how run down or underfunded its facilities, no matter how little it was meeting local needs, they refused to budge from this one consideration that Glasgow Green was somehow an inviolable part of the city's history. This was a purely emotional response which failed to take account of the potential advantages of the proposed new facilities and the attendant upgrading of the whole of the Green. It was clear to all those who had actually thought about Glasgow Green and how it was being used that the park should not be preserved as it was. Instead, we should have transformed all our parks into the kind of facilities that people would want in this day and age.

Now the Glasgow District Labour Party entered the fray. This was too good a row for them to keep out. They too were all for leaving the Green substantially as it was. There is invariably a conflict in local government between those in the party but outside the administration, who consider themselves responsible for policy, and those within the administration, the elected members representing and working on behalf of – in the case of Glasgow – 700,000 citizens.

Much of the argument against the Glasgow Green proposals implied that somehow, in undertaking its duty towards the electorate in a responsible manner, the Council was being undemocratic. I decided that we should put the issue to the people. After all, we firmly believed that we were working in the interests of Glasgow's citizens. So I agreed that the *Evening Times* could run a poll and I would abide by its decision.

There are certain situations in which you just can't do anything right. I had been accused of being undemocratic, even on occasion *anti*-democratic. But now I was making the most democratic gesture possible, there was a great furore.

The campaigners, mostly unrepresentative zealots, succeeded in linking the Fleshers' Haugh and Elspeth King issues in the public imagination. I was cast as the big bad Council leader trampling down the defenceless. The fact that these quite separate issues were now inextricably linked in the public mind meant that when the *Evening Times* ran its poll, to which less than 1,500 people responded, 88 per cent of them were against the proposed development.

True to my word, I accepted the result of the poll and the matter was dropped. Fleshers' Haugh remains to this day a collection of little-used red blaes football pitches, and Glasgow Green as a whole, in spite of some improvements, much as it was in 1988 when the issue was first raised. There is some hope for the future, however. The pall of neglect will be lifted when the Lottery-funded Millennium project for Glasgow Green proceeds. This will include new planting, upgrading of children's play facilities and the restoration of the impressive terracotta fountain which was gifted to Glasgow by the Doulton company in 1888. Undoubted improvements, but, alas, not enough.

CHAPTER NINE

As 1990, our year of triumphs and traumas, proceeded towards its close, one event gave me enormous personal satisfaction. On 5 October, in the presence of the Princess Royal and an audience of more than two thousand, the new Glasgow Concert Hall opened.

In June the European Community's Strathclyde Integrated Development Fund had, much to our delight, awarded £10 million to Glasgow projects. £8½ million of this sum went to the concert hall, reducing the charge on the City itself and allowing us to spend the balance on the refurbishment of the McLellan Galleries.

In early September, the Queen recognised the significance of the concert hall by allowing the word 'Royal' to be used in its name. The *Daily Record*'s banner headline was 'The Lally Palais', and underneath, in much smaller lettering, 'Or as the Queen calls it, the Glasgow Royal Concert Hall'. Ever since that headline, most folk have given the *Record* the credit for the concert hall's nickname, but I'm sure Tom Shields could put them right.

Strangely, although Michael Tumelty, the *Glasgow Herald*'s music correspondent, had roundly condemned the hall's previous moniker when we were still using the word 'International' and had criticised the acronym 'GICH', he had nothing negative to say about the new name. When the hall was handed over by the contractors at the end of August, I was happy to remind a news conference of Mr Tumelty's bet of a bottle of whisky that the hall would not be ready in time for its royal opening in October. As an honourable man, Mr Tumelty handed over a gallon of whisky, which was happily received by the Castlemilk pensioners. Being a journalist, he didn't buy the whisky himself. It was gifted by Gloags, producers of a well-known, indeed famous, brand of the amber nectar. As Mr Tumelty's column recorded:

The problem wasn't the wager – I won't grouse about that. It was the relentless and staggering impecuniosity of *Herald*'s music man.

He continued:

It was a very large gallon bottle which yesterday, with a twang of the heartstrings (I've never held a gallon of whisky before), the *Herald* presented to Pat Lally. The bottle will be delivered smartly by Councillor Lally to the Castlemilk Pensioners Action Committee. The *Herald* music department's immediate application for membership was declined.

Mr Tumelty wasn't aware of this at the time, but a major factor in our decision to seek the approval of the Palace was his repeated criticism of GICH. I may have won the bet, but I hope Mr Tumelty can now take some small pleasure in the fact that he was instrumental in our concert hall becoming the Glasgow Royal Concert Hall.

The opening day, 5 October, was actually the day after the anniversary of the burning-down of the old St Andrew's Halls. While we had aimed for the exact day, it was more important that the Princess Royal should be able to join us. She was delighted with the hall and very happy to participate. A facility that the city had lacked for so long and needed so badly was, at long last, open. Glasgow was now in a position to provide state-of-the-art facilities for international performers in a 2,500-seater auditorium. It was a magnificent new asset, and all those people who had said it would never be finished in time had been proven wrong.

It must, however, be admitted that not all the great ventures of 1990 turned out to be successes. In early December, BBC TV's *Focal Point* reviewed our year as European Capital of Culture under the title 'A Tale of Two Cities'. The programme considered the extent to which the Glasgow of 1990 had been a contradiction of the alternative notion of the city promulgated by the little group of Scotia Bar Trotskyites and anarchists who paraded under the banner 'Workers City'. The Scotia, in Stockwell Street, a short distance from the River Clyde, is one of the pubs which claims to be the oldest in Glasgow. It is the haunt of writers, folk music fans and off-beat politicians of the armchair variety. Of *Glasgow's Glasgow*, the presenter, George Hume, asked, 'Did you buy a lemon?' With regret I had to conceed that the description was apt, 'We bought a lemon.' This ambitious exhibition did not live up to expectation.

The concept of *Glasgow's Glasgow* – to present the city's history in a contemporary, inter-active way – was fine. To have had a year-long cultural celebration without an exhibition on Glasgow would have been wholly unacceptable. The plan originally outlined to us dealt with Glasgow's relationships with the world, particularly the development of the new world, Glasgow's industry, the exportation of trains, the volume of our shipbuilding and the history of Glasgow's people. The intention was to reflect all aspects of Glasgow's development, including the fundamental role of the workers in trade and industry and in the development of the city.

The exhibition's location under Central Station was innovative, and the Scottish Development Agency put substantial resources into ensuring that this inspired but difficult location would work. In 1989 we became fearful that Doug Clelland and his cohorts weren't able to deliver it within a realistic budget. As we had already invested a very great deal, the only solution was to put some of our own senior officers on the *Glasgow's Glasgow* board to ensure that work on the exhibition progressed as efficiently as possible. Our Director of Museums, Julian Spalding, was particularly critical of the organisation of the event. Although by this time it was already an exercise in damage limitation, the Policy and Resources Committee of the City Council agreed that the exhibition should proceed. Cancellation would have left us with a substantial debt and nothing to show for it.

Part of the way through the exhibition's run we insisted on a further change. The exhibition had been charging £4 a head, but we decided that this should be cut to £1 with accompanied children getting in free. This greatly boosted the number of visitors, but it would have had to increase fourfold to equal the income brought in at the previous price. The price cut was about access rather than income. It was important that the exhibition should be available to as many people as possible.

In total *Glasgow's Glasgow* cost over £4.5 million. Financially it was the biggest disaster of 1990, but there were compensations. Not only had it launched, in the Arches, a fine new multi-use venue, but also, by its close, it had attracted over half a million people. It was by far the most successful post-war exhibition to have taken place in Glasgow. Those who visited really liked it, so it may have been a lemon, but it was a fairly juicy one.

Somehow, it wouldn't have seemed right if 1990 had ended without a massive dispute and the press calling for my head. The year had been a massive success. The perception of Glasgow throughout the world had changed for good. Glasgow's people were now the proud possessors of a new concert hall of international quality and many of them had witnessed a succession of world-class stars who by their presence had endorsed Glasgow's hard-fought place on the cultural map.

The year would end with me once again embroiled in controversy and the subject of attacks in the press. Strathclyde Regional Council had put up £500,000 towards the cost of the concert hall. The money was to be used in the furbishment of an area that would become known as the Strathclyde Suite. I remember commenting at the time that, for half a million pounds, I would have called it Disneyland if they'd wanted. The Regional Council then suggested that an expanse of blank wall in the lower foyer of the concert hall should be decorated with paintings. They would spend £50,000 holding a competition to select an artist. In principle, I was quite happy with that, as we needed something other than bare walls.

I have learned subsequently that to achieve an appropriate result in an art competition you have to exercise control over those who are selected to enter. If I were asked now, I would suggest a limited competition between people who could do the type of job required – not that you shouldn't allow one or two unknowns to become involved, as you might get a magnificent surprise. I was apprehensive about how the proposed competition might turn out, and among the conditions we laid down was that we should have the ultimate say over what was appropriate for the hall.

Charlie Gray, then Leader of Strathclyde Regional Council, doesn't like modern art, and Strathclyde Region took a hands-off approach. They appointed the architect in charge of the concert hall project, John Richards, to be chairman of a judging panel that also included the heads of painting at the Glasgow and Edinburgh schools of art and the artists Jacki Parry and Barbara Rae.

The open invitation for artists to submit applications attracted over 150 ideas, including entries from the USA and Europe. The only major developing figure to get on to the shortlist was Steven Campbell. I was reassured to hear that he was included. However, when the entries came in Steven had not worked up his preliminary design, which effectively ruled him out. It was a great pity and I was bitterly disappointed.

The judges' favourite design was by Iain McCulloch. I commented that I didn't like it and that it was extremely garish. John Richards assured me that it could be toned down, but I wasn't convinced – I had never heard of a real artist toning down a painting. So I reminded Charlie Gray that although the Region might agree on a winner of their competition, we would decide what went up in the concert hall. I didn't want to embarrass the Region by imposing our right of sanction. It was a mistake because they went ahead with their press conference, against my advice, and announced that Iain McCulloch was the winner. It seemed extraordinary that, having trawled the whole world for an appropriate artist, they'd managed to find one in Lenzie, a charming middle-class satellite of Glasgow about ten miles from the city centre which was, I think, established in Victorian times.

Foolishly, I then deferred to John Richards and his panel of judges. These were people, after all, with a great deal more experience of the art world than myself. I suppose I was naïvely hoping that, in the translation from sketches to full-sized murals, McCulloch's designs would eventually fit in to the ambience of our new concert hall, but it was not to be. Shortly after they went up, the director of the concert hall, Cameron McNicol, commented wryly that everybody who saw the murals had a religious experience. I looked slightly bemused, and he continued, 'Well, you see, Pat, everyone who comes up the stairs is stopped in their tracks and they invariably exclaim either "Oh my God!" or "Jesus Christ!" '

The dinner to inaugurate McCulloch's work was planned for the night of Monday 10 December. The murals created such a discordant note within our new concert hall that I decided I had no choice but to be bold. At the dinner I thanked Strathclyde Region for their generous contribution to the concert hall. I then indicated that the paintings would remain in situ for the whole of the concert hall's inaugural year, making my point clear with the words: 'Nothing in this life is permanent.' Iain McCulloch had brought along sketches of his work to present to various people on the occasion. I never did find out if he'd brought one for me, because with all the dignity he could muster he got up and left the dinner after my speech. The next day the press was full of it.

In a letter to the *Glasgow Herald* McCulloch, who had presumably attended the Michael Donnelly school of socialist invective, described my attitude to his paintings as 'an attack upon freedom itself'. He went on to argue that his work was intended to:

> Bear witness to the struggle of mankind for freedom: freedom in the first instance from blind nature; freedom from superstition; freedom from the brutalities attendant upon the doctrine of the divine right to rule; freedom from religious and political dogma; until at the end of the cycle man emerges dominant but rightfully fearful of his future. That is what these paintings are about and that is what is being suppressed.

All that was very well, but in the setting of the Glasgow Royal Concert Hall all of this invective, expressed in paint on canvas, looked bloody awful.

The critic Clare Henry, writing in the *Glasgow Herald*, gave an accurate description of the pictures:

> The design comprises two panels, each addressing the theme of Strathclyde seen at different periods of time and social development. Raw black outlines his parade of heroic characters and seething personal bestiary which includes Mary Queen of Scots after the defeat at the battle of Langside, Christ on the ass at Palm Sunday, and an industrial-modern Adam with a spanner tongue.

She continued:

> McCulloch believes art has a purpose. He confronts serious issues with gusto. He doesn't try to soften contradiction, provide easy solutions or eschew violence. His art, theatrical, dramatic and ironic, acts as a parable of our plight. It speaks highly of the power of his work that Pat Lally is so determined to remove his paintings.

The misunderstanding lay in the assumption that the issue had anything to do with power – either the power of art or the powers that were vested in me as Leader of the Council. It was simply a question of what was appropriate. Iain McCulloch is a very considerable artist whose work has a great deal to say, in the right setting. In spite of Strathclyde Region's attempts to argue that there was a case in law for the murals to remain, I had them taken down and erected in the Tramway, our avant-garde exhibition venue, where they did not look out of place.

Throughout 1990, and into 1991, the *Glasgow Herald* had been consistently critical of the Council and particularly of me. They had chosen to personalise the Elspeth King issue, so that although the decision not to appoint her had been clearly the responsibility of our Director of Museums, I was made the subject of the *Herald*'s attack. The same was true in the case of Fleshers' Haugh and the concert hall murals: they were running a sustained campaign.

When I met the *Glasgow Herald*'s then editor, Arnold Kemp, at a reception in the Burrell Gallery, I decided that this was an opportunity for a little chat. I made it clear that he could continue his campaign of vitriol and invective against me as long as he liked, but I would continue to do what I believed to be right for the city, whether that met with his approval or not. I made it quite clear that I would not be swayed by the *Herald*'s attacks. The way I had operated in the past was the way I intended to continue. Our discussion did get a little heated, but Mr Kemp and I now had an understanding. The *Herald*'s tone subsequently changed. The criticism did not cease, but now it was much more reasoned, which, as a politician, was all I could reasonably expect. Overt sycophancy would have been nice, but balanced criticism was quite acceptable.

Early in the new year, I was preoccupied by two electoral issues; one affecting Scotland, the other more specific to Glasgow. I became Vice-Convenor of the Scottish Labour Campaign for Electoral Success. This organisation had been set up to work against the introduction of proportional representation. Such an electoral system could, we felt, only lead to instability. As a Scottish Assembly seemed inevitable and depended only upon the election of a Labour government, something else which seemed only a matter of time, it was important to examine the implications of PR. In an 'Outsider' piece in the *Glasgow Herald*, I emphasised that:

> The Labour Party exists to exercise the power of government as socialists on behalf of working people. As such, we surely believe that a non-Labour government in Edinburgh would be just as damaging to the interests of this country and its people as a UK one at Westminster.

As no party had won more than 50 per cent of the Scottish vote since the Tories in 1955, PR would reduce the likelihood of a majority Labour government to zero. On the assumption that a coalition with the SNP or the Tories could never happen, it was, therefore, inevitable that the only government arising out of such a process would be a coalition between Labour and the Liberal Democrats.

The prospect, for the Liberal Democrats, was that they could be in government without 'the inconvenience of ever having to win a single seat outright'. I concluded my argument by stressing that, with Labour in its best position for nearly twenty years to win a general election, we should be seeking to use the power of government to serve the country according to our own programme endorsed by the electorate.

PR would be 'a historical betrayal of our voters and our members, and, in the end, Scotland'. I warned against the creation of a Scottish Assembly arising out of a promise of Labour policies but created under an electoral system which would prevent those policies from being carried out. In any case, the notion that PR was in some way more democratic than the first-past-the-post system overlooked the inevitable distortion which PR would introduce.

By empowering the central party machines to create the electoral lists, PR would effectively condemn the electorate to the choice of the apparatchiks. Unfortunately all that I predicted in 1991, came to pass in 1999. Scotland's first assembly resulted in the creation of an uneasy Labour/Liberal Democrat coalition, and the top-up lists, particularly from the Labour Party, had a number of sycophantic, time-serving hacks, selected by the Party centrally.

In April 1991, the Conservative Government presented its proposals for restructuring the Scottish local authorities. The Scottish local government minister, Allan Stewart, presumably to redress the balance after our earlier proposal of a larger Glasgow, suggested that the city should be divided into four new authorities. I commented, 'This is a Lilliputian solution to reorganisation of local government. It's thought up by small men with small minds who think small.' Stewart was simply following the path that Margaret Thatcher had taken in London, when she destroyed the Greater London Council and deprived the capital of an international voice. London ended up without representation and now Allan Stewart was trying to introduce similar proposals in Glasgow which would silence Scotland's largest city.

Stewart clearly believed that his own constituency, Eastwood, was the centre of the universe and that the creation of more Eastwoods would be a good thing. He obviously hoped it would be a good thing for the Tory Party. As it turned out, when the new authorities were eventually created, although the boundaries were further compromised, the situation was nothing like as bad as Stewart's absurd proposals. Glasgow may have been compromised, but at least it was substantially intact.

Another issue which arose early in 1991 and which, like the Scottish Parliament, would find a resolution in the last months of the millennium, was the new Hampden. There was a proposal to move Scotland's national stadium outside Glasgow, where, it was argued, it would be much easier to provide the level of car-parking and support facilities required.

I put my weight behind the *Evening Times* campaign for building a new stadium at Hampden, citing the success of our twinned cities, Nuremburg and Dalian, in building new stadia; Turin, with whom Glasgow had a friendship link, had been given a stadium wholly funded by central government. Glasgow had little hope of government finance and the Council was compromised by its borrowing limits. The new

Hampden was eventually built, but only after the invention of the National Lottery and the Millennium Fund.

As we moved towards the Council's leadership elections in May 1991, I felt that a challenge to my leadership of the Labour Group was inevitable. Over the previous year, hardly a day had gone by without some attack on myself in the press. Despite the undoubted success of Glasgow's year as the European Capital of Culture, politicians tended to focus on negative press coverage. But when the challenge did come, even I was surprised at some of those ranged against me.

CHAPTER TEN

The headline in the *Evening Times* read 'Secret Plot to Oust Lally'. It was May Day 1991, somehow a symbolic date for the knives to be out. The paper announced that the first challenge to my leadership in five years would be led by Councillor Charles McCafferty, affectionately known as 'Chic'. This was no surprise. McCafferty was a close ally of Jean McFadden and someone who had hung around on the fringes for a number of years. In 1989, he had been elected to the Labour Group Executive, although he failed to hang on to the position the following year.

McCafferty's challenge was not surprising, unlike the identity of two of his cohorts. The other members, of what the *Evening Times* somewhat predictably described as the 'Gang of Four', were Bill Butler, Marjory O'Neill and Margaret Sinclair. Both Madge O'Neill and Margaret Sinclair were friends and supporters of mine: now here they were challenging my leadership of the Group. Ironically, they justified their challenge by arguing that my leadership style was too autocratic – exactly the same argument I had used against Jean McFadden five years previously. The only difference was that in her case it was true. By speaking to the press the 'Gang of Four' were breaking the Labour Group rule concerning the public communication of internal matters, which stipulated who was authorised to talk to the press. They were eventually reprimanded and warned about their future conduct.

On 15 May I beat Chic McCafferty for the leadership by six votes. This was in effect a warning shot from my fellow councillors, as was made clear when McCafferty didn't even get voted on to the Executive. You've got to watch politicians – sometimes they can be awful devious.

With a renewed mandate, I was able to proceed both with rectifying past mistakes and, although we were no longer the European Capital of Culture, to pursue new prizes for the city. In June we were happy to announce that the prominent Scottish artist Peter Howson had agreed to produce replacements for the thoroughly inappropriate paintings in the concert hall. His pictures, which were to have cost £60,000 were being financed by Scottish Amicable, one of Scotland's leading life assurance companies. Unfortunately, but perhaps inevitably, the furore over the murals flared up again and Howson eventually bowed out.

The Poll Tax caused further internal strife within the Labour Group when five members opposed the Labour Group's agreed policy that Glaswegians should be advised to pay their tax. Jim McVicar, Chic Stevenson, Larry Flanagan, Archie Simpson and Bill Butler were subsequently censured for their actions. Councillors McVicar, Stevenson and Flanagan were suspended without limit of time, which meant they could not stand as Labour candidates at the subsequent election in May 1992. McVicar and Stevenson left the Labour Party and stood as Militant candidates. Archie Simpson was suspended for nine months and subsequently left the Labour Party to stand as an SNP candidate. Bill Butler was suspended for six months.

Another saga which, like the Poll Tax, would run and run, was prompted by the announcement that Edinburgh was the favoured location for the proposed new National Gallery of Scottish Art. My reaction was swift – I identified an alternative site in Glasgow (opposite the concert hall) and even produced an indicative design. Edinburgh was, after all, already the home of the Royal Museum, the National Gallery, the National Gallery of Modern Art and the National Portrait Gallery – an overabundance of museums funded by all the people of Scotland but substantially benefiting the Edinburgh economy.

The *Herald*'s editorial on 23 August was strongly supportive of our position – perhaps Arnold Kemp was trying to make amends. Arguing that Glasgow had half the population of Scotland within travelling distance, it derided the demonstrable lack of other Government investment in the city, and expressed the opinion that Edinburgh already had galleries enough. It was not a question of any rivalry, real or imagined, between Glasgow and Edinburgh, but simply a need to redress the balance. The editorial concluded 'this scurvy treatment of Glasgow is gratuitous probably political, and a growing scandal which must be challenged'. For once the *Herald* was being overtly partisan in backing me on a key issue for the city. Partisan but absolutely right.

The Trustees of the National Galleries of Scotland were, it seems, swayed by our arguments. The matter went into abeyance and we were able to regroup, fully consider the site options and strengthen our arguments in favour of the gallery being in Glasgow. By early 1992 we were able to offer alternative sites including Pollok Park near the Burrell

Gallery and the superb former Sheriff Court building right in the heart of the city. We were also able to show that without access to major collections held by the City of Glasgow, the proposed gallery would be woefully inadequate. Glasgow held a number of works by Scottish painters in which the National Collection was weak. We also had an unrivalled collection of work by Charles Rennie Mackintosh. Together these considerations created an extremely powerful argument in our favour.

Our bid to become the UK City of Visual Arts in 1996 also centred round a gallery issue. This time, what was proposed was the conversion of the former Royal Exchange – which had more recently served as Stirlings Library – into a gallery of modern art. I had been sitting in my office one day, mulling over what might be done to ensure the long-term future of the building, when I began to wonder whether it could be transformed into a gallery of modern art. My next move was to check our capital programme. I established that we had £4.6 million yet to be allocated. I then talked to our Director of Architecture, Chris Purslow, explained what I wanted to do and suggested that he go along to have a look at the building to see whether it could be converted to a gallery of modern art. I also asked him not to tell the library staff the purpose of his visit.

The Royal Exchange is a superb Georgian building. It was actually built around an earlier mansion house which is still visible if you know where to look. The lofty portico and the magnificent Exchange Room itself were added in the 1820s to create one of the most impressive civic buildings in Glasgow.

The fact that the Royal Exchange sits at the end of Ingram Street and is the centrepiece of a beautiful Georgian square simply adds to the impressive effect. Yet this magnificent civic building, which had been owned by the City for many years, was largely neglected. The ground floor was occupied by the library, which was popular and well-used. The basement, which extended beyond the footprint of the building, had suffered badly from water penetration resulting from damage caused by heavy vehicles parking on the pavement above. Part of this area was occupied by Mayfest. But the rest of the building lay empty. Some years before, there had been a serious outbreak of dry rot on the upper floors, but this had been eradicated.

Because of the various extensions to the original mansion house, the Exchange was a curious mixture of levels that had never been properly integrated. So it was a difficult building to utilise. Indeed, in the early eighties, the Royal Exchange was almost lost to the City of Glasgow.

It had been proposed that, in view of its under-use, the building should be sold. Almost immediately a building society offered a million pounds. I was on the Labour Group Executive at the time, and argued that this was a civic structure which should be used for a civic purpose. This argument was sufficient to dissuade my colleagues from disposing of the building, although at the time I had no idea what a proper civic purpose for the building might be.

Chris Purslow inspected the building and reported that not only could it be converted into a gallery with the necessary offices, shop and restaurant that such a public facility would require, but it could be done within the extraordinarily tight budget available.

The next problem was rehousing the library. It was a popular library that would have to be relocated somewhere central. I talked to the Director of Finance, who told me that the Council was selling some of its property in Miller Street to a developer. So, in exchange for the property, the developer could build the new library for us. It was an ideal solution.

When the proposal was explained to our Convenor of Arts and Culture, Councillor Charles Davidson, he was enthusiastic and agreed to give his support. Our Director of Museums and Art Galleries, Julian Spalding, was then brought in to work with Chris Purslow on the plans for the gallery. After the necessary papers were drawn up, committee approval sought and achieved, the future of one of Glasgow's finest buildings was assured.

Our acquisitions fund had already created a superb collection that included work from artists such as John Bellany, Ken Currie, David Hockney and Peter Howson. Now we had the building to house it and we were confident that we could gather the funding to create a superb facility. We went into the competition for the City of Visual Arts full of confidence.

The title UK City of Visual Arts was one of a number of annual prizes that the Arts Council of Great Britain planned to award in the years leading up to the Millennium. The then Chairman of the Arts Council, Peter Palumbo, had been hugely impressed when he visited Glasgow in 1990. He decided that each year up until the year 2000 would be identified with a particular art form and these would be the focus of year-long festivals in cities throughout the UK.

Our 133-page submission for the Visual Arts festival in 1996 was very impressive. I was convinced that no competitor could come close, but, as these things are never absolutely certain, I hedged my bets by indicating that, win or lose, we would organise a festival of the visual arts in 1996. In addition to the new Gallery of Modern Art, we proposed major exhibitions at the McLellan Galleries, a Mackintosh exhibition which would tour the United States and a series of community-based arts initiatives.

When we met the selection panel, they were obviously enormously impressed by our proposals, and we got the impression that they viewed our submission as the best. However, we had been European Capital of Culture in 1990, and they seemed to feel that their job was to give the award to the area that needed it most rather than pick the best candidate. When Peter Palumbo created Arts 2000, I'm quite sure that he didn't see it as a sort of arts-led version of social security.

The peculiar amalgam of Cumbria, Northumberland, Durham, Tyneside and Teeside, styling itself the North Region, became the focus of the Year of Visual Arts. We were disappointed but bullish. As time would tell, Glasgow's celebrations of 1996 would be on a much more substantial scale and leave a more enduring legacy than anything in Durham or Tyneside.

Early in 1992, the great value of our cultural endeavours, which were aimed at creating a new momentum for the city of Glasgow, was confirmed by the publication of a study by the economist John Myerscough. It revealed that around 12 million people had attended our events during 1990 and nearly 6,000 extra jobs were created for the city. His report emphasised that unless we continued to generate new projects, there was a danger of the momentum of 1990 being dissipated. I was determined that so long as my leadership continued, there would be no risk of this happening. But just a couple of months after Myerscough's confirmation that my work on behalf of the city had generated real change, Jean McFadden challenged me for the leadership – and won!

In the local government elections for the city in early May, I was returned with a reduced but still healthy majority. The Labour Party was enormously successful, so clearly the electorate appreciated the way Glasgow was being run. But the influx of new councillors worked to Jean McFadden's advantage. Over the years I had noticed that on the various occasions when Jean McFadden and I challenged for particular posts, newcomers would invariably support the Duchess at first but come round to supporting me once they had got to know us and the way the Council worked. I think this was partly because Jean McFadden enjoyed a closer relationship with the City and Central Labour parties. By contrast, I had been at odds with the party machine on several occasions. Rather than pander to a party line that had nothing to do with its manifesto, I pursued whatever was in the interests of the people of Glasgow, believing this to be in the long-term interest of the Party.

On 27 May 1992, I was beaten thirty-one votes to twenty-three by Jean McFadden for the leadership of the Group. I was not, however, entirely out in the cold. Jean's stalking horse from the year before, Chic McCafferty, challenged me for the position of Depute Leader. The vote was as close as I had anticipated. On the first count, we both polled twenty-seven votes. After two more rounds produced ties, we agreed that the only way to resolve matters was to trust to luck and toss a coin. I won.

Speaking to the BBC immediately after my defeat for the leadership, I promised a comeback. The interviewer asked if, in my new role as Jean McFadden's Depute, I would be supportive. My response, with a smile, was 'I'll give her the same support she gave me'. Jean McFadden was then asked if in her triumph she would be magnanimous to her Depute. Through a smile that I'm convinced was forced, she responded, 'I'll give him the same loyalty he gave me.' But she didn't.

I was Depute Leader of Glasgow City Council but had no specific responsibility. In a way, the situation was similar to that of Peter Mandelson, when he became minister without portfolio. I'm sure that Councillor McFadden would even have taken away my chairmanship of the Concert Hall Board but for the fear that this move might backfire. It struck me as ironic that in a similar situation six years previously, I had ensured that she became City Treasurer, a position with a good deal of influence. However, in such situations, there's nothing to be done, so I carried on with my constituency duties and making contributions to Council and Group meetings when it was appropriate.

Shortly after the Council's elections, the Region also voted for a new Leader. Charles Gray had, like myself, been Leader for six years. Over that time, he had, I think, steered the Region skilfully and always with an eye to what was in the best interests of the electorate. However, in the months leading up to the election he had been a little intemperate on a number of issues, and it was this brusqueness of manner which led to his being challenged.

The challenger, Bob Gould, was a former railwayman. The Depute Leader of the Regional Council, he was little-known outside political circles. One newspaper questioned 'Bob Who?' Despite his fine head of grey hair, Bob never looked well. He was overweight, with a sallow complexion, and a slight stoop. But, on 1 June, he still managed to beat Gray by forty-eight votes to thirty-seven. One of his colleagues was quoted in the *Evening Times* as saying 'he is a quiet, methodical man, who believes in making decisions through talking and discussion, rather than confrontation'. But some years later, Bob Gould's style of politics would lead the City of Glasgow into deep and profound crisis.

Happily, although I was no longer Leader, the momentum on a number of key projects was maintained by others, mainly outwith the Council. The recently established Glasgow Development Agency, led by its Chief Executive, Stuart Gulliver, was beginning to realise the potential of the city's key industrial sites, as it pursued the infrastructure and cultural projects that I had for so long seen as fundamental to Glasgow's future prosperity. The developers John Sheridan and Douglas Loan, who had been responsible for the superb Italian Centre, promoted their plans for transforming the former Sheriff Court building on Ingram Street into the National Gallery of Scottish Art. This was a superb idea and would have brought much-needed investment right into the heart of the Merchant City. This key area had been the focus of a great deal of expenditure in the mid-eighties but, with recession and the move away from such urban projects by the Glasgow Development Agency's predecessor, the Scottish Development Agency, progress had slowed markedly.

A minor arts issue arose over the purchase by the City of an eleven-foot-high statue of me by the renowned neo-classical sculptor Sandy Stoddart. The piece was created in a response to an article by the *Glasgow Herald*'s art critic, Clare Henry, on the concert hall murals. Stoddart had taken exception to Clare Henry's suggestion that I had a predilection for a sort of chocolate box cliché of historic art. In her article she had mentioned blue skies, swallows and shepherdesses. So Stoddart placed a sculpture of my head on a massive plinth which bore the German inscriptions 'Blauer Himmel' (blue skies), 'Schwalben' (swallows), 'Schaferinnen' (shepherdesses), 'Girlanden' (garlands) and, finally, 'Biderlally' – 'honest Lally'. While I had my doubts about the swallows and shepherdesses, I could not disagree with Mr Stoddart's final assessment of his subject.

The fuss was caused not by the statue itself but by Julian Spalding's decision to buy it. At £10,000 it was a snip for such a substantial work by a well-known artist. But those in power at the time didn't quite see it that way. They challenged Julian Spalding over the issue, only to find that he had already entered a legal agreement and the purchase was a *fait accompli*. Julian Spalding never discussed the matter with me, but if he had, I would have told him that it was none of my business. When we set up the Contemporary Art Fund, it was quite clear that works would not be chosen by committee. The Council employed a highly qualified and well-paid visual arts expert to take such decisions. The Director of Museums and Galleries had the necessary experience and knowledge, so the acquisition fund was his to manage. There are certain areas of activity which I don't think committees should get involved in. I'm constantly reminded of the old adage about a camel being a horse designed by committee, although I do quite like the Glasgow architect Isi Metzstein's take on that: 'a committee is a decision-making body designed by a camel'!

Some people – particularly critics like Clare Henry – had suggested that a panel of experts should be established, but the vast majority were happy with the arrangement as it stood. So when Spalding bought the 'Biderlally' he was operating within his delegated authority. Whether I felt the statue was good, bad or indifferent, it was his decision to purchase it. I enjoyed one *Sunday Mail* headline, 'Statue Pat?' While the hat does wonders for my hairline, if you look at the bust closely, it's much too jowly. It makes me look old.

I remember being part of a City delegation to Russia for a Burns Supper. On the way back, one of the plane's engines blew out, which caused some trepidation. One of my fellow delegates, the senior Conservative John Young, commented that if we didn't make it back, at least I was assured a little bit of immortality through the bust. So posterity will have an image of me in a silly hat – oh well!

I was reminded all too poignantly of my mortality when, in April 1993, my brother Robert died of a stroke at the age of sixty-four. Robert was a constant friend and supporter. He never married and, as I became increasingly active in public life, he became a major contributor to our family life. He visited the house almost every day and was in constant contact by phone. One evening when I arrived home, Peggy was very upset and indicated that Robert hadn't been in touch and she couldn't get him on the phone.

I drove down to Toryglen where Robert lived. When I got to his house, it was all in darkness, which seemed strange. I peered through the blinds and saw him stretched across his bed. I had to call the police to gain entry and they arrived very quickly. When we got in we discovered that Robert was unconscious and he was taken by ambulance to the Victoria Infirmary. He had suffered a massive stroke and never regained consciousness. He died a few days later. As well as being my brother, Robert was also my best friend from childhood onwards. I have always regretted that I was not able to say farewell and let him know just how much I cared.

After Robert's funeral, I was thrust once more into the political fray.

Before the Group elections in 1993, the *Evening Times* ran the headline, 'It's Lazarus Lally'. The piece confidently predicted that I was 'set to make a spectacular comeback bid'. I wasn't, and I didn't, and in the elections I was even beaten for the Depute Leadership by Chic McCafferty. Once again, he got the all-too familiar twenty-seven votes, but on this occasion no coin-tossing was required, as I only got twenty-four.

So once again, it was time to hunker down and get on with it. Two major events were looming. The city was proceeding, albeit with rather less gusto than I would have liked, towards its festival of visual arts in 1996 and we were also in the running for the 1999 City of Architecture and Design award.

By December 1993, the *Evening Times* was dusting off its Lazarus headlines again. This time it assumed that the nickname was well-enough known to stand on its own. Its piece, which was simply headed 'Lazarus set for Council takeover', reported that I was 'set to mount a sensational takeover coup in Glasgow City Chambers within months'. The election of my supporter Paul Martin for the Alexandra Park ward was seen as a boost to my chances of election. Although Jean McFadden refrained from commenting, her Depute, Chic McCafferty, had no doubts: 'I don't think there's any likelihood of Jean being defeated.'

As the 1994 Council elections approached, several people in Jean McFadden's coterie, faction, or gang or whatever you might like to call it, were dissatisfied with her *modus operandi*. They felt that her approach lacked drive and leadership: she was never good at making decisions; there always seemed to be somebody else to consult.

I'm convinced that many of the Council's officers were frustrated at not being able to act because key decisions hadn't been made, and when there is frustration among the officers, the elected members tend to pick it up. An essential of local government, perhaps of all government, is direction in order to achieve change – it is the opportunity to bring about change that attracts people to politics in the first place. So as the leadership's lack of direction became obvious, I received increasing support from both old and new members of the Council. I am sure that many would also have started to worry about their chances in the next Council elections. There is nothing like a bit of enlightened self-interest to focus the mind.

CHAPTER ELEVEN

On 18 May 1994 I defeated Jean McFadden for the Group leadership by two votes. In an interview with the BBC I expressed my delight at being able to resume my activities on behalf of Glasgow, which had been so rudely interrupted two years before. Reflecting on Jean McFadden's relative inaction during her time as Leader, and presuming that most folk would have had quite enough of the Lazarus references, I also added playfully, 'Action man is back in action'. The next morning, the *Daily Record*'s brilliant headline was 'Action Man gubs the Ice Maiden'. The *Glaswegian* speculated that it would be difficult for Jean McFadden to make a future comeback. It also suggested that 'she will receive the eventual call, as an establishment figure, to sit in the Lords'. I am sure that the irony of the 'Duchess' actually becoming Lady Jean was not lost on the *Glaswegian*'s columnist.

Now that I was Leader again, one of my first tasks was to decide what attitude I should take towards Mrs McFadden. The first time I became Leader, I saw to it that she became City Treasurer, one of the most important posts in the Council. But when she in turn became Leader, she gave me no post at all. Those, it seemed, were the new rules.

As Leader, she had represented the Council on the Board of the Glasgow Development Agency. It would have been petty and inappropriate to remove her from that post. But she had also represented the Council on the Convention of Scottish Local Authorities (CoSLA), where she had served the city well but for rather a long time. Here I felt it was appropriate to have a new representative. So accordingly, I moved that her term on CoSLA should end.

I could understand Jean McFadden being aggrieved at not retaining the leadership, I could even sympathise with her frustration at our proposal that she stand down from CoSLA. But the response of her supporters to these reverses of fortune was quite unexpected.

The meeting to elect the Lord Provost took place two weeks after the leadership elections. It was three short of the required quorum of members. While Jean McFadden and three of her closest colleagues were present, the rest of her supporters had, it seemed, succumbed to an extraordinary variety of illnesses and personal mishaps. I adjourned the meeting and indicated that we would reconvene at six p.m. I then asked the Group whip, Madge O'Neill, and the Secretary, Pat Chalmers, to contact all of those who were absent, irrespective of their reasons.

When we reconvened, the meeting was still inquorate. I adjourned until the following day. By this time, matters were becoming completely farcical. Jean McFadden's supporters might have been making a point on the first occasion, but when the third meeting without a quorum occurred I indicated that unless the matter was resolved I would suspend all of those who had chosen to be absent pending a Labour Party inquiry. They each received a letter drawing their attention to Group rules. Such was my frustration that I described them in the press as 'a bunch of spoilt weans'. Jean McFadden's colleagues were peevishly preventing those who had won the leadership in a fair contest from getting on with the business of running the city. After my threat attitudes changed.

Jean McFadden had adopted the role of spokesman for our absent colleagues during the meeting. As I had suspected, she was clearly upset by her removal from CoSLA. She argued that, because she had instigated grievance procedures following allegations of bullying and sexual harassment within the organisation, she should continue as a delegate. I agreed to stand down as a delegate to CoSLA until October, to allow her to finalise this inquiry. I made it a condition that she should consult me on other agenda matters, but she never consulted me on anything. Indeed, the individual concerned resigned from CoSLA and the inquiry petered out.

Jean McFadden also wanted Alan Duncan, one of her supporters, to have a place on the new Community Action Committee. I happily granted this request and also agreed that we should seek the view of the City Party with regard to the terms of reference and membership of the Community Action Committee. Peace and harmony was restored. Jimmy Shields was appointed Lord Provost with Tommy Dingwall as his Depute. We were able to get on with the business at hand – or so I thought!

The excuses from those who didn't attend the Group meetings gave us some light relief amid all the frustration and anger. Doubtless the then Group Whip Madge O'Neil still has them on file. If they survive, they will certainly give future historians a chuckle. One member's excuse was that his freezer had broken down and he had to take out a wedding cake and store it in the freezer of a relative who lived outside Glasgow. His car then broke down en route, but we never learned what happened to the wedding cake. Another member wrote that he had injured his back lifting a roller shutter. It all seemed like a new addition to the 'Carry On' series: 'Carry On Up The Council'. Sadly, Jean McFadden bears little relation to Barbara Windsor, and these people were not comedians: they were supposed to be elected representatives of the people and behave with the responsibility that this implied.

Another, quite extraordinary, outcome of the whole situation over the Provostship vote was the subsequent request from, it seems, a number of Jean McFadden's supporters that the Scottish Labour Party should investigate the running of the Council and my role as Leader. Given that these were the same people who were guilty of thwarting the proper process of government the notion of them complaining to the Party did, I suppose, have a certain Alice in Wonderland piquancy about it.

When I lost the leadership I accepted this as the decision of the Labour Group. I continued to work on the business of my constituency and, as far as I was able, that of the Council. Some of the Duchess's supporters on the other hand sought to frustrate the process of government by ensuring that we didn't have a quorum for decision-making. I felt that if there was any investigating to be done, it should surely be of those who were unwilling to accept the democratic will of the Group.

In September I met Jack McConnell, the General Secretary of the Scottish Labour Party. It was an opportunity to discuss how we might overcome the petty factionalism which had damaged the Council's Labour Group earlier in the summer. We had a useful conversation, and I suggested that he should consider calling in the folk who had been at the root of our problems. His lack of enthusiasm for this idea was perhaps a foretaste of things to come.

Sadly, a foretaste of things that weren't to come was the list of goals that I set out shortly after my appointment. Each was achievable and should still be on Glasgow's agenda.

I was keen to give some renewed momentum to the idea of a National Gallery of Scottish Art. Progress on this seemed to have slowed, and I was keen to restart the process. The former Sheriff Court had always been my favourite setting for the new gallery. I felt that the Glasgow Development Agency's proposal to put the gallery in Kelvingrove Park would have the advantage of being close to our own superb facility at Kelvingrove, but the landscape there was carefully planned and any alteration would have been hugely disruptive. After the furore that greeted my attempts to redevelop Fleshers' Haugh, I knew that the disruption to the carefully landscaped parkland in the West End might not be popular with the general public.

A much more achievable aspiration for one of the city's parks was the proposal to create a Millennium tower at Bellahouston. This idea emerged in 1991 when Jim Waugh, whom I knew from his role in our press office for 1990, and his colleague Neil Baxter, brought an outline plan to me. Their proposal was to recreate Tait's Tower from the Empire Exhibition of 1938. While I thought this was a great idea I had to point out that the original tower was built from corrugated steel and close-up it looked pretty nasty.

Their concept was quite different: a sleek, very modern building which would follow the form of the original, with bars and restaurants in a great, glazed curve at its foot, and three viewing balconies which would, they assured me, allow 450 people to see right over the city. There would also be a funicular railway to take people up the hill and, around the base of the tower, in what was effectively an unused area of the park, they were going to ask architects and designers to create safe and fun children's play facilities. The proposal would have transformed the park and provided a tremendous boost for Glasgow.

These ideas, and the plans for a new Scottish National Theatre, could have been realised if we had the support of our partners in the Glasgow Development Agency and Europe. Unfortunately, the impending reorganisation of local government limited my ability to promote such ideas. But I strongly believe that bold objectives should be set even if they are unlikely to come to fruition in the next months or even few years. To move forward, the city must have a vision. There was, however, one vision which we all shared at that time and which was achievable.

Glasgow, along with Edinburgh and Liverpool, had been shortlisted for the award of UK City of Architecture and Design 1999. From my previous experience of an Arts 2000 bid, I knew that ours, when I took over the leadership, was doomed to failure. Replete with high ideals and airy promises, it was phrased in flowery and extravagant language. I felt it failed to give those who would be responsible for judging it enough real information and to make the promises of tangible change which would enable them to decide in Glasgow's favour.

I wasn't the only one who felt our bid was too nebulous. Some of those from the City and its partners from the Glasgow Development Agency and the private sector were concerned as well. The journalist Ruth Wishart had also been asked to create a bid document. Her work was sharper-edged and more focused, but was a synopsis of the original document which cleared out all the wordy clutter. Something more powerful was needed in the very clear, unambiguous language for which Ruth Wishart is justifiably respected.

I requested that the officers concerned should produce a document which maintained the strength of Ruth's writing, but I also emphasised that they should place considerable stress on our intention to democratise the decision-making process and give the ordinary people of Glasgow a voice in determining the nature of the city as it developed in the future. This, I felt, would not only reflect the reality of Glasgow but also put some clear blue water between ourselves and the other bidders.

I understood that Edinburgh and, to a lesser extent, Liverpool, were treating the award as a sort of architectural beauty contest and concentrating on capital projects. If we could demonstrate that we were listening to the voices of ordinary people as well as the experts, I was convinced that this would give us an edge.

As the judges' visit to Glasgow approached, our bid manager, Director of Planning, Mike Hayes, and his team worked hard to make sure that they would have an impressive, stimulating and convincing day. We opened a bid shop and exhibition space in Princes Square, a smart shopping centre right in the heart of the city. The unit we got had been a dance studio and was very stylishly decorated, in a combination of wood, brushed steel and white paint. We simply converted what was there and the shop looked tremendous.

Another great idea, developed by a young architect called David Mason and his senior colleague in our Department of Architecture, Jim Cook, was what they called the 'Big Model'. This was something of a secret weapon. One problem which had perplexed me was the lack of public engagement with what we were doing, despite its importance for the city.

The Big Model, which sat in Princes Square's central, covered courtyard, was made up of bits and pieces of scaled-down buildings and scaled-up design objects. So models of a Mackintosh chair or an IBM computer were placed in the same Glasgow landscape as the tower from Alexander 'Greek' Thomson's St Vincent Street Church or the Waverley, the world's last ocean-going paddle steamer, sitting on the River Clyde. All this was made of wood and acrylic, and looked very impressive.

The idea of the Big Model was to get the public to ask 'What the heck's that?' A masterstroke in the middle of this display was the model of the Finnieston Crane, from which was hanging a straw locomotive. In 1988, for the Glasgow Garden Festival, the sculptor George Wyllie had created a full-size straw locomotive suspended from the real crane. It was a powerful symbol of the heavy industries that had made Glasgow a world force in Victorian times.

Another venture in support of the bid – which raised a few eyebrows – was my trip to Edinburgh during the Edinburgh International Festival. When our attempts to promote our rival bid on Edinburgh's buses were thwarted, I decided that we should take our own bus to Edinburgh. On 1 September, our number 99 double-decker bus, destination Glasgow, made its way along Princes Street. We stopped at the Mound where I held a press conference. Of course, all of the UK's arts media were there and the press interest was tremendous. It was, I suppose, a sort of Glasgow performance art. In response to a question which implied that our visit to Edinburgh was perhaps a little impolite given that we were in competition, I replied that, given that the world's media was in Edinburgh for the Festival, we had decided to come to them. I have to say that all the officers and even the private-sector advisors who were working on the bid cautioned against my visit to Edinburgh. When one of my colleagues, Craig Roberton, called it a very high risk strategy, I replied that it was not as high a risk as doing nothing. Our bid manager, Mike Hayes, who also doubted the wisdom of the trip, did his best to hide himself at the back of the bus. But later he acknowledged that I was right and that my Edinburgh foray had put the spotlight on Glasgow's bid.

Edinburgh's civic leaders were less than thrilled. Their Lord Provost, Norman Irons, complained to Labour's Scottish Secretary, Jack McConnell, and Lesley Hinds, Edinburgh's Leader, expressed the view that our visit was provocative, which of course it was. In press interviews we had frequently described our bid as lighting the blue touch paper, so the *Scotsman*'s cartoon on the occasion was a delight: it depicted a massive firework trailing the words 'Glasgow City of Architecture and Design 99' in the night sky over Edinburgh Castle. I regarded it as a confident prediction of things to come. After that, people were certainly aware that Glasgow was fighting hard to win the City of Architecture prize.

But the organisers of Edinburgh's bid were very confident. Their submission had been driven by one of their most prominent councillors, George Kerevan. Their bid manager was Peter Wilson, who had been involved in the latter stages of the 'lemon' of an exhibition we had mounted for 1990, *Glasgow's Glasgow*. Edinburgh had spent a fortune on expensive marketing and ensuring that their various capital projects, particularly their architecture centre, were ready to start if they won the prize.

One estimate put Edinburgh's expenditure as high as £1.5 million. By the end of our campaign, we had spent only a relatively modest £200,000. The prize itself may have been only £400,000, but the purpose of winning the award was to help address a much more substantial agenda. Infrastructure would be improved and new capital projects generated, but it would also be a lever for a fundamental reappraisal of all aspects of the planning and building process. Both tourists and local people would be able to enjoy the final festival. It was a lot to fight for.

A few days before the official visit from the judges on 26 October 1994, I got a call from the press. The inquiry was in that peculiar, challenging tone which journalists adopt when they imagine that somebody's got one over on you. It seemed that Edinburgh had just announced that they had received official permission from the Queen to use Holyrood Palace for their presentation. If the intention was to disturb my composure, it was unsuccessful. 'That's excellent,' I replied. 'Our presentation will be up a tenement close in Dennistoun.' And I was being utterly sincere! Dennistoun is a housing area in the East End of Glasgow with a mixture of traditional turn-of-the-century tenements and more modern post-war tenemental housing.

We learned that the organisers of Edinburgh's bid intended to take the judges up in a helicopter. So when they came to us the day before, Mike Hayes made a point of telling them that we had contemplated taking them up in a helicopter but felt that this was much too ostentatious. Of course, Edinburgh's plans were top secret, so when the helicopter trip was announced on the following day, the judges immediately marked Edinburgh down as just a little ostentatious.

We had also thought it would be inevitable that, after the judges had seen our extremely elegant, restrained and sophisticated shop and exhibition space, they would ask to see Edinburgh's equivalent. They did and Edinburgh was wrong-footed. There was apparently a great flurry of activity to change the programme and make ready the little, former woollens shop in the Canongate which had been used as the city's bid office.

In Glasgow the judges had enjoyed a long and stimulating day. We showed off all the best that Glasgow was doing in the fields of architecture and design, and introduced them to many representatives of our housing associations. We made sure that there were plenty of surprises and a lot to ponder. They must have been pretty tired when they got on the train to go to Edinburgh in the evening, and doubtless they were impressed by British Rail's generosity in supplying them with ample measures of spirits to speed them on their way. Very civilised! Of course, we picked up the tab for this hospitality.

Our visit to the Royal Academy in London to hear the announcement of the award-winner was very exciting. I was convinced that we had a very good chance, as I think were all of those who had contributed and who went to London to hear the announcement at the Royal Academy. We felt we'd produced the best proposals and we knew that the judges had been impressed by their visit to Glasgow.

We'd delivered our bid as a team, in which the City had co-operated with its various partners. I also felt that we had met the objectives laid down by the Arts Council. The others had perhaps tended to ignore the conditions, stating instead what they believed the year should be about and trying too hard to shoe-horn the bid into their city's agenda rather than adjusting their own agenda to comply with the bid conditions. We were also fortunate in that our views about public participation and the Arts Council's coincided so closely.

At the Royal Academy it was like being at a cup final. The teams were all excited, there was a great build-up and the tension was exhilarating. Sir Terence Conran, the chairman of the judging panel, delivered a little speech about how every city had offered different things and each had unique merits. It was exactly the sort of speech which was required and expected, but no one was really concentrating.

Sir Terence finished his preamble and announced simply, 'And the winner is . . .' Then an interminable time seemed to go by as he opened the gilt envelope. 'Glasgow!' he shouted, and the room went wild. Glaswegians, who unlike the representatives from Edinburgh and Liverpool, had stayed at the back of the room, were leaping around and embracing each other.

One or two members of our party even started a thoroughly inappropriate football chant: 'Easy! Easy!' They were soon hushed. After all, we had to be magnanimous in victory, and in fact, their chant wasn't even accurate – it hadn't been easy. But we knew it had been worth the effort.

Our rivals were devastated. The Liverpudlians took their defeat in good part. A number of them gave mock punches to their former Director of Planning, who had subsequently, as our Director of Planning and bid manager, found himself competing against his native city. But Edinburgh, perhaps less steeled for defeat, took it badly. So convinced had the East Coast team been that they were going to win that they'd invited the world's press and media to a big party in Edinburgh. The reaction of their Lord Provost, Norman Irons, on receiving the news was relayed on television. One of the things you learn in politics is to congratulate opponents and keep smiling. That night, Norman Irons showed the strain, as he had been placed in a difficult and embarrassing position. The champagne was packed away and I believe the celebration cake was sold off in the City Council's canteen the next day for thirty-five pence a slice. And the media set off to travel forty-five miles along the motorway to a city which had just started to party.

After Conran's announcement, I got up on to the stage to accept the award. I had made preparations by taking a 'Glasgow's Miles Better' car sticker. Mr Happy, Glasgow's famous smiling face logo, had been resurrected only the week before. This would be his first major appearance in the national media since his return. Somehow, I empathised with Mr Happy.

I put my hand in my pocket to discover to my horror that the sticker I thought I had carefully folded wasn't there. My triumphal gesture would be thwarted. Fortunately I looked down at the crowd of smiling Glaswegians and caught the eye of the Labour Group secretary, Pat Chalmers. One of the great advantages that Glaswegians have over the rest of humanity is telepathy. Pat immediately knew what I wanted, and delved into her handbag to emerge triumphantly waving a 'Glasgow's Miles Better' sticker. Within seconds, I was holding it proudly over my head. It was a shot which appeared in innumerable newspapers.

The difference between the award for City of Architecture and Design and that of City of Culture was that in 1990 the Arts Minister Richard Luce had made the announcement at a distance. For the 1999 award, the whole team was together. That, coupled with the presence of our rivals and the conviction that this was the last big prize of the Millennium made it an extraordinarily dramatic moment. I have no idea how I would have felt if we hadn't won, and I couldn't help but feel sorry for the Edinburgh team who had invested far too much both financially and emotionally. Their key players, particularly George Kerevan, were devastated.

At the end of the evening, the whole Glasgow contingent headed off to a Chinese restaurant called Zen and Now. It was designed by the architect Rick Mather who some years later would make a notable contribution to Glasgow's celebrations as the UK's City of Architecture and Design.

CHAPTER TWELVE

It's extraordinary how often, when you're on a high, fate brings you back down to earth. After our euphoria in London two events conspired to do just that. The first was rather insignificant, only really memorable because it happened so immediately after my return. A couple of days after our famous victory, my car, a modest little Mini Metro, was stolen from outside our house, driven to the bottom of the hill and torched. Never one to be downed by adversity, I decided to put the insurance money to good use. Instead of replacing the car, I used the £1,200 to buy shares. This wasn't a conversion to gross capitalism, but an emotional investment. The shares, of which I am still the proud owner, were in Celtic Football Club. Ever since my father first took me along to a cup final when I was too young really to understand what was going on, I have been a fan of Celtic. Unfortunately, because spending most of my working life in retail meant working on Saturdays, I couldn't get to as many games as I would like. Most years the only football match I got to see was the New Year's Day Celtic–Rangers match – a match that many other folk avoided. I did get to the odd evening game, but my attendance inevitably diminished as my political career took up more and more of my time. So while I've always been keen on Celtic and a supporter for nearly seventy years, I couldn't be described as an avid fan – consistent but not avid.

The second event, which followed soon after winning the 1999 award, was the tragically untimely death of our Lord Provost, Jim Shields. Jim, who like myself came from the Gorbals, had first been elected on to the Council in 1971 and been a popular choice for Lord Provost. Jim was one of my oldest friends in politics. Years before, after Party meetings in the Gorbals, we would often walk up the road together and talk about all the changes which had to take place in society to make life better for people. One morning, I got a request to come along to see him in his office. Very calm and very philosophical, he told me that he had cancer and that he only had a short time to live, probably about three months. I was deeply shocked as I had not even been aware that he was unwell. I suppose I also felt a little guilty that I hadn't noticed, but he looked so healthy and hadn't given the least hint.

Jim was very much at peace with himself and determined to carry on with his duties as Lord Provost for as long as possible. In the weeks he had left, with his wife Barbara by his side, he continued to work hard to promote the city and, particularly, the children and disabled groups for whom he had worked throughout his career. I visited him in hospital on the night he passed away. Once again, I was immensely impressed by his dignity and his lack of bitterness.

Jim's funeral service was held in the banqueting hall of the City Chambers. Its magnificent fresco paintings depicting the nobility of labour made it seem a thoroughly appropriate venue and gave all those who had worked with him the opportunity to say a final farewell. He was a Lord Provost who served with distinction, a credit to the city, and his death was a great loss. Perhaps those who had tried to thwart his election felt just a little pang of guilt when he passed away.

The new Lord Provost was Jim Shields' Depute, Tommy Dingwall. Tommy, who represented Maryhill on the Council, was quite a different character from Jim Shields. While he could, on occasion, be highly entertaining, he also had a fairly volatile temperament. Like myself he had participated in the Tribune Group. For many years he would have described himself as among my supporters, but he was never particularly consistent. I suppose you could describe his behaviour as erratic.

The first time I met Tommy Dingwall was when we were both delegates at a Scottish Labour Party conference at Perth Town Hall. He was a member of the Amalgamated Engineering Union delegation, and I was a delegate from Cathcart Constituency Labour Party. The engineers' union had a large delegation and occupied a very long table. Cathcart's four delegates had seats at the end of their table. During the course of the conference Tommy, who is well known for snide but sometimes quite witty comments, made a number of humorous cracks about the Amalgamated Engineering Union's leadership.

I didn't meet Tommy again until a number of years later when he was elected to the Council for the Maryhill area. In due course, he decided that he would participate in the Tribune Group. He was always a bit of a loose cannon, however, and had a fearsome temper. Periodically he would explode. On one occasion, at the close of a Labour Group meeting, he had a violent difference of opinion with Councillor Larry Flanagan.

The meeting ended but their argument continued and Tommy head-butted Larry. This was deplorable behaviour, and prompted a meeting of the Labour Group Executive. However, Tommy apologised and Larry graciously accepted his apology. There were hints in the press that there had been an incident, but they were unable to get any clear information. The incident was hushed up.

The only time there was ever a vote on anything in the Tribune Group was when Tommy was competing with Jim Mutter for the position of Depute Lord Provost, or Depute Chairman of the Council as it was described at that time. Before the ballot, he made it known that if he didn't get the position he wouldn't be supporting any of the group members at the AGM. Understandably, this behaviour upset a number of members. He carried the vote, but I can't say I was overly impressed.

Sadly, once installed as Lord Provost, Tommy did not demonstrate the same respect for the role as his predecessor. For over forty years, it has been the tradition that at the penultimate performance of the Edinburgh Military Tattoo, the salute is taken by the Lord Provost of Glasgow. Over the years, this has been used as an opportunity for the Lord Provost to entertain guests, including senior representatives of the business community and important organisations within Glasgow. The difference with Tommy was that many of his guests had no connection with the Council. When one of his staff delicately questioned his choice of guests, he was curtly told that, as Lord Provost, Tommy would decide who was invited.

On two occasions during his Provostship, Tommy was taken by a Council limousine to Rothesay – not on official business but because Tommy has a flat there. These visits allowed him to change the linen and clean the windows. Doubtless the Council limousine and driver would have impressed the neighbours.

Later, towards the end of his period as Lord Provost, Tommy organised a Sunday lunch in the Chambers for thirty-four people. This was not a civic event approved by the General Purposes Committee although, as Lord Provost, Tommy did have the authority to approve such a function himself. The only indication left on file with regard to this event is an instruction to provide good wines – the guest list is no longer on record. Of course, the Council picked up the tab. Each of these activities might charitably be dismissed as minor, though perhaps not entirely selfless. However, the real extent of Tommy's self-interest was yet to reveal itself.

As our new Lord Provost, Tommy Dingwall had, I suppose, at least one virtue. He is a man who likes to keep his appearance sharp. In his immaculately tailored suits he undoubtedly looked the part.

As we approached the Council elections of 1995, we were moving, once again, into one of those odd situations where the election was effectively for a council-in-waiting, pending the abolition in April 1996 of the regional councils and the creation of unitary authorities.

Strathclyde Region had been a huge and powerful organisation. The new City Council that was going to replace it would be a combination of those who had served on the Region and the District – a pooling of knowledge, experience and expertise which, as this was politics, inevitably meant a fight.

As Bob Gould was Leader of Strathclyde Regional Council, and I was Leader of Glasgow District Council, we agreed that we should get together to consider the political implications of reorganisation. It was important to establish if we could reach an acceptable accommodation relating to control of the new Council. We arranged to meet at the Casa d'Italia. Formerly the Glasgow Italian Club, this magnificent building had been acquired by Strathclyde Regional Council and converted into a centre for civil marriages. The setting was wholly appropriate. We were, after all, seeking to negotiate a political marriage between our two groups, but there was perhaps also a darker symbolism in this gloriously Italianate setting for a meeting between politicians. While we didn't wear Homburg hats or carry violin cases, this was a meeting between seasoned members of two political families to agree the future of the dynasty.

Present at the meeting from the District Council were my Depute Leader Gordon Macdiarmid and Councillor Mutter, while Bob Gould had brought along his Regional colleagues Gerry McGrath, the Depute Leader, and Willie O'Rourke.

I was concerned that the Region and the District represented two distinctive groups who might each try to create their own power base rather than integrate. The result would be instability and a reduction in the service which we had been elected to provide in the people of Glasgow. Historically, although it had never amounted to open warfare, there had always been political sensitivity between the two organisations, and over the years there had been a number of issues where matters had become quite fragile.

I suggested that in the new combined authority those services which had been the responsibility of the Region should be managed by a committee whose Convenor had a Regional background, while the Vice-Convenor would be from the District and vice versa in the case of

District services. This would ensure continuity of knowledge and experience as well as an appropriate training mechanism, which would integrate the two organisations and ensure that lines of succession were not restricted. My proposals were accepted and in due course largely implemented.

We went on to consider if we could agree a slate for officers and members of the Labour Group Executive. At this stage, we didn't want to determine a hard-and-fast list, but merely a basis for agreement that we could take back to our respective memberships.

In the Council elections, on 6 April 1995, to my delight my own majority nearly doubled and the result for Labour as a whole exceeded even our own expectations. The Party took seventy-seven of the eighty-three seats. The Tories were reduced to three councillors while Scottish Militant Labour, the Scottish Liberal Democrats and the SNP had one seat each. The Labour victory was heralded as a sign of what was to come in the general election. We even got a visit from a triumphant Tony Blair.

The bulk of the members of the new Labour Group were from the former Glasgow District Council. The difference in numbers between those who had historically supported Jean McFadden and those who had supported me was minimal, but there were a number of newcomers who in the traditional way of these things gave their initial support to Mrs McFadden. The incomers from Strathclyde Regional Council, although relatively few in number, effectively held the balance of power.

As I had been Leader of the District Council through eight turbulent but on the whole very successful years, it seemed to me a good time to stand down. I thought that a fitting conclusion to my long political career working for the people of Glasgow would be to become the first Lord Provost of the new Glasgow City Council. It would also be an opportunity to do what most politicians usually declare they intend to do on resigning or retiring – spend more time with my family, or at least with Peggy, because as Lady Provost she would assume a prominent role as an ambassador for the city by my side. Honouring Peggy in this way would, I felt, be only appropriate after her many years of support and sacrifice.

Bob Gould agreed that if I did not oppose him as Leader he would lend his support to my nomination as Lord Provost. He was keen that Gerry McGrath should become Depute Lord Provost. To balance the equation, Gordon McDiarmid would be Depute Leader of the Council. All this was confirmed at a succession of meetings, at which we also agreed on who might be nominated to the Executive of the Labour Group and to the convenorships of the various key committees.

Had all parties adhered to the agreement, it could have been delivered amicably and successfully. Unfortunately, Bob Gould was also, unbeknown to the rest of us, negotiating with Jean McFadden, who had been authorised by her group to meet with him. Not that we didn't have our suspicions.

When it came to the elections for the new unitary authority, Bob Gould made no effort to deliver our agreement. While he was elected unopposed, Jean McFadden was elected Shadow Convenor of the new Council, a role that many interpreted as Lord Provost in waiting. She received thirty-nine votes to my thirty-seven. The Labour Party's Scottish Executive had already stipulated that office bearers would be required to seek re-election in twelve months, and there would therefore be a further election before roles in the new authority were actually finalised, but Bob Gould indicated that he might seek the approval of Labour's National Executive to extend this election period to two years. For obvious reasons, Jean McFadden also approved of this idea. 'What we want to get in this new council is stability.'

There was clearly more than one arrangement in place. Bob Gould had done deals with both myself and Jean McFadden. Presumably he felt that his position as Leader would be more secure if I were off the pitch. Once secure in her own position, Jean McFadden supported her own close ally, Gerry Carroll, for the role of Vice-Convenor and he was elected. Happily, Gordon Macdiarmid succeeded in becoming Depute Group Leader.

In all of this Bob Gould did not emerge with any honour. At the time, one councillor remarked on the process of double-dealing and back-stabbing which had taken place. Even at this early stage, it was clear that although Labour had a huge majority, this wasn't going to be an easy ride. The whole process of the elections to the shadow authority did not cover anyone with glory.

Shortly after the Group election for the shadow council the *Scotsman* reviewed the various occasions on which Jean McFadden and I had stood against each other, describing our relationship as a 'feud'. I was quoted in the piece pointing out that although we were in the habit of competing for the same jobs, it was not a feud. The article described how I had offered Jean McFadden the post of Treasurer when I first became Leader. Asked if she had supported me in the same way, she said, 'Pat has a very selective memory and he must have forgotten he remained as Depute Group Leader when I took over.' This was the occasion when the Deputeship was decided on the toss of a coin. Jean McFadden was being just a little disingenuous when she suggested that this was in some way the result of her patronage.

Two weeks after the Shadow Council elections, a group of councillors convened to determine the appointment of the Chief Executive to the new authority. Given that the new organisation was only a pale shadow of its future self, and that people still considered themselves to be part of the Region or the District, it was inevitable that any decision would be split along District versus Regional lines. The balance was in favour of the District, with councillors Baird, Gray, Macdiarmid, McFadden and Young (the sole Conservative) from the District and Gould, McGrath, McNulty and Marshall from the Region.

The candidates for the post were John Anderson, the former Depute Chief Executive of Strathclyde Region and Glasgow's Town Clerk and Chief Executive, Tom Monaghan. John Anderson had already failed to become the Chief Executive of another of the new authorities, and there was a general feeling in the council and the city that Tom Monaghan was the more credible candidate. He was better qualified, more experienced and certainly one of the finest officers I had encountered over the three decades of my work with Glasgow District Council. On interview they both gave credible performances.

When it came to the vote, the split was much as would be expected, with the Regional councillors voting for Anderson, and those from the District for Monaghan, with one exception. Jean McFadden deferred her vote until everyone else had made their preference clear and then voted for John Anderson, who was duly appointed Glasgow's new Chief Executive. This conduct did nothing to enhance Mrs McFadden's standing with the Council as a whole.

When the appointment was announced and the press asked for comments, Tom behaved with his usual professionalism and dignity. But questions were being asked. It did seem odd that among those interviewing the two candidates was John Anderson's referee, Bob Gould. The situation was not improved when, at the Labour Group Executive meeting on 2 May, Bob Gould invited John Anderson into the meeting so that he might be introduced as the new Chief Executive to the future ruling body of the City Council.

One of the councillors on the Executive made it clear that the Executive's permission for such an invitation should be sought first. So Glasgow's £96,000-a-year, new Chief Executive sat and waited for nearly an hour outside the room while a heated debate ensued about the appropriateness of his appointment. Having delegated authority to the selection panel, the Executive was on dangerous ground legally if it decided to rescind the decision. John Anderson's appointment was endorsed, but many felt that Jean McFadden had done herself no favours.

While all this shadow play went on behind the scenes, I remained Leader of the District Council. In October, one of the seemingly never-ending stories of my leadership once more hit the press. The McCulloch murals were long gone from the Royal Concert Hall, and we had commissioned four internationally-renowned Glasgow artists to replace them – Steven Campbell, Ken Currie, Peter Howson and Adrian Wiszniewski.

Each artist had been asked to prepare a large work on an appropriate theme for the space. Unfortunately Howson's failed to fulfil the one vital stipulation of the brief, that the work should be vertical. As the press conference to unveil the pictures had already been announced, I had the unenviable task of revealing that only three out of the four artists had come up with the goods. There was nothing for it but to indulge in a little bit of theatre, quite appropriate in the concert hall. Pulling back the curtain to reveal the blank space where Howson's painting should have hung, I commented, 'This is a minimalist painting by a famous Glasgow artist called How Soon. And the question is, how soon will Peter Howson's painting arrive in Glasgow so that we can put it on display?' Soon afterwards Peter Howson finished a new canvas to complete the concert hall's quartet. The saga of the concert hall murals was happily at long last concluded.

In late October, I was again privileged to be the guest of the Mayor of Dalian, Bo Xi Lai. Mayor Bo is an impressive figure whom I've known for six years. He was Vice-Mayor of Dalian when we first met, and is much taller than most Chinese and very athletic-looking. He is married with one young son, as is the policy in China. His father, who is still alive, is one of the Chinese Immortals. Bo Yi Bo was Deng Xiao Ping's best friend. They usually holidayed together.

Mayor Bo speaks good English, not quite fluent because he doesn't get much practice. His aim is to make Dalian not the biggest city in China but the best. He is something of a human dynamo, always on the move, who mixes very freely with the people of his city, who regard him with affection and respect.

Bo Xi Lai promotes Dalian as the Hong Kong of the North. Not only is the city becoming more economically successful, but also it is becoming increasingly attractive with flourishing greenery and floral displays.

Bo Xi Lai has visited Glasgow twice, once with the largest Chinese trade delegation ever to visit the United Kingdom. On that occasion, we arranged a visit to Ibrox Park, courtesy of Campbell Ogilvy. Bo was very impressed with the trophy room. Out on the pitch with Tommy Dingwall and myself in goal, he sent a drive screaming into the back of the net from about twenty-five yards. Jorg Albertz would have been proud of the shot!

Given the relationship between Glasgow and Dalian, it is worth explaining something more of the relationship between the two cities. Dalian is a port with a coast not entirely unlike the Clyde coast, with sandy beaches and offshore islands. The city itself is much like Glasgow was in the early part of the twentieth century. They build ships, they manufacture locomotives, and they are strong in heavy engineering, clothing, textiles, glassware and electrical goods.

In addition to this raft of traditional industrial manufacturing, Dalian is becoming increasingly important as a centre for pharmaceutical and high-tech sunrise industries. On the fringes of the city there are mines for industrial diamonds and gem stones; Dalian is one of China's most significant suppliers. The city also has important fruit and agricultural areas, and a large fishing fleet trading in both the Persian Gulf and the USA. In terms of national trade the city is the most important port in China, its port area is currently doubling in size.

Dalian is a young city which celebrated its centenary in 1999. Its people are warm, friendly and hospitable. Their sense of humour is superb, even on matters which we in the West might imagine they would be sensitive about. On all my visits to China I've never felt restricted or inhibited about anywhere I wanted to go or see. Apart, that is, from one significant exception.

Talking one day to Bo Xi Lai about the cultural life of the city, I commented that I was surprised that they didn't have a museum. He pointed out that Dalian was a very young city, and although they were very strong in music, dance and the performing arts, they only had one museum, which was outside the city.

A little while later, I spoke to one of the representatives from the Dalian Foreign Affairs Office who cared for us on our visits. Sen Jun, the leader of the office, was among the group of four who first visited Glasgow to discuss the possibility of a twinning arrangement. He became a close friend and when I used to joke with him about being one of the 'Gang of Four' he would hold up his hands in mock horror and say 'Oh don't call me that!' He didn't speak any English, nor I any Chinese, but this was no impediment to our friendship. Sen was a lawyer by training and one of the pioneers of the revolution. In our day-to-day dealings, nothing was ever too much trouble. He always wanted to show us as much as possible and worked hard to ensure that the relationship between Glasgow and Dalian succeeded and developed.

I asked one of Sen Jun's colleagues in the Foreign Affairs Office about the museum and he told me that it was in Lushun, an area outside the city proper. I intimated that I would very much appreciate a visit if it could be arranged, as museums and galleries had long been a particular interest of mine, but he replied that the area was forbidden to foreigners. On my suggestion that, as Glasgow and Dalian were twin cities, Glaswegians might perhaps be considered as a special case, he promised to check to see whether this could be done. A couple of days later he informed me that it was impossible.

On a subsequent visit to Dalian, they honoured me by making me an Honorary Director of the Dalian Chinese Association for Friendship with Foreign Countries. I was delighted. The following day I asked my new friend in the Foreign Affairs Office whether, given that I had now been honoured by this association, I might be able to visit the museum at Lushun. Once again, he said he would enquire whether it was possible. Again the answer was no.

Prior to my next visit, I had received word that Mayor Bo wanted to make me an honorary citizen of the city. This was totally unexpected and a huge honour, which I was the first European to enjoy. At a banquet in my honour I was presented with a scroll, and my name was inscribed in Chinese script on a large monument outside Dalian's town hall – Patrick Lally, a citizen of Dalian.

Nothing if not persistent, I asked my friend in the Foreign Affairs Office whether, given that I was now a citizen, I could go to the Lushun museum. He promised to find out, and when he came back, he had a smile on his face. The visit was duly arranged.

It was with an extraordinary sense of anticipation that we set out for the Lushun museum. It is quite possible that I am the first outsider to have visited the township since the area was liberated from the Japanese. Lushun is one of a number of townships within Dalian's administrative area. I had previously visited Fushun, the location of a coal-fired power station built by the Gibson Group from Glasgow, and the diamond-producing area within Dalian province. I had also gone to the economic and technical development zone, a new town about twenty miles from the city proper which did not have a separate name.

We set off by car on a warm, sunny morning, travelling through fruit-growing areas. Lushun is located up the coast from Dalian, and takes a couple of hours to reach by car. The museum was impressive – its architecture was not in the traditional Chinese style but was twentieth-century classicism with, I thought, a touch of Greek Thomson. It is set in a small, landscaped area. Despite this exterior, the building was disappointing inside. The exhibits would certainly have benefited from better lighting and presentation, while the artefacts themselves were traditional items on the scope and scale of a folk museum. It could not compare with the magnificent museums in the Forbidden City, the Ming tombs in Beijing or the terracotta warriors in Xian.

However, Dalian is a very young city which was only founded in 1899. As a consequence, it has had neither the opportunity nor the incentive to build up museum exhibits of the same standard as those in better-known collections elsewhere in China. One unique, if somewhat macabre, collection in the Lushun museum was a group of mummified human figures. Apparently these had arrived overland at Lushun to be exported overseas. Quite where they came from or why they didn't manage their emigration I don't know, but they did make Lushun museum fairly memorable.

After my visit to the museum, I met the local Mayor, who showed me comprehensive models of plans for the development of the area. The proposals for economic and commercial expansion were impressive and, as Lushun is part of Dalian, I am sure they will be delivered. Thereafter, we had a meal and enjoyed typical, generous Chinese hospitality before returning to Dalian city.

After my return from China I focused on our preparations for the 1996 Festival of Visual Arts and the 1999 Festival of Architecture and Design. In early December an interview panel composed of Bob Gould, Stuart Gulliver, Chief Executive of the Glasgow Development Agency, Andrew Wright, President of the Royal Incorporation of Architects in Scotland, and myself, advised by Bob Palmer, Director of Performing Arts and Venues and Mike Hayes, Director of Planning, convened to select the Director of the 1999 festival. Competition was keen, and the Glasgow Development Agency engaged a London firm of headhunters to review the candidates for the post. In the list of five there were two locals. Given that the festival was an event of national importance, we were pleased that out of over a hundred initial applicants two local applicants managed to make it on to the short-list of five candidates.

Each of the candidates was asked to deliver a ten-minute vision of how they would run the festival. Victoria Thornton, then head of the Royal Institute of British Architects Architecture Centre, and one of the Arts Council's judges who had given us the 1999 award, was unwell but made a brave effort. Rory Coonan, Head of Architecture at the Arts Council, was surprisingly uninspiring. Frank Binnie, who was the Design Council's Scottish Director, seemed to me to lack the breadth of understanding of the subject that we felt to be vital.

The other local candidate, Neil Baxter, had first come to my attention with his proposal to rebuild Tait's Tower, and he was subsequently a consultant on our 1999 bid. His ideas for the festival were ambitious and well presented. However, the journalist Deyan Sudjic's presentation undoubtedly offered an imaginative vision for the festival. It would also, through the creation of an impressive housing development and other planned capital projects, draw visitors and new investment to the city.

After a fairly lengthy discussion, we finally decided to appoint Deyan Sudjic. His ideas were not fully formed but they were imaginative and seemed to offer the most practical benefit to the city. At the time I described the appointment of Deyan Sudjic as an 'act of faith'. I proposed that Neil Baxter's impressive performance made him an ideal candidate for the Depute Directorship, but the consensus of the panel was that we should go through the usual process of seeking applications. Some time later I learned that Deyan Sudjic was very resistant to the idea of Neil Baxter being appointed, which is a pity. The job of Depute Director was never actually advertised, but in time was filled by Eleanor McAllister, a secondee from the Council with a well-founded reputation for delivering major capital projects.

CHAPTER THIRTEEN

That strange year in which we awaited the advent of the unitary authority was a time for introspection. In addition to being the last Leader of the District Council, I was the Shadow Planning Convenor for the new authority. The responsibilities of this new body would require changes in the administrative mechanisms of the Council. But I was not impressed by the early proposals of our new Chief Executive. In attempting to streamline the administration of the Council, he wanted to amalgamate activities under new, catch-all directorships. This would create portfolios so broad that directors would inevitably be covering areas of activity about which they knew nothing.

Elections to the key positions within the new authority were due on 18 March 1996. A year earlier, we had elected the shadow Leader and Convenor (the legislation did not permit us to elect a Shadow Lord Provost, so the title Convenor was adopted instead). Jean McFadden had won the convenorship from me by two votes. Some outside the Council imagined that at the outset of the new unitary authority all the previous year's appointments would merely be ratified, but those more closely involved knew that the translation from Convenor into Lord Provost was quite different from the other positions on the new authority. The Lord Provostship uniquely combines the role of ambassador with that of Chairman of the Council – effectively the equivalent of the Speaker of the House of Commons. It also carries substantial prestige.

Jean McFadden may have beaten me by two votes the year before, but twelve months is a very long time in politics and the newcomers were now fully informed on the qualities and capabilities of the candidates for the Provostship. In addition, a number of prominent councillors with influence felt that Jean McFadden's vote against Tom Monaghan had been ill-advised. A few days before the election, the *Herald*'s municipal correspondent John MacCalman reported that in spite of these considerations, 'the result is still expected to be extremely close'.

Jean McFadden was extremely confident. She had come to an arrangement with her employer, the University of Strathclyde, to have time off to undertake her duties as the new Lord Provost. When the result of the ballot emerged, even I was surprised by the scale of my victory. In the past when we had competed for key positions there was rarely more than two or three votes in it. This time I won an unprecedented majority of twenty-seven and was duly elected the first Lord Provost of the new Glasgow City Council.

Alex Mosson was elected as my Depute. As expected, Bob Gould retained the Leadership, and Gordon Macdiarmid the Depute Leadership, both unchallenged.

Asked if she was disappointed at not being elected Lord Provost, Jean McFadden dismissed her defeat. She hadn't really wanted the Provostship, she said. It was, after all, 'just a knife and fork job'. It was too good an opportunity to resist. At my inauguration as Lord Provost, I announced, with all due solemnity, 'Here I stand, knife and fork at the ready, in the service of my city!'

The long-planned Festival of Visual Arts was now upon us. This impressive series of exhibitions, educational initiatives and business promotions to celebrate the year stood in stark contrast to the rigorous cuts we had to impose in our educational and social provision. Such contrasts are an inevitable feature of managing a city, and because events of a widely differing nature receive equal prominence in the media there is often confusion in people's minds.

Expenditure on promoting the city through cultural initiatives represents a very small proportion of overall budgeting. Social work, education and housing are all enormously costly items but because they are not considered 'sexy' receive little coverage by comparison with artistic events.

Over the years, Glasgow has worked hard and drawn in money from numerous outside sources to create new cultural attractions. The benefits to the city's economy in terms of income generation is many times that spent on the funding of such activity. As in 1990, the 1996 festival attracted designers, entrepreneurs and tourists. It also marked the opening of one of the city's most significant cultural attractions.

The opening of the Gallery of Modern Art was scheduled for 31 March 1996. It was the last glorious act of Glasgow District Council. The new Glasgow City Council would assume power the next day, 1 April, a date which, in retrospect, has a certain irony. However, on 31 March, the District was determined to go out in style. The opening ceremony was performed by Her Majesty the Queen, accompanied by His Royal Highness Prince Philip, the Duke of Edinburgh. It was a pleasantly warm, sunny day.

In the morning I looked round the gallery just to make sure that everything was ready for the royal visit. On my way out, I spotted the visitors' book and pen on a small table close to the exit. Years of experience with pens in this kind of situation has taught me that they very rarely, if ever, work. Assured that the pen had been fully tested and was working, I insisted that none the less another pen should be provided, just in case.

The appointed hour came, our royal guests arrived, and the formal opening took place. The plaque was unveiled, and Her Majesty toured the gallery. She seemed to be impressed with the building and to enjoy the exhibits. We then all had a cup of tea and Her Majesty and Prince Philip chatted amiably to the guests. Then it was time to go, and I led them to the visitors' book.

The Queen sat down, and started to write – or, more precisely, started to try to write. The pen wouldn't work and, in spite of my instructions, there was no other pen. I was not happy. Her Majesty did not complain and struggled to produce a legible signature. At one point, the Duke of Edinburgh said 'that's all right', but the Queen was most insistent that it should be done properly. Eventually she succeeded. I was extremely embarrassed.

The plan was that the Queen would go off to Edinburgh, to Holyrood Palace, while the Duke would visit the Royal Infirmary with me accompanying him. The Queen moved over to talk to the throng of people lining Exchange Square, and I went with her. Prince Philip waited in his car for a while and then took off for the Royal Infirmary, leaving me and his security people stranded. Eventually they sped off to catch up with him.

I escorted the Queen to her car, and bade her farewell, then caught up with the Duke at the Infirmary. 'So you have this job as Lord Provost for three years with no time off for good conduct,' he commented. I replied that I doubted that losing the Duke of Edinburgh came under the heading of 'good conduct'. He laughed, and told me not to worry. It had been a day not entirely without incident, but a good one for Glasgow.

The reaction of the art critics was sniffy, but the vast majority of visitors to the new gallery loved it and appreciated the extraordinary variety of work on display. This included paintings by the so-called 'New Glasgow Boys', extraordinary papier-mâché Mexican sculptures on macabre themes and the strange Sharmanka kinetic sculptures by a Russian emigré artist who had settled in Glasgow and opened his own gallery at the instigation of our Director of Museums.

With the new unitary authority at last established, I was happy that the City of Glasgow's bank balance was in the black. It wasn't to remain so for long, as, in its final year, Strathclyde Region had approved a budget overspend. It therefore closed with a substantial deficit which was then inherited by the new authorities. Thankfully my primary responsibility as Lord Provost was not for the city finances, but I was aware that we had problems ahead.

The duties of the Lord Provost are extraordinarily varied. During my first months as Provost two events in particular gave me a great deal of pleasure.

Just a couple of months after I became Lord Provost of the city of Glasgow, I was privileged to play host to my old friend the former Mayor of Paris. Monsieur Chirac had, in the interim, become President of France, but he and I had kept in touch. As part of the itinerary of his State Visit to the UK in 1996, Monsieur Chirac requested a visit to Glasgow. I met him, and His Royal Highness Prince Charles, at Glasgow Airport. The first thing the President said to me, as a personal aside, was that the trip to Glasgow had been his idea, not the Prince's. His comment confirmed a previous call from a contact at the British Embassy in Paris which had informed me that the President wanted to schedule a visit to Glasgow during his State Visit.

I first met Jacques Chirac in April 1989 when he was Mayor of Paris. The city was celebrating both its year as European Capital of Culture and the bicentenary of the French Revolution – the latter of far greater significance as far as the people of France were concerned.

My invitation to Paris arose because my close friend Susan Baird, who was then Lord Provost of Glasgow, was visiting Japan on behalf of the city. As Leader of the Council, I deputised for her at the Parisian event. Susan was an extremely popular Lord Provost and a lady of great personal charm, able to get on with people at every level in society. She has always been a very close friend and I greatly value our relationship.

I'd never been to Paris before and found both the city and the celebrations fascinating. The high point – literally – was dinner at the top of the Eiffel Tower. This was preceded by a film in a marquee at the foot of the tower – Abel Gance's superb black-and-white epic *Napoleon* with the Orchestre de Paris providing a live soundtrack. The meal was superb. I had the opportunity to chat to Monsieur Chirac about Glasgow's impending Year of Culture and the celebrations then taking place in Paris. One very odd aspect of the whole proceeding which struck me as extremely disconcerting was the fact that, throughout our meal, Monsieur Chirac was surrounded by photographers. There were four of them, two on each side of the Mayor. I'm convinced that they photographed every mouthful of food that he ate. He totally ignored them, which couldn't have been easy. I have never seen anything quite like it.

After out *dîner en haut*, there was a fireworks display at the Trocadero, and at the end of this evening of extraordinary sensations, I felt very privileged to have been Glasgow's representative.

The following year Mayor Chirac joined us in Glasgow to hand over the title of European Capital of Culture. He was delightful company, and I was aware that our relationship was moving from diplomatic acquaintance into friendship. Both our then Lord Provost, Susan Baird, and Monsieur Chirac played their formal parts in the proceedings magnificently.

Jacques Chirac, now President, returned to Glasgow in 1996. His day in the city began in Easterhouse with a number of community visits, including one to the Prince's Trust, which were instigated by the Prince of Wales, who does a tremendous job in supporting community-based activities throughout the UK. After Easterhouse, we headed into the city centre for lunch in the City Chambers.

In my civic welcome, I complimented Monsieur Chirac on his growing regard for Glasgow and remarked upon the personal contacts that we had had over the years. I also made mention of the 'auld alliance', the treaty struck between Scotland and France in 1245. There is a replica of the treaty with its seals and signatures on the wall in the Lord Provost's office. But I don't think the President was particularly impressed; after all, he has the original in Paris.

'Long Live the Auld Alliance!' I said in conclusion. I wondered what Prince Charles made of this. This alliance had, after all, been between the French and the Scots against the English. The President made this point rather humorously in his reply and Prince Charles didn't seem to be too put out. Then to my delight the President declared me to be a Commander of the French National Order of Merit, a very considerable honour.

After lunch, the Prince, the President and Madame Chirac joined me in my office. There was an awkward mishap when a button came off the President's jacket. Madame Chirac was very upset – it obviously wouldn't do for the President of France to go out with a button missing – but my personal assistant, Ian Easton, came to the rescue. He borrowed a needle and thread from my private secretary, Bernadine Blair, and sewed on the button himself. I don't know how good Ian's sewing is, but the button stayed on until the President was safely out of Glasgow. Honour was saved.

In the afternoon the Prince, the President and I went on a successful but uneventful visit to Pilkingtons, one of Glasgow's major exporting companies. My wife Peggy the Lady Provost and Madame Chirac visited the Burrell Gallery, where they had a much more exciting time. The gallery sits gently in the rolling landscape of Pollok Park. A long, clear glass wall at the back of the gallery looks directly out on to grass and woodland only a few feet away.

Madame Chirac admired this woodland scene, and turned to view the exhibits. Two youths on bicycles passed in front of the window. One of them got off his bike and, adjusting his angle for maximum visibility, started to urinate against a tree while waving in a friendly fashion to horrified onlookers in the gallery. This was, I suppose, a Glasgow version of *cloche-merle*.

The Glaswegians were keenly aware that their task was to ensure that Madame Chirac's gaze was averted from the glass wall during this proceeding. The walkie-talkies were getting red hot. The youth then finished peeing, calmly zipped himself up and got back on his bike, still waving to the onlookers. He got as far as the end of the wall before being grabbed by the police and hustled away.

Madame Chirac enjoyed her visit to the Burrell so much that she over-ran her schedule, Peggy reported that the incident of the urinating youth was an experience she could have done without, but her relation of the tale, including her description of the trauma of trying to ensure that Madame Chirac saw nothing, caused endless amusement in the Lord Provost's office afterwards. I never did find out what happened to the culprit. Happily the event didn't make Tom Shields' Diary in the *Herald*.

A further little incident is worth mentioning. When Prince Charles, the President, Madame Chirac and their entourage were leaving from Glasgow Airport to return to London and continue their State Visit, the Prince drew me to one side. With a smile but in a voice with just a hint of wry chastisement, he muttered 'Long live the Auld Alliance!' I laughed and shrugged my shoulders. We shook hands and said our fond farewells.

The President's visit clearly demonstrated that Glasgow was a truly international city. For too long, we had been held back by the misconception that, even in the UK, we were somehow in the second league. If my political career demonstrated anything, it was that Glasgow was limited only by its own aspirations. We had had the self-belief to become the

European Capital of Culture, then went on to win the title of UK City of Architecture and Design. In my new role as Lord Provost, I was determined to continue to promote Glasgow's role as an international player.

On 9 August I welcomed competitors and officials from the 1996 World Rowing Championships to a civic reception in the City Chambers. In my speech, I observed that with twenty-four events and two thousand competitors the world regatta was much larger than the Olympic regatta at Atlanta, which consisted of only ten events. I then suggested that, with the combined resources of Glasgow and Edinburgh, Scotland could aspire to host the Olympic Games in 2008 or 2012.

I noted that with the advent of Lottery funding, finance from central government was not as critical as it had been in the past. None the less, John Major's government had demonstrated a lamentable lack of real commitment to sporting activity, and I welcomed Tony Blair's undertaking that a future Labour government would make investment in sport a major national priority.

My speech created a flurry of interest. The *Evening Times* commented that my dreams had 'the uncanny knack of coming true', and echoed my fundamental belief that 'big ideas bring big rewards'.

Some people dismissed my mention of the Olympics as being too big an idea. But the City of Edinburgh immediately offered to back a feasibility study into a joint bid. Their Tory leader, Daphne Sleigh, commented, 'It's an interesting idea, and Edinburgh could be a successful venue for the Olympics. It's certainly more prestigious than Atlanta.' Their Lord Provost, Eric Milligan, was also positive: 'Neither city could consider staging them alone – perhaps together we could put forward a successful bid, especially with the advent of Lottery funding.'

In the same *Edinburgh Evening News* article in which the above quotes appeared I pointed out that as Tokyo and Seoul would be joint hosts of the World Cup Finals in 2002, there was a precedent for such a joint bid. Sadly, Glasgow's Leader Bob Gould saw matters differently. 'There were more pressing needs,' he said. But the balance of press comment was positive.

The Times commended the idea, not least because of the effect it would have in creating a united Scotland. 'The cities complement each other in the same manner as the iodine tang of an Islay malt is best tempered by cool ice. The combination of Edinburgh's bourgeoise propriety and Glasgow's exuberant proletarianism should enhance any event shared by the two.' The *Daily Mail* comment column awarded me a gold medal for optimism.

An association with Edinburgh of much longer standing was the annual visit to the Military Tattoo. Towards the end of August, Peggy and I, accompanied by twenty-two guests, set out for Edinburgh. The numbers were fewer than in previous years. I was concerned to ensure that our guests were only those appropriately qualified by dint of their work for the city, rather than, as sadly had sometimes been the case in the past, a larger group of previous Lord Provosts' friends or members of the press. Michael Kelly's guest list had been particularly notable for the number of editors of prominent newspapers which it contained.

The evening went very well, although it was chilly and the service in our indifferent hotel on the outskirts of Edinburgh was rather slow. We were very tired when we finally arrived back in Glasgow, but I was horrified later to read in the *Herald* and the *Daily Record* of complaints about the visit. This, after all, was a traditional event which brought Glasgow and Edinburgh a little closer together every year. It was also funded from the Common Good Fund and therefore did not draw upon our council tax payers.

The press articles quoted the Conservative Bailie John Young and Councillor Tommy Sheridan, a member of Militant, but I knew that the source of the information must be somebody within the Labour Group. I was very angry, even more so when I discovered from John Anderson, the Chief Executive, that the only person who had approached him for information about the Tattoo trip was the Group Leader, Bob Gould. I subsequently spoke to Bob Gould, who informed me that his colleague Bailie O'Rourke had raised the matter with him, which I presume had precipitated his further research and then his directing the matter to the press.

Bob Gould was perfectly well aware that this visit was a fixed part of the Lord Provost's annual calendar, and an important civic duty, and, as I stated in my letter of 30 August to the Labour Group Secretary, his conduct in contacting the press was potentially very damaging to the Labour Party:

> If the Group Leader is unhappy about any of the Council's activities, the place to raise it is in the Labour Group and not in the columns of the Press or the Media who are only too happy to clobber the Labour Party if the opportunity is presented to them. I, myself, will make no public criticism of the Group Leader in response to attacks on me made by him.

The press coverage continued for a couple of days, but the focus, intriguingly, shifted on to the supposed 'rift' between Bob Gould and myself. It was clear that channels of communication between the Council Leader and the press were still open. The *Herald* usefully pointed out, however, that the root cause of this little disagreement might well be the difference in styles between the City and the Region. The City had always maintained a programme of liaison with other Scottish, UK and international cities and promoted events that encouraged trade. Early the following year we were to discover just how little Bob Gould actually understood about the controls, checks and balances which were a well-established part of the system.

Over the next few weeks there continued to be substantial support of my Olympics proposal, but Glasgow's leadership was distinctly apathetic. While John Major asked to be kept posted and the Edinburgh City Fathers were keen, the mood in Glasgow couldn't even be described as lukewarm. To the detractors, I pointed out that overseas tourism in Glasgow had grown by well over 100 per cent in the last decade and that 22,000 jobs depended on tourism. An annual expenditure of over £400 million made this industry a major aspect of our economy. Set against this, UK tourism had grown by only 35 per cent overall. So Glasgow was well ahead of the game, I thought, although it was nowhere near exploiting its full potential.

As is always the case with big ideas, for all those who are willing to try, and run the risk of failing, there are many more who are convinced in advance that failure is inevitable and won't make even the least effort. Sadly, that was the prevailing mood in the City Council. As Lord Provost I had put as much as I could into the idea. To adopt a sporting metaphor, it had been up to others to grab the baton and run with it. Sadly, it wasn't even a fumbled transfer. After making good speed on the first leg of the race, I had held out the baton to discover there was nobody there to receive it. At least the initiative raised our profile in the press.

In early November, to my enormous personal pleasure, I was invited by Strathclyde University to receive an Honorary Doctorate in Law. Not too many Gorbals boys who left school at thirteen have been recognised in this way.

John Arbuthnott – now Sir John – the Principal and Vice-Chancellor of the University and his wife Eleanor, have been consistently supportive of my work in the city. While I'm quite sure that the invitation was agreed by the University Senate, I'm convinced that Sir John played an important part in their decision.

At the presentation ceremony on 6 November 1996 I had the privilege of listening to an oration by Lord Goold, the Lord Lieutenant of

Renfrewshire. The Lord Lieutenancy of Glasgow was one aspect of my responsibilities as Lord Provost which consistently gave me enormous pleasure. I have always been an unashamed supporter of the Royal Family: I believe they do a marvellous job for the country, and to be their representative in Glasgow was a considerable honour and a responsibility which I hope I administered appropriately throughout my Provostship.

Lord Goold was Chairman of Strathclyde University Court. He was also a former chairman of the Scottish Conservative Party. I had in the past watched him on television and listened to him on radio extolling the virtues of Margaret Thatcher's Government. Quite frankly, I couldn't stand him. I would listen to his careful exposition of policies with which I disagreed fundamentally, and on occasion get very angry. But now here we were, some years on, the former Chairman of the Scottish Tories and the former Leader of Glasgow's Labour administration, and he was saying nice things about me.

As I got to know him personally, I came to see quite a different side of Jim Goold, and it wasn't simply because he had volunteered to honour me. He was very sincere in his kind comments and in his love for, and interest in, the city of Glasgow. I met him only on a few occasions after that, but he completely confounded my earlier impression of him. He was a kindly and generous man. I grew to like him enormously, although sadly I didn't know him for long before he became unwell and died. Strathclyde University has named a new Hall of Residence after him. It is an honour thoroughly deserved.

A continuing saga was the plan for a Glasgow-based National Gallery of Scottish Art. For some time, the preferred venue had been the former headquarters of the Post Office in George Square. In mid-November 1995, the building had been secured by the Glasgow Development Agency, which took a one-year option in the hope that we could secure the agreement of the National Gallery trustees and put together the necessary funding.

Early in 1996, an impressive shortlist of seven European architectural practices competed for the job of designing the new gallery within the existing building. We were delighted when the Glasgow practice, Page & Park Architects, won. It demonstrated that local talent could take on the best in the world and, by applying the special knowledge and enthusiasm for the task which arise out of living in a city, understanding it and wishing to create within it, could come up with by far the best design. In fairness, the second-best design was also by a Scottish practice, from Edinburgh.

Sadly at the end of November our application to the National Lottery Heritage Fund was rejected. Unbowed, we reviewed our plans and agreed that early in the new year I would meet Lord Rothschild, chairman of the Heritage Fund and Angus Grossart, chairman of the National Gallery Trustees, to determine a way forward.

By the end of 1996, I was settling into the extraordinarily busy and demanding regime of the Lord Provostship. I had been honoured by the Chinese, by the French and by Strathclyde University. I was flattered and humbled by all this extraordinary recognition, and also felt very pleased that at long last Peggy could be a real participant in my work for the city.

Early in the new year, in relaxed mood, Peggy and I set off for a holiday in the Canary Islands. Going on holiday was a relatively recent experience, and I have to admit I was beginning to like it. Until the boys were teenagers, I never went on holiday. Peggy and the boys used to go away, quite often to Peggy's aunt at Canvey Island near Southend, or to Spain. I was too busy and travelled only as part of my civic duties.

The Canary Islands, the sunshine and the beach were a new experience. It was a welcome change to be away from Glasgow and spared the busy schedule of meetings with politicians and business people. But while we were relaxing on a beach in Gran Canaria, our world was about to be turned upside down.

CHAPTER FOURTEEN

The *Evening Times* headline read 'Give us a trip and we'll vote for you'. The beleaguered Leader of the City Council, Bob Gould, had decided to vent his frustration with his Council colleagues by talking to the press. For the next eighteen months we were destined, as my friends in Dalian might put it, to live in interesting times.

My earliest memories of Bob Gould were of his fairly lack-lustre career as a councillor in the old Glasgow Corporation. He was a rail worker and one of the National Union of Railwaymen's group of councillors who were allowed time off for council duties by British Railways. This group co-operated with the Amalgamated Engineering Union's elected council members. Both groups normally acted in concert and were a sizeable voting block at Labour Group annual general meetings. Today they would be described as a 'faction'. They had significant influence and their representatives filled a number of important Council positions.

When Strathclyde Region was formed, Bob Gould became the Regional councillor for a Springburn seat. He subsequently failed in his bid for reselection for Springburn but was selected for the Renfrewshire ward. At the Region, he spent a number of years as Personnel Convenor. This job involved a lot of travel to Edinburgh and London, representing the local authorities in negotiation with local government trade unions.

It was an important job, but a dead end for any politician who wanted to improve the quality of life for his constituents or change society for the better. It seemed to me odd that he should have spent virtually his entire political career in such a role, but the opportunities for travel were pretty good and maybe Bob just liked trains. Ultimately Bob became Leader of the Region, a role which would have given him greater scope for achieving positive change.

Perhaps being Leader of Glasgow City Council required different skills from the Leadership of Strathclyde Region – it was an extraordinarily demanding job. I have to admit that sometimes I resented the amount of time it required, and the frequent occasions when it kept me away from Peggy and my family. If I was resentful, you should have heard Peggy on the subject.

Bob Gould, by contrast, was very laid-back. He referred much of what came before him to the Chief Executive, John Anderson.

I remember on one occasion bumping into Bob in the councillors' corridor and walking with him in the direction of my office. It was about three o'clock in the afternoon. To make conversation, I asked him where he was off to and he told me he was going home. He found it hard to put in the time, he said. This was someone who could easily have spent all day every day just representing the interests of his Pollokshaws constituents, never mind carrying out his duties as Leader.

The view that Bob Gould lacked the drive, vision and energy to be Leader gathered strength as his first year in the job wore on. There was a general acceptance that it was extremely unlikely that he would continue to be Leader after the next annual general meeting, which was scheduled for May 1997. Most people felt that Gordon Macdiarmid, the Depute Leader, would undoubtedly be the next Leader of the City Council.

Bob Gould knew that his time as Leader was limited and it was apparent that, rather than acknowledge that his attitude to the job might be a contributing factor to this, he began to develop a persecution complex. He became convinced that his leadership was being undermined. Most folk, however, were aware that undermining Bob Gould would be a complete waste of energy. He was doing a good enough job all by himself.

As I was still on holiday, it was only when I telephoned in to the office that I learned that Bob Gould had been making ridiculous statements about 'votes for trips' to the press. I was concerned to find out whether his allegations had named individual colleagues. I was reassured to discover that no specific names had been given. It wasn't until I returned from my holiday that I got a detailed account of everything that had unravelled in my absence.

The issue which had precipitated the affair was the inevitably vexatious one of budget cuts. The unitary authority carried a huge burden of responsibility and massive overheads which simply could not be funded from our rates and the monies allocated by the government. In the 1996 budget round Bob Gould had resisted cuts of around £20 million in education which would have necessitated school closures. This simply made matters worse for 1997. However, Gould was gambling on an incoming Labour Government picking up the tab. I think he was the only one to imagine that this was a realistic chance. Gordon Brown, the Shadow Chancellor, had effectively ruled it out when he declared in 1996 there would be 'no more cash' for the beleaguered local authorities. Now, faced with having to slash a total of something like £80 million from our overall budget and the potential loss of two thousand jobs, Bob Gould came up with a plan which he felt would avoid compulsory redundancies.

As a trade-union man, he felt that the best approach would be to negotiate a deal with the unions whereby council employees would waive their agreed 2½ per cent pay increase. Even if this was realistic, it would simply have delayed the inevitable. It would also have put Glasgow at a considerable disadvantage. Our employees would be on a different payscale from Council workers doing the same jobs elsewhere in Scotland.

At the meeting of the Labour Group Executive the idea was firmly rejected by eleven votes to four. Not satisfied with the view of the Executive, Bob decided to take the issue to the meeting of the full Labour Group. This was an extremely unusual move, and not one likely to end in success. But he was being remarkably pig-headed on the issue. This time, after a very heated meeting, he was defeated by an unbelievable sixty-four votes to three.

After consulting with his long-time colleague and supporter Des McNulty, Secretary of the Labour Group, Gould declared that he was resigning as Leader and walked out of the room. When he was stopped by Tommy Dingwall, who probably advised him not to make decisions in the heat of the moment, he continued on his way with the parting shot, 'I'm not taking any more of this crap!'

As the Labour Group was more or less united in the view that his arguments and proposals were totally unacceptable, his public resignation could not have been better timed. So what did they do? At the instigation of Jean McFadden, they hastily reconvened a meeting with Councillor Gould and pleaded with him not to resign. This had to be one of the most spectacularly daft decisions ever made by an organisation which had had its moments in the past.

It was the next day that Bob Gould talked to the press, presumably still smarting from his maltreatment. His comment, to Vic Roderick of the *Evening Times*, that councillors were willing to trade their support for trips, was complete nonsense but it made a very good headline, as a politician of Bob Gould's experience must surely have known.

It was later suggested that the 'votes for trips' claim was simply a throw-away comment after the formal interview was over. But Bob Gould knew exactly what he was doing, he just hadn't thought it through. There could, after all, be only one outcome of such an unsubstantiated accusation. Unless he could provide evidence, his comments would bring the Glasgow Labour Group and the Party itself into disrepute. In such a situation Gould could not survive as Leader – indeed it had to be questioned whether he was sufficiently responsible to continue serving the Party at all.

The next day, 5 February, Bob Gould called in sick with flu. He knew what the papers were going to say. When the *Evening Times* came out at lunchtime, with the allegations spread all over the front page, the Council went into meltdown. A large number of councillors requested a specially convened Group meeting, which took place just after four o'clock that afternoon.

By late afternoon, the General Secretary of the Scottish Labour Party, Jack McConnell, and his senior officer, Lesley Quinn, had issued an invitation to the Group for a meeting with senior office bearers the next day. By an unhappy coincidence, 5 February was the day for Scottish Questions in the House of Commons. It gave the Scottish Secretary, Michael Forsyth, and his local government minister, George Kynoch, a wonderful opportunity to mock the Labour opposition, glorying in the fact that, for once, an accusation of sleaze did not concern the sexual or financial affairs of a senior Tory.

After a rapid recovery from his flu, Bob Gould appeared, somewhat sheepishly, on the Thursday morning. At eleven forty-five he and his fellow councillors Gordon Macdiarmid, Des McNulty, Jean McFadden and the Group Whip, Bob Marshall, shared a taxi to the Labour Party's Scottish headquarters at Keir Hardie House in Lynedoch Place, among the attractive Victorian terraces of the Park area. It can't have been a pleasant ride. Even though he had at least two long-standing supporters with him, nobody in that taxi would have been particularly happy with Mr Gould.

The headlines that day included the *Daily Mail*'s 'Labour's Junkets for Votes Scandal'; and the *Herald*'s 'Glasgow: The Shame – Councils must be protected from hoodlums'. But there were also signs that Gould was seeking to backtrack on his original assertions. In the *Herald* he commented: 'No one ever asked me for trips in exchange for votes. I couldn't get involved in that. I want to run this city efficiently and honestly.' He continued: 'I was simply discussing what members were saying to each other in the councillors' corridor. I'm delighted that the Labour Party is to have an investigation.'

Now he was indicating that his previous accusations were mere rumour, yet he was suggesting that the Labour Party should proceed with an investigation anyway. This notion of an investigation into tittle-tattle was strange unless Bob Gould had already discussed the matter with the Scottish Labour Party. If that was the case, then he had blurted out his accusations prematurely.

Oddly, the day after the *Evening Times* first ran Bob Gould's accusations, their columnist Michael Kelly, the well-known former Lord Provost, a friend of Jean McFadden and public relations entrepreneur turned journalist, wrote a long piece under the headline 'If Gould goes, Jean's in line to heal the rift'.

Kelly's article rightly pointed out that Bob Gould's first task should be to 'name names, specify dates and list the precise trips and conferences involved'. This would then, he suggested, 'in the absence of a satisfactory explanation, require the resignations of every councillor, however senior, involved'. If, he argued, Bob Gould couldn't support his allegations, he should be asked to resign. Kelly then referred to his old colleague Bob Gould as 'a likeable, dedicated man who has put all of his honest energy into council work'. But as poor old Bob had not succeeded in the leadership, Kelly suggested that he might make use of his long-established skills in labour relations as Chairman of the Personnel Committee.

It was extremely magnanimous of Kelly to suggest such a handy lifeline, particularly as Gould's allegations had prompted the biggest scandal since Dick Dynes maliciously suggested that all was not in order with the Council's housing procedures.

Michael Kelly then suggested a remarkable solution to the whole problem. While Gordon Macdiarmid was the acknowledged favourite for the leadership, he was 'from the "district" side of the great divide'. So who might be the saviour? Well, Jean McFadden, of course. But she was also from the District. Well, yes, but it seems she'd often said nice things about the Region, so in Kelly's somewhat questionable logic that made her the ideal choice. He concluded that, while Jean certainly wouldn't want the job of Leader, it was her duty and the Labour Group should appoint her unanimously. All this notwithstanding the fact that, if Gould's accusations were true, then there was as much chance of Jean McFadden being among the guilty parties as anyone else. Altogether, a remarkable little commentary.

One little incident which happened around this time was Jean McFadden's suggestion of an interesting two-tier solution to the requirement for cost savings through redundancies. She advocated that council employees who lived within the city should be favoured over those who resided outside Glasgow's boundaries. If this ill-conceived suggestion was intended to demonstrate that Mrs McFadden was the appropriate person to steer the Council out of its political and financial difficulties, it failed miserably.

Mrs McFadden's proposal failed to take into account the usual factors affecting redundancy, such as length of service and the importance of the job within the new structure, and it stood a very good chance of being illegal. It was a quaint diversion which somewhat undermined Michael Kelly's argument that Jean McFadden was the only person who could give the city the intelligent leadership it required.

As for the Labour Party, you would have expected them to be guarded in their response after such extraordinary and highly questionable accusations. In the *Evening Times* headline piece on 5 February, Jack McConnell was quoted: 'If any action is required, that action will be ruthless.' A more guarded response might have been, 'Action will be carefully considered', or 'Action will be based on due analysis of the facts.' Instead Mr McConnell was determined to be 'ruthless'. His phraseology lacked the circumspection which might have been expected of the Secretary of the Scottish Labour Party.

After Gould's meeting with McConnell and Quinn the day after he made his forthright comments, suddenly shy of publicity, he left by the back door. One outcome of that meeting was a gag on all members of the Labour Group: they were told not to discuss the allegations. Jack McConnell promised a 'full and frank' inquiry, saying that he didn't care what impact this would have on the General Election.

He might not have cared, but the last thing Party headquarters in London wanted before an election which they were set fair to win was a potentially acrimonious inquiry into alleged abuses of power in one of the Party's strongest areas of support. It was announced that the planned inquiry would be undertaken by a member of Labour's National Executive Committee. But the Party was, presumably, all too aware that with an election looming the short-term priority was damage limitation.

I returned from my holiday to find growing concern in the Council Labour Group that the Party would suppress matters until after the General Election. As all Glasgow's councillors were under a cloud of suspicion, we decided that an independent inquiry was a necessity. The Scottish Labour Party interpreted this as defiance of their rule, but it had taken no action in the previous ten days and members of the Council were increasingly concerned to clear their names.

Perhaps our threat to hold an inquiry prompted action from the Party.

It had previously indicated that a member of the National Executive Committee would conduct the investigation, but now it sent a troubleshooter in the shape of Mrs Eileen Murfin, the Party's Constitutional Officer.

Mrs Murfin, a slim bespectacled lady in her fifties, had been involved with the ousting of the Militant Tendency on Merseyside in the early 1980s. Neil Kinnock then brought her into the National Constitutional Office with a brief to tackle issues that might potentially bring the Party into disrepute. It was in response to the Labour Party's troubles on Merseyside that its disciplinary arm, the National Constitutional Committee, was established. Mrs Murfin would go on to be involved in investigations in Birmingham and in the messy selection battle for Glasgow Govan between Mike Watson, the sitting MP, and Mohammad Sarwar, where allegations of racism were flying around.

On her first one-day visit to Glasgow, Mrs Murfin had a preliminary meeting with Jack McConnell. Then she and Lesley Quinn, her equivalent in the Scottish Labour Party, met Gordon Macdiarmid, Jean McFadden, Des McNulty and Bob Marshall. Her visit appeared to be a fact-finding mission which would be the preamble to a fuller, exhaustive investigation to clear up the matter.

Two days earlier I had written to Jack McConnell expressing my anger at Bob Gould's suggestion that 'votes for trips' was common practice under previous administrations. 'I find the whole proposition totally ludicrous and insulting to decent, active members of the Labour Party and the Group. I am astonished that such allegations have been raised in the media and not in the Labour Group where procedures exist to allow such matters to be investigated and persons guilty of misbehaviour to be dealt with.' I made it clear that at no time during my eight years as Leader of Glasgow District Council had this ever been the case. I also stated that I was sure that Councillor McFadden, who had also been a Leader of the District Council, would similarly reject such allegations relating to her period as Leader. My letter to Jack McConnell was the first of a number I would write to which I would receive no reply.

Another very significant event took place in the early spring of 1997. A very unpleasant protest by Scottish Militant Labour disrupted a key Council meeting, which centred on substantial and painful budget cuts, mainly resulting from the new responsibility of the city authority for education. The cuts were necessary because of changes in local populations, but also because our funding from central government was insufficient to maintain the scale of the service we had inherited. It was the old story of the Council taking the blame for Government cutbacks. A noisy rabble of around two hundred people stormed the City Chambers and prevented our meeting from convening. The police had been forewarned of an attempt to occupy the building, and staff were only opening the quadrangle gate to allow vehicles in and out. Councillor Tommy Sheridan, who represented Scottish Militant Labour on the Council, had parked his car in the central courtyard of the City Chambers. He drove to the exit and when he was half way through the gate got out to fetch something he had left in his office. With the car preventing the gate from being closed, as if on cue, the protesters rushed past and gained entry to the building. Once inside, they pushed Council officers aside and blocked entry to the Council Chamber.

Several councillors and council employees were physically intimidated by protesters. The corridors of the Chambers rang with shouting, swearing and threatening taunts. It was unpleasant and unnecessary. Most of the councillors, after all, had real sympathy with the protesters' position. However, common sense and financial reality demanded that hard decisions be made, otherwise the consequences for all of Glasgow's working people would be drastic reductions in all Council services.

At the end of a frustrating delay, some of us managed to get into the Council Chamber via a fairly circuitous route and a door which is normally kept locked. The meeting proceeded against a background of chanting and banging on the door. We managed to conclude our business and the protesters eventually went home. There were no arrests but it was a close-run thing.

Immediately after the meeting, I wrote to John Orr, the Chief Constable of Strathclyde Police. I got to know John when I was the Leader of the Council. I've known five or six Chief Constables of Glasgow or Strathclyde. All of them have been admirable men, but John Orr is exceptional. Not only is he a very good policeman, as an examination of Strathclyde's crime statistics demonstrates, but he undertakes his demanding job in an easy and relaxed manner. He is similarly relaxed at functions and, indeed, with the public at large. I have the impression that his own staff, the members of the Strathclyde Police Service, not only respect him but hold him in some affection, which must be unusual for somebody in such a job.

On this occasion I was writing to him as the Lord Provost and Chairman of the Council to express concern that the protest had meant that only twenty-four out of a possible eighty-three councillors had been able to attend the 1997/8 budget meeting. I pointed out that a number of councillors who had wanted to attend the meeting were not helped by the police to do so. I urged the Chief Constable to review procedures in order to prevent any recurrence.

The Leader of the Council, Bob Gould, also took up the matter. John Orr wrote back that he planned to meet Gould, myself and the Convenor of the Joint Police Board. He also indicated that a full written report would be submitted to the Council as soon as possible. He was true to his word and new police procedures were instituted for Council meetings, particularly when there was any prior intimation of potential protest.

The Council made their disapproval of Councillor Sheridan's actions clear and agreed that in future he would not be permitted to hold meetings within the City Chambers. In the circumstances, he got off lightly.

With the Labour Party busily campaigning towards the General Election, little progress was made with the inquiry. But my work as Lord Provost continued as usual, with the opening of our new Tourism Information Centre in George Square and the judging of the annual Lord Provost's Prize, Scotland's most prestigious award for work by contemporary artists. In mid-March, Peggy was delighted with a profile in the *Herald* which focused upon her charitable work within the city. It gave her an opportunity to explain her particular concern for and understanding of the role of carers.

Peggy has spent many years caring for her aunt and then her mother Dolly, both sufferers from Alzheimer's Disease. The article also gave her the opportunity to promote the charity fashion show that she was organising with Marks & Spencer. The idea for the event had come about when Anne McBryan of the Prince and Princess of Wales' Hospice had chatted to Peggy about the difficulty of raising funds to keep the thing going. She was deeply concerned that, while everybody was sympathetic, there were so many demands on people to contribute to a whole range of charities that the needs of the terminally ill sometimes got overlooked.

Peggy had immediately approached Bill Neish, of Marks & Spencer, who was only too willing to help. Bill is a quiet and effective individual, the first Chairman of the Glasgow City Centre Association, a big man who, in my experience, was unfailingly generous. Peggy explained how she hoped the Lady Provost's Fashion Show would become an annual event in aid of the hospice. It was certainly to continue throughout her term as Lady Provost.

Towards the end of March we shifted our preference for a site for the proposed National Gallery of Scottish Art from the Post Office, which had been favoured for some time, back to the old Sheriff Court building in the Merchant City. This had become available again after a company which had been trying for some time to raise the finance to put a hotel into the building eventually gave up.

While in some ways a return to the very first proposed site for the Gallery took us back to square one, we had at long last started to get positive indications from the Government. The Scottish Secretary Michael Forsyth approved the plans and offered support for revenue costs. Now the National Gallery trustees only had to raise the finance and Glasgow would have its first National Gallery.

CHAPTER FIFTEEN

At the end of March, a month after Eileen Murfin's first visit to Glasgow, it was announced that six councillors would face disciplinary action, and that further interviews would take place in May (after the General Election). Who these councillors were and why they would be facing disciplinary action was not explained.

Jack McConnell defended this noncommittal announcement: 'We promised a report, we delivered a report, we have delivered action, and we will ensure that the highest standards exist in Glasgow City Council regardless of the actions we have to take to ensure that.'

He presumably hoped that a strident declaration that something was happening would be enough to obscure the fact that not very much was happening. The press did its best to whip things into something like a story, but other than raking over old ground there wasn't much to be said.

In mid-April, the Scottish Labour Party wrote to Des McNulty, ordering that the Group annual general meeting, scheduled for 12 May, should be postponed until further notice. That meant that all the office bearers would stay in office for the time being, despite the fact that it was apparent that, having started the whole stramash and not subsequently substantiated his allegations, Bob Gould did not have the confidence of the Group.

Towards the end of May, the Council's Labour Group was advised that the remit for the investigation by the National Executive Committee's inquiry team had been agreed. The first stage would be for a four-member panel to conduct investigations. This group would review the allegations against councillors through both interviews and written evidence. Every member of the Labour Group would be summoned to appear before the panel.

In the event the panel consisted of just three members of the Scottish Executive: Margaret McCulloch, Rhona Brankin and Sylvia Tudhope, while Noel Foy, one of the junior officers of the Scottish Labour Party, would be secretary to the panel, with Eileen Murfin and Lesley Quinn giving support as required. While it was indicated that all members of the then seventy-six strong Labour Group on the Council would be interviewed by the panel, in fact only thirty-seven of the seventy-six members of the Labour Group were contacted and asked to meet the panel. No explanation was given why less than half the sitting councillors were summoned, and what should have been an objective inquiry began to look very partisan indeed. Only Rhona Brankin and Sylvia Tudhope were present at my interview. So much for the NEC's 'four-strong panel'.

The *Evening Times*, which seemed to have particularly good channels of communication with the Scottish Labour Party, provided a new twist with their headline on 22 May: 'Labour Purge on City Chambers Old Guard'. From the original accusation in February of 'votes for trips', we were now, it seemed, embroiled in a Labour party enquiry into 'corruption, abuse or wrongdoing' and 'around a dozen councillors could face the axe'. While the source of the *Evening Times* story wasn't clear, it did quote Scottish General Secretary Jack McConnell whose instructions, the article implied, had come from the highest level. Mr McConell was quoted as saying he had authority from the new Prime Minister, Tony Blair, to embark upon a 'ruthless clear-out'.

In mid-June Glasgow welcomed 24,000 Rotarians from around the world to their annual convention. It was the largest conference Scotland had ever seen. The logistics were extraordinary. Hotels throughout the central belt were fully occupied and 400 coaches took delegates to and from the conference each day. However, the rewards more than justified this huge effort, with an estimated income of £19 million for Glasgow, and £13 million for elsewhere in Scotland.

At the opening ceremony a thousand performers entertained the delegates at Ibrox Park, and throughout the conference the city was seen at its very best. Peggy and I were rushed off our feet, attending several events each day and representing the city for anything up to fourteen hours continually. By the end of the conference we were exhausted, but we knew that Glasgow had made a lasting impression. The delegates returned to the 122 countries which they represented with 'Haste ye back' ringing in their ears.

Life was beginning to take on a slightly surreal quality with the press schizophrenically reporting superb events and the city's real successes against a recurring theme of scandal. The investigations were paralysing the effective administration of the city, and in early July Jean McFadden urged that the pace of the inquiry be speeded up.

I suppose I was fortunate that much of my duty was ceremonial.

Several initiatives announced that summer were part of our preparations for our role as City of Architecture in 1999. Over the summer months we launched the Partnership Fund: an initial figure of £450,000 was to be spent on community projects throughout the city. We also published the designs for the Lighthouse, the extension and refurbishment of Charles Rennie Mackintosh's 'A'-listed former *Glasgow Herald* building in Mitchell Street. It was to be a venue for exhibitions and conferences.

Millennium Spaces was a scheme to redevelop several locations throughout the city in conjunction with local associations to improve the local environment for individual communities. The final large capital project for 1999 would be the creation of a unique development of new housing for sale and rent on Greendyke Street beside Glasgow Green and next to the recently developed St Andrew's Square. All these projects set up for 1999 would, we hoped, create an impressive, year-long festival.

At the time I was campaigning for Glasgow as a home for the Scottish Parliament. I realised we had only an outside chance, but it was a case of 'nothing ventured, nothing gained'. We offered the Co-op's former headquarters in Morrison Street and Strathclyde Region's former head-quarters at Charing Cross, but also outlined options for building a new parliament. In the end, unfortunately, nothing was gained.

The 'votes for trips' inquiry rumbled on in the background. The inquiry panel had asked many councillors about their attendance at charitable dinners. So in late June I wrote to Lesley Quinn to explain the basis upon which the Council supported charitable events. In respect of the dinners, I outlined the policy concerning donations, which were modest, usually of around £100, and the purchase of tables for the Council's guests, which I confirmed that either I as Lord Provost or a Bailie of the City would host. Other invitees would include Bailies, Group officers, elected members, the Council's chief officers and representatives of organisations in the city including the Lord Dean of Guild and Deacon Convenor, along with representatives of the Greater Glasgow and Clyde Valley Tourist Board and the business community.

I also outlined the other support that the Council offered non-profit-making organisations. This included the provision of facilities within the City Chambers and the attendance of the Lord Provost or a Bailie to lend individual charities support on behalf of the City.

Lesley Quinn wrote back indicating that 'all matters discussed within the panel hearings are confidential'. She also suggested that some of the councillors who had already been interviewed might have misrepresented their discussions. She implied that, although a number had requested that the Lord Provost's office, which was responsible for allocating places at charitable events, should clarify the matter, she really didn't welcome this information. Her assertion of confidentiality was reassuring in the short term but, given what was to follow, it seems that this was a case of one law for the Party and quite another for its representatives in Glasgow.

Shortly afterwards I received a letter inviting me to meet the NEC's inquiry team. This meeting was arranged for Wednesday 9 July. The letter asking me to attend didn't specify what would be discussed. It certainly didn't indicate that at the meeting I would be questioned closely on issues which had been raised with the inquiry team by members of the Group whom they had met beforehand.

I attended the meeting unaccompanied as I assumed I was simply being asked to give information and advice on the operation of the Lord Provost's office to assist with the background to the inquiry. But in the event the inquiry panel – just two members with Noel Foy acting as secretary – questioned me on all aspects concerning the City Council's Labour Group. Ms Brankin and Ms Tudhope wanted to know about discipline and harmony within the Group, the Council's financial position, the appointment of Bailies, attendance at conferences, factionalism, the administration of the Common Good Fund, relations between councillors and officers. While much of this was beyond the direct remit of the Lord Provost's office, I endeavoured to give as clear a picture as I could as an experienced, informed and active councillor.

Over the next two and a half months press speculation about the inquiry team's investigation continued. In mid-August, I received an extraordinary fax from the *Scotsman*'s Glasgow office which contained a list of questions that indicated either an extraordinarily vivid imagination or, and this seemed more likely, inside information. What price the confidentiality on which Lesley Quinn had insisted?

The *Scotsman*'s questions indicated that I was 'the target of serious allegations made by various councillors'. It expanded on this theme to suggest that I had abused funds: 'among items mentioned was the use of public funds authorised by you in connection with your attendance at the 1996 Edinburgh Tattoo', and 'we understand other allegations were made concerning use of funds to pay for councillors' expenses such as the purchase of a table at a charity event'. According to the *Scotsman*, 'the inquiry team has recommended that disciplinary action be taken against you', and it wanted to know if I would be able to carry on as Lord Provost.

The fax went on: 'You may be aware that your long-standing colleague Councillor Macdiarmid was interviewed several times by the inquiry team. They are recommending action against him and several other colleagues known to be political associates of yours.' And the fax

153

confirmed what was already very apparent: 'Clearly our sources are within the Labour Party. What is your reaction to Labour Party colleagues leaking details of the inquiry team's recommendations?'

After a list of ten allegations and questions, the journalist indicated that, as my answers to these questions would be in breach of the Labour Party's 'no comment' rule, the *Scotsman* would be prepared to attribute my response to 'sources'.

In spite of urging confidentiality, the Labour Party itself was clearly leaking like the proverbial sieve, with information from the very highest level being supplied to the *Scotsman* and, I suspect, also the *Evening Times*. It was the first real indication of a witch-hunt against me and my Tribune Group colleagues. Aware that any contact with the press would be in breach of Party rules, I copied the fax to Lesley Quinn at the Scottish Labour Party's headquarters. In my covering letter I expressed my astonishment and made it clear that I would not be speaking to the press. Again there was no reply from Lesley Quinn.

During the early months of the Labour Party's inquiry the Labour Group continued to approve foreign visits as necessary. Being intimidated into a close-down would have disrupted existing relations with international authorities and organisations and would have been potentially damaging for Glasgow trade.

One proposed trip rightly raised eyebrows. Bob Gould intimated his intention to attend a five-day urban regeneration conference in Portugal accompanied by the Chief Executive, John Anderson. The *Evening Times* ran the story under the headline 'Junket Genie Leaps Back Out Of The Bottle', and the Scottish Labour Party imposed a clamp-down on councillors' travel shortly after the visit was approved.

In spite of their insistence that councillors should maintain confidentiality, the Scottish Labour Party continued to give off-the-record press briefings. On 7 September under the headline 'Provost Faces Suspension in Sleaze Row', the *Sunday Times Scotland* reported that the Scottish Executive Committee recommended that Pat Lally, 'credited with spearheading the city's renaissance at the turn of the decade' and eleven other councillors be suspended pending disciplinary action. The paper named them as Dierdre Gaughan, Bob Gould, Gordon Macdiarmid, Alex Mosson, James Mutter, Steven Purcell, Heather Ritchie, George Ryan, Jim Sharkey, Elaine Smith, David Stevenson.

The rest of September was a blur of press speculation, most of it focused on Bob Gould as the original 'whistle-blower' and myself. The national leadership of the Labour Party declared itself 'angered' by the leaking of the inquiry report. It vowed that it would find the 'mole', but in practice did very little. If they had really wanted to, finding their 'mole' would have been very easy – we all knew where the leaks were coming from.

For those of us who were the subject of an increasingly vicious and seemingly well-informed series of press articles, this was a particularly frustrating time. The Scottish Labour Party insisted, at least in any communications with us, that they had to maintain the confidentiality of their interviews with what was a highly selective, perhaps specially selected, group of councillors.

But while we were being told nothing, a continuous stream of information, innuendo and accusation was being fed to the press. Headlines such as: 'Candidates for the Carpet' (*Herald*, 8 September 1997), 'Council Crisis at Boiling Point' (*Glaswegian*, 11 September), 'Lord Provost Faces Axe Over Sleaze' (*Mirror*, 20 September), 'Blair Sharpens Glasgow Axe' (*Express*, 20 September), 'Lally's Head on Block in Sleaze Purge' (*Record*, 20 September), 'Lally to be Suspended in Sleaze Crackdown' (*Scotsman*, 23 September), and 'Labour to Purge the City Fathers' (*Herald*, 23 September) left us in little doubt as to who were the targets of the Labour Party's reported 'purge'.

In the *Scotsman* of 20 September, under the headline 'Labour Keeps Silent on Reports of Councillors about to be Expelled', Euan McColm reported:

> The Labour Party remained silent last night over reports that seven Glasgow councillors are to be expelled next week.
>
> Officials stuck doggedly to the line that they knew nothing about the contents of a report into claims of junketing and rule-breaking among elected members.

However, the article did make mention of 'a series of high-profile leaks'. It also reported that 'according to insiders, Mr Gould is among those facing discipline for bringing the Party into disrepute by making his initial allegations'. But this gave us scant comfort.

While we were being subjected to a constant barrage of accusation, indeed condemnation in the press, the Scottish Labour Party maintained its line of mock propriety. The findings of its inquiry would remain confidential. Considering the accusations that were being made, this withholding of information from us was disgraceful.

While we had no idea of what specific accusations were being made against us, the press continued to write about these charges in a vague but vituperative fashion. Clearly confident in their sources, endless column inches and even editorial comment suggested a cut-and-dried case.

The *Scotsman*'s editorial of 23 September was particularly forthright:

> In the meantime, the Party must continue to show that it will no longer tolerate dirty little municipal secrets. If Tony Blair wishes to show that there is a real difference between New Labour and Old, he must dismantle entrenched, unscrupulous local regimes wherever he encounters them. Labour was born as a party of principle, in which self-interest yielded, as a matter of principle, to the greater good. In Scotland's second city that principle has been soiled beyond recognition. Those who fouled Glasgow's name deserve all they get.

I may not be a newspaper editor, but for someone to publish with such absolute clarity and certainty they presumably must have absolute confidence in their sources. Wherever the leaks were coming from within the Labour Party machine, it wasn't at low level. For the editors to be quite so gung-ho they had to be getting their information from the very top. While the Party's press spokesman, Angus Macleod, gave off-the-record briefings, he could not have acted without the approval of the General Secretary, Jack McConnell.

There was one small crumb of comfort in an article written by Ron MacKenna in the *Herald* on 24 September. Under the heading 'Political Rivals May Bury This Lazarus at Their Peril' he commented:

> Short of driving a stake through his heart, the Labour establishment over the years has done everything in its power to try to finish him off. His high profile, abrasive, but at times extremely successful leadership had party leaders wringing their hands over its political incorrectness.
>
> For a while in the City Chambers he ran rings around his ideologically sound, but practically hopeless opponents, gleefully ignoring the edicts of Labour's unelected party bureaucrats.
>
> For a few heady years, he was simultaneously public enemy number one and the city's saviour. His style was labelled 'Stalinist', and Glasgow was dubbed 'Lallygrad'. Yet the Garden Festival, Glasgow's reign as European City of Culture in 1990 and the building of the Royal Concert Hall, now immortalised as the 'Lally Palais', all bear his imprint.
>
> Ironically, given his current difficulties, his leadership which mixed political reality with keeping a tight rein over his colleagues, appears to have smacked more than anything of Blairite tendencies.

And all this time, as Lord and Lady Provost, Peggy and I continued to undertake our civic duties. We went out every day and every night, attended three or four functions a day. We weren't running away, we had nothing to run away from. Peggy was extraordinarily brave. In private she would cry, but in public she was always there by my side. Occasionally we would walk into a room and be greeted with a sudden hush. People were so surprised to see us attend their event. They just assumed that the barrage of vile press speculation would have sent us into hiding.

Yet even when the press coverage was at its most vicious, people would come up and shake our hands. Their 'it's nice to see you' and their sympathy with our ill-treatment was genuine. There were, of course, one or two who skulked in corners muttering, but the vast majority were obviously with us. This ability of the average Glaswegian to see through even the nastiest journalistic speculation was hugely encouraging to both of us.

On 24 September the *Herald* reported that 'London sources' had confirmed that I was to be suspended from the Labour Group. The Council Leader Bob Gould, the Depute Leader Gordon Macdiarmid, the Depute Lord Provost, Bailie Alex Mosson, and Bailie James Mutter were to share the same fate. Four councillors, Dierdre Gaughan, Elaine Smith, Heather Ritchie and James Sharkey faced expulsion. Three councillors, David Stevenson, Steven Purcell and George Ryan, would be questioned further.

On the same day, I was officially notified by letter. David Gardner, Assistant Secretary of the Labour Party, advised me that I would be suspended from membership of the Council's Labour Group, on the grounds that the 'initial investigation had identified a *prima facie* case of breach of Labour Group rules'. It was alleged that I had failed to operate within 'accepted Party procedures and thereby sought to undermine the Group Leadership'. It was also alleged that I had adopted 'an inappropriate stance towards council employees and procedures' and as such I had 'failed to maintain the standards required of a public representative of the Party'.

Upon receipt of the letter, I consulted my legal representative, Glasgow's famous former Lord Provost, Peter McCann. Peter, having established that he would be able to act on my behalf, wrote to the General Secretary of the Labour Party to make clear that from now on they wouldn't be fighting just one septuagenarian – there would be two of us!

CHAPTER SIXTEEN

On 24 September, Tom Sawyer, the London-based General Secretary of the Labour Party – a man rarely as amusing as his literary namesake – produced a press release describing the 'tough action' that the Party was taking in Glasgow. The report of the NEC's inquiry team, he argued, was 'thorough, fair and far-reaching' and the Party 'would leave no stone unturned'. Both assertions were questionable. Even at this stage it was apparent that only the views of a selected group of Glasgow councillors had been sought. Mr Sawyer went on to indicate that the Party intended 'to eliminate all bad practice in the Labour Group and Council', and pledged that 'those councillors named today will, following further investigation, have charges laid against them'. These charges would, in turn, be presented to the Party's National Constitutional Committee, which would consider 'appropriate disciplinary action, if any'. Mr Sawyer affirmed that, now that the report was completed, 'our primary task is to eliminate all bad practice in the Labour Group and Council so that the good reputation of Glasgow Council can be restored'.

The recommendations which accompanied the press release were extracted from the report of the NEC inquiry team, but the report itself, being 'private and confidential', was not included. Thus the press were effectively given the sentences without any intimation of the crime. The recommendations stated:

> In four cases, it is considered that there is sufficient *prima facie* evidence of breaches of Party rules and Group rules to justify instructing the General Secretary to arrange for the drawing up of charges for presentation to the NCC for appropriate disciplinary action to be considered.

In five more cases, the recommendations continued in a separate paragraph:

It is considered that there is already sufficient *prima facie* evidence
of breaches of Party rules and Group rules to justify instructing
the General Secretary to arrange for the drawing up of charges for
presentation to the NCC for appropriate disciplinary action to be
considered.

The two paragraphs were nearly exactly the same. The difference
between there being 'sufficient evidence' and 'already sufficient evidence'
escapes me. Yet this was the sort of gobbledegook which the Labour
Party deemed it appropriate to send out with a press release. Sadly,
however, nobody in the press chose to expose this material for what it
was, bureaucratic nonsense.

In three other cases, the extract from the report continued, there was
'sufficient concern about evidence' to prompt further action. It noted
two resignations, those of Councillor Yvonne Anderson and Councillor
Gordon Archer. It went on to advise that the Glasgow Labour Group
adopt new Standing Orders, hold elections for Group and civic vacancies
which would arise from the suspensions, and, in general, tighten up and
observe existing rules. In particular, it recommended the setting up of
a 'Special Panel' to approve visits outside the city. The extract from the
report concluded with a thoroughly paternalistic footnote recommending that 'potential officers undertake appropriate training in
advance of the elections' and 'the implementation of the process would
itself be used as a development opportunity for the Labour Group'.

The findings of the 'private and confidential' report itself highlighted
'an almost total absence of good working relationships within the
Labour Group' and 'fierce factionalism'. The report did not consider
specifics, but under headings including 'Conduct of Members' and
'Group Management' it alluded to 'unsatisfactory dealings and working
relationships between local authority employees and some members of
the Labour Group' and 'unsatisfactory political, operational and organ-
isational management'. A further heading 'Exercise and Receipt of
"Patronage"' indicated that 'the team fully explored the question of
alleged inappropriate attendances'.

The report was vague and general which, given that it was largely based
upon interviews, is hardly surprising. They had clearly talked to a lot of
people with a lot of axes to grind, and that had resulted in a woolly report.
At any given time, if you chose to explore the innards of any political
grouping, particularly a party of government, I am quite sure you would
discover many people with a gripe. The gripes might change from day to
day and week to week, but there will always be gripes, people feeling ill

159

done by and people who attribute the preferment of others to all sorts of motives or agendas, very rarely to the fact that the preferred individual might have qualities which gave them an edge on the competition.

Much of the responsibility for the constant and highly damaging press coverage could be laid, fair and square, at the door of the Scottish Labour Party. This fact made one of the findings of the inquiry team's report particularly ludicrous. Under the heading 'Media Attention' it highlighted the adverse press coverage that had occurred throughout the UK as well as in Scotland. 'This publicity,' the report continued, 'formed the basis for a discourse between the team and members giving evidence, on the impact of the press coverage and the damaged reputation the Labour Party had suffered as a consequence.'

But the bulk of the press coverage was of the Party's own making. The best way for it to dam the stream of adverse publicity was simply to tell the truth – to instruct their spin-doctors and those issuing the non-attributable briefings to reveal how very little they'd actually discovered in Glasgow. Try as they might to shroud the fact in bureaucratic doublespeak, there was no substance to the allegations.

My suspicion was that the Labour Party's spin-doctors were working hard to generate adverse publicity about yours truly, presumably so that when I was ultimately beaten into submission by the sheer tedium of the bureaucratic onslaught, or left the field of play due to press-induced stress, they could claim a great moral victory. Unhappily for them, I had long since determined that quitting just wasn't my style.

The Scottish Labour Party also issued a press release, headed 'Dewar Welcomes Glasgow Report'. Donald Dewar was quoted as saying:

> The Labour Party has said all along that we were determined to conduct a thorough, fair and far-reaching review into the allegations surrounding Glasgow City Council. The tough nature of the recommendations contained in today's report shows how seriously we have taken this.

As a lawyer, Dewar should perhaps have been more aware of the high standards demanded by Scots Law. His comments suggested that, like those at Party headquarters in London, he believed that the Party's vague, unsubstantiated allegations were acceptable. When some time later, in a speech to the Law Society, I joked that I probably spent more time in the courts than most of my audience, Dewar made the less than humorous comment that it was no bad thing that some people had to spend so much time in the courts.

In view of what was to come, Donald Dewar might feel that he should have been more circumspect in his comments. The general view of Donald Dewar is that he is a decent man. But would a decent man have allowed the shoddy and unjustifiable action by the Labour Party against me to continue? Or would he have stopped the whole process in its tracks? Dewar must, after all, have been fully aware of exactly what was happening at every point.

The preliminary investigation by the NEC's inquiry team was, it seemed, simply a preamble to a fuller investigation. I met Lesley Quinn on 24 September in Committee Room One in Glasgow City Chambers at 12.55pm. At this meeting Ms Quinn agreed that I deserved to know who was making allegations against me. I never got the information and she subsequently denied saying this. Meanwhile, I and eight others were suspended. As predicted, among these were the whistle-blower, Bob Gould, his Depute Gordon Macdiarmid and my own Depute, Alex Mosson. Both Alex and I immediately announced that we would be seeking an adjudication on the matter in the Scottish courts. My precise words were reported in *The Times* on 25 September:

> I will also be further consulting with my solicitor in order to ensure that we obtain full disclosure of the allegations and the names of the persons making the allegations because clearly all of the information that was dealt with by the inquiry committee created the climate that led to today's suspensions. I do not think it's a terribly just way of dealing with things.

While my colleagues, Messrs Gould and Macdiarmid, were effectively removed from their Group roles and thereby their positions within the government of Glasgow, the legal position for the Lord Provost was quite different. Rather like the Speaker in the House of Commons, the Lord Provostship is an apolitical appointment. The Lord Provost represents the City, not the Labour Group. Theoretically it would be quite possible for a representative of a party other than the ruling group to become Lord Provost, in fact there have been instances in other Scottish local authorities where just that has happened. Norman Irons, Lord Provost of Edinburgh from 1992 to 1996, was a member of the Scottish National Party in an authority under Labour control. While I might have been suspended from the Group, neither the Scottish Labour Party nor Tony Blair himself had the authority to remove me from the Lord Provostship.

Of course, such legal niceties did nothing to stop the oft-quoted 'senior Labour sources' from maintaining their intimidation through the press. The *Express* claimed an exclusive. It reported that I was to be axed from the Provostship and my 'arch-rival' Jean McFadden installed in my place. In the words of 'senior Party sources', councillors who supported me would 'have to consider their future carefully'. The *Express* also reported that 'for legal reasons, Labour has not revealed what specific charges have been brought against the nine suspended councillors'. This particular line would become very familiar. Rather more helpfully, it also pointed out that 'given that the complaints obviously covered a period going back a number of years, it seemed to have taken the Labour Party a very long time to do anything'.

Touchingly, the *Daily Mail* revived my habitual moniker, but concluded 'this time Lazarus may decide to settle comfortably into his grave'. What a very depressing prospect – not a chance!

On 25 September I had a long meeting with my lawyer, the feisty Peter McCann. The Labour Party, doubtless aware that their case was flimsy, had been playing on the public perception that 'if it's in the papers, then it must be true', not something I've believed for a very long time. Together Peter and I reviewed the minutiae of the report and judged it to be flawed on numerous counts. In addition to its circumlocutory style, we discovered many factual inaccuracies. We came out fighting. Alex Mosson meanwhile had taken the legal process even further and was visiting the Court of Session to try to get his suspension lifted.

To ensure that the Council ran smoothly, and applying the total objectivity for which the Scottish Labour Party is a byword, to no one's great surprise, Jean McFadden was appointed as what they termed an 'interim' Leader. Her message in the *Mirror* must have allowed innumerable Glaswegians to sleep comfortably in their beds, 'I want to reassure you. The city will recover.' A further, fascinating diversion was the publication on 26 September by the *Evening Times* of the NEC inquiry team's entire report. How it got this 'private and confidential' document was not explained, but then for months the press had been full of information from unexplained sources, 'reliable sources' and 'senior Labour Party sources', and very rarely did any of these 'sources' have a name. 'We publish the damning document in its entirety,' commented the *Evening Times*'s editorial. 'The reasons why the NEC acted as it did in suspending the Lord Provost, Council Leader, their deputies and five of the key figures are spelled out in plain English.' The *Evening Times* surely has a better grasp of what 'plain English' is than that.

A couple of days later, Glasgow City Council's estimable new Leader, who someone rather uncharitably described to me as the 'warmed-up left-overs of one of our old leaders', spoke on Radio Scotland's *Eye to Eye* programme. She said: 'I'm fairly clear in my own mind that what the Labour Party, the NEC of the Labour Party, wants the Group to do is remove from office those of the nine which actually hold office including the Lord Provost and the Depute Convenor of the Council. There are procedures for putting that in motion.'

Mrs McFadden's comment was both confusing and completely wrong. As time would tell, there were no such procedures.

Michael Kelly more or less endorsed Mrs McFadden's view in the *Scotsman*. He did, however, note that removing me from office would take 'someone with a thorough understanding of the law and standing orders'. He also dismissed Frank McAveety out of hand. Frank was the councillor who appeared to be the Blairite challenger for the leadership after Jean's spell as interim Leader was through. Kelly strongly advocated that 'the Party hierarchy should make it clear that its councillors are expected to endorse its choice of Leader' i.e. Mrs McFadden. After all, why let a little thing like democracy get in the way of what the Scottish Labour Party wanted. It hadn't up until now.

It must have been very frustrating for Mr McConnell and his colleagues in the Scottish Labour Party. They had demolished most of the Tribune group on Glasgow City Council. They'd installed their choice as Leader and yet one of the main suspended Tribunites was still there as Lord Provost, First Citizen of the City and Lord Lieutenant, representing Her Majesty the Queen in Glasgow. There didn't seem to be any legal mechanism to shift me. The new leadership of the Labour Group was similarly vexed. They too put their heads together and remarkably, despite the acknowledged intellectual might of the Scottish Labour Party, it was their non-elected puppet executive which came up with the solution first. All they had to do was kill me.

Not that there was any suggestion of literally rubbing me out. Instead, they would simply pretend I was dead. Somebody had noticed that on previous occasions – and sadly there had been a couple in recent years – when a Lord Provost died he also, well, ceased to be the Lord Provost. Perhaps this was the solution to their problem. As the Council's Standing Orders did not allow the removal of a Lord Provost during his term of office, this notion of a pretend death offered possibilities.

Jean McFadden, with the keen legal brain which had won her a first class honours degree, gave a candid interview to the *Scotsman*. She would, she said, talk to the Council's Chief Executive John Anderson, who, like herself, was a lawyer so he'd know what to do. Clearly, to Mrs McFadden the possibility of death and the effect it might have on one's career prospects was a revelation: 'New Lord Provosts have been elected during a term when someone has died and that has not been a problem.'

Having a chat based upon a 'what if he was dead' scenario and consulting the Chief Executive without realising that it was a completely loony-tunes notion was embarrassing but at least kept it confidential. Mentioning the idea to outsiders would have been unwise, but to discuss it with the press struck me as an early sign of madness.

Despite the fact that the Labour Party was now living in some sort of alternative universe, Alex Mosson's test case against his suspension did not succeed. The Court of Session ruled that the suspensions were valid. It was a setback, but the beginning of October brought glimmers of hope. The Labour Party had, it seemed, taken legal advice and discovered that you couldn't simply unseat a Lord Provost. Even pretending he was dead wasn't going to work. There were dissatisfied mutterings among councillors about the 'guilty until proven innocent' verdicts which had been imposed upon the suspended councillors. It had also been agreed that the appointment of an interim Group Leader, elected rather than selected this time, would take place on 10 October. Frank McAveety was seen as a dark horse in this particular race, in which the favourite was Jean McFadden, but then she had been the favourite a number of times before. Things were looking up.

In the leadership election Frank McAveety displaced the Duchess, and Charlie Gordon was chosen as his Depute.

On 15 October 1997 something quite unexpected and almost unprecedented happened. I got a letter from the Labour Party. Eileen Murfin wrote to invite me to attend for interview on either Wednesday 22 or Thursday 23 October at Keir Hardie House.

According to the letter, the purpose of the interview was to seek my response to 'various matters which emerged during the NEC's recent preliminary investigation in Glasgow'. It would be conducted by herself and Noel Foy, and full notes would be taken. The meeting would 'enable you to be informed of the substance of matters which have been alleged against you and to give you the opportunity, if you wish, to respond to them, but you need not do so'. I was pleased to note that 'the interview is not a "trial" or hearing of any issue or allegation'.

The letter continued that the allegations and my responses would form the basis of a report to the National Executive Committee which would then take a decision on whether there was a disciplinary case to be referred to the National Constitutional Committee.

Mrs Murfin listed a number of matters as the proposed content of the meeting. It was alleged that I had breached Group rules by failing to operate within Party procedures and thereby sought to undermine the Group Leadership. Cited in support of this allegation was Glasgow's Chief Constable John Orr's letter to Bob Gould in March 1997. Objections from the Chairman of the Roads and Transportation Committee alleged that I had manipulated procedures of business when bus shelter contracts were being considered. Another odd allegation, listed in Mrs Murfin's letter, came from the Group Leader Bob Gould himself. Mr Gould is a man whose friendship with a well-known developer in the city has been reported in the press. He was implying some impropriety in the fact that I had met a developer. Mention was also made of the conduct of Labour Group meetings, although as Lord Provost I had no control over this. Indeed, Jean McFadden was Convenor of the Group, so perhaps she too should have been invited to my meeting with Mrs Murfin 'to be informed of the substance of matters . . .'

Then I was accused of interfering in the management of the Service and Personnel Department procedures concerning chauffeur services; and of supporting a councillor who'd assaulted a senior local government officer. Finally, issues had been raised regarding the operation of the Common Good Fund. Mrs Murfin's conclusion to her letter, 'I look forward to meeting you in Glasgow next week', somehow lacked any real sincerity.

On Wednesday 22 October, shortly before three o'clock in the afternoon, I arrived at Keir Hardie House, armed with a point-by-point refutation of the relatively minor and inconsequential charges enumerated in Eileen Murfin's letter. Although Mrs Murfin's letter explicitly stated that this meeting was 'not a "trial"', by this time, being a little jaded with the machinations of the Labour Party, I decided, that irrespective of how the hearing had been set up, that I was not going to be. I arrived accompanied by my estimable lawyer, Peter McCann.

CHAPTER SEVENTEEN

On admission to Keir Hardie House we were met by Noel Foy, a Labour Party Scottish organiser who had acted as secretary to the initial inquiry, and led into a committee room where we were met by Eileen Murfin. Mr Foy would be taking notes.

According to Mrs Murfin's letter, my responses to the allegations detailed in her letter would form the basis of a report to the National Executive Committee. Her letter included the words 'if any' in parenthesis with regard to my responses, almost implying that I might not have any valid response to her inquiry into the charges. If Mrs Murfin had imagined that I would present a thin defence, she was proved very wrong. Peter McCann and I didn't leave Keir Hardie House until nearly six o'clock that evening, by which time Mrs Murfin's final appointment of the day, Jim Sharkey, had arrived for his four o'clock meeting, waited an hour, and left.

To counter Mrs Murfin's letter, I tabled eleven productions and asked that these be copied to the National Executive Committee to assist in their deliberations.

My first submission was my own CV. It felt it important that the inquiry agent and subsequently the members of the National Executive Committee should know that I had served as a councillor almost continuously for three decades and had held a succession of senior posts. My CV enumerated twelve directorships, many of which, at the time of meeting the NEC's officers, I still held. Of these twelve organisations, I was chairman of five. My CV also listed fourteen organisations of which I was patron or honorary president, and some ten honours and awards including those I had received from Strathclyde University, the city of Dalian and the President of France. I felt it was important that the inquiry agent, who was after all a parachutist from Labour Party HQ in London, and subsequently the members of the National Executive Committee, should be fully aware both of my career and of those organisations which had seen fit to involve me in their management and, of course, the others which had considered that I had deserved honours.

I countered the assertion that I had 'sought to undermine the Group Leadership' with a number of submissions. I provided a copy of a letter I had written to the Secretary of the Labour Group, Des McNulty, in March 1996.

In the approach to the Provostship election, there had been all sorts of rumours flying around in the Group. While one usually ignores tittle-tattle, I was particularly aggrieved that statements to the effect that I intended to remove a number of councillors from their convenorships were being spread by senior members of the Group.

I had received a telephone call from Bill Timoney, Convenor of the Police Committee, informing me that Bob Gray, the former Lord Provost and long-term friend of Jean McFadden, had told him that I intended to remove him and Councillors McCarron and Green from their present convenorships. I assured Bill Timoney that the rumour was entirely untrue, which he accepted. I then phoned up Bob Gray to confront him with this completely unfounded allegation.

It looked very much as if the intention of such rumours was to weaken my support in the Provostship vote. In the letter I wrote to Des McNulty I informed him that this behaviour was outrageous, but that I would not be naming names. The purpose of my letter was to have the Group condemn such muck-raking, not to indulge in further muck-raking. I revealed to him that I had heard that promises had been made to certain councillors in return for their votes. I expressed the hope that such stories were untrue, commenting that those who elected us 'would demand higher standards of behaviour than this'. Far from undermining the leadership, I copied the letter to Bob Gould as I was sure that, as Leader, he could not possibly condone such sharp practice in the Group.

Along with the letter I also submitted to Mrs Murfin the minute from the Labour Group's Annual General Meeting on 18 March 1996. The Secretary of the Labour Group, Des McNulty, had intimated the content of my letter at the opening of the meeting and it had been noted. Then, of course, I had gone on to score a resounding victory in the Provostship election.

Another submission to Mrs Murfin was the letter I had written to Jack McConnell after my return from holiday. In response to Bob Gould's original allegations in the *Evening Times*, this letter had indicated 'quite categorically' that votes for trips was not a practice that existed under my administration. I had also suggested that Mrs

McFadden would be able to confirm that she too had not presided over a Labour Group where such activity took place.

I also submitted a short paper I had written in June on the conduct of the NEC inquiry. In it I expressed my conviction that the disciplinary procedures laid down in the constitution of the Glasgow Labour Group were the appropriate mechanism for handling the matter. By circumventing these procedures, the Party had prevented the issues from being addressed expeditiously and effectively. The decision of the Party to take control had resulted in Labour members of the Council being vilified by the media, damaging their reputations and that of the Party. I made clear my profound concern that Glasgow's reputation as the United Kingdom's leading post-industrial city had been severely damaged.

When I wrote this paper, the matter had already been running for eighteen weeks, and I pointed out that the Scottish Labour Party's anonymous spokespersons' off-the-record statements to the media had caused considerable damage to the Glasgow Labour Group, which was now thoroughly demoralised. Furthermore, the Party's imposition of ponderously slow procedures to examine the case from on high meant that the Glasgow councillors were unable to defend themselves, 'either individually or collectively'.

I observed that in the time the Labour Party had spent on *not* dealing with a relatively minor issue in Glasgow, Tony Blair had mounted an election campaign, won a huge victory, 'taken up the reins of government, filled all the Offices of State, and established and enhanced the reputations of the Parliamentary Labour Party and the Labour Government, both nationally and internationally'. The submission concluded with my plaintive enquiry, 'if all that can be achieved, why is Glasgow still suffering?' That complaint had been written in early June, and here we were on 22 October and no further on.

In support of the allegation that I had undermined the leadership, Eileen Murfin's letter of 15 October raised the following specific items: (1) a letter from the Chief Constable to Bob Gould indicating the Chief Constable's intention to meet me; (2) an objection from the Chairman of the Roads and Transportation Committee that I had interfered in business concerning bus shelter contracts; (3) a meeting I had had with a property developer; and (4) conduct of Group meetings.

I took each point in turn and addressed each individually, verbally and by other productions. (1) The suggestion that, in indicating that he intended to meet myself as well as the Leader, the Chief Constable was somehow an unwitting accessory in my undermining of Bob Gould was just daft. I had written to John Orr because I happen to be the Chairman of the Council meeting nearly prevented by the Militant mob. As Chairman, I wanted to ensure that members could attend the meeting safely. This was my only reason for seeing him.

(2) On the roads and transportation issue, my intention was not to interfere but to clear up an inconsistency. Having read the March papers of the Labour Group and the Roads and Transportation Committee within ten minutes of each other, I noticed that they contradicted each other. I merely wrote to the Chairman of the Roads and Transportation Committee to point this out. I could see no more appropriate way of acting in the circumstances. Far from undermining the Chairman's authority, my letter, by drawing attention to the oversight, helped his committee to act in keeping with the wishes of the Labour Group Executive. I expressed no opinion on what action should be taken; I merely suggested that the conflict between the papers be resolved at the Labour Group.

(3) My meeting with the property developer was held not at my request but the developer's. I made sure that also present at the meeting were the Depute Chief Executive and a senior officer from the Department of Planning and Development. There was little more I could do to ensure that the matter was handled in an appropriately businesslike way. The developer's purpose in asking to meet me was to give assurances that he shared the aims for the city centre that I had long espoused. He seemed concerned to refute rumours that he would try to thwart important developments in the city centre in order to smooth the way to planning permission for a large peripheral site. I accepted his denial of these rumours and was pleased to note that he would be working towards positive development in the city centre. On the matter of other developments, I indicated that the Planning Department had its own well-established and proper procedures for dealing with such matters. The meeting ended amicably but, apart from being an intriguing interlude, had no real significance until it became part of Mrs Murfin's investigation.

(4) The conduct of Group meetings was under the convenorship of Mrs McFadden. So the manner in which they were conducted was her responsibility and not something I could properly comment upon.

As I made the above points, I was not sure whether or not Mrs Murfin appreciated the import of the arguments and evidence I had brought before her.

The second 'charge' against me was that I had adopted an inappropriate stance towards Council employees and procedures. Three matters were listed: (1) interference in the management of the Service and Personnel Department procedures regarding the provision of driver/chauffeur services; (2) support of a councillor who had assaulted a senior local government officer; (3) and general concerns expressed in verbal evidence and press coverage regarding the operation of the Common Good Fund.

I tabled four letters in strong contradiction of the broad accusation that I had 'adopted an inappropriate stance towards Council employees'. These were in the form of four very touching character references that I had recently received from Council employees with whom I worked most closely on a daily basis. Katie McGhee, my assistant PA, was the first to write, on 26 September 1997. Her letter was short and to the point, indicating her support and that she was 'particularly appalled' at reports in the press which had repeated the statements in Mrs Murfin's letter about my attitude towards Council staff. Katie made it clear that I habitually treated staff 'with courtesy, fairness and respect'.

My PA, Ian Easton, wrote on 30 September in reaction to the publication of the NEC inquiry team's report in the *Evening Times*. Ian was upset by the implication that there seemed to be improper control of expenditure with regard to civic hospitality. Given that control of this aspect of our work was a significant part of his job, and that he is a most meticulous officer, he was understandably somewhat put out by the suggestion of any impropriety, as this necessarily impugned his own professionalism. In his letter he outlined the approvals process, and the necessity for the Council to have a mechanism to ensure that hospitality is provided for visiting VIPs or members of the Royal Family, acknowledging the security implications of such events. He underlined the role of the Lord Provost as Lord Lieutenant on these occasions. Greatly perturbed by the accusation that I had not acted properly in my relationship with Council employees, he confirmed that my relationships with staff were 'professional and friendly'. He had copied the *Evening Times* information to his colleagues who all shared his views on the matter.

My personal secretary, Bernadine Blair, wrote in early October that, having worked with me for three and a half years, she had never witnessed me treating my colleagues or visitors with anything other than 'the utmost respect and courtesy'. She continued, 'It has been a pleasure and a privilege to work for someone whom I both respect and admire. I have witnessed first hand the vast amount of work undertaken by yourself in both your roles as Leader and Lord Provost of Glasgow City Council and I have never doubted your professional integrity.' Like her colleagues, Bernadine offered her support.

The final letter came from Jim Clark, who had been my personal assistant when I was the Leader and now served within the Lord Provost's staff. Jim had recently married and had actually been away on his honeymoon when I received notification of the Party's accusations against me. Jim professed himself 'astonished and angered at the "charges" levelled against you by the Party'. Like his colleagues, he was highly complimentary about the quality of my work and, like them, indicated that he would be happy to support me if this was appropriate during the Labour Party's deliberations.

Jim concluded his letter with a kindly and perceptive analysis of how I was feeling. 'Knowing you as I do, I realise that the personal hurt you must feel about these allegations will not be as strong as the anger you feel as a result of the damage they are causing to the reputation of the city of Glasgow itself. Equally I know that you will work twice as hard in the coming months to repair the said damage.'

If that little lot wasn't enough to blow away any suggestion of my adopting an inappropriate stance towards Council employees, I don't known what would be. However, for good measure, I also provided documentation which refuted each of the specific allegations enumerated under this heading.

(1) I presented as evidence a short report to show that my behaviour concerning the provision of driver/chauffeur services had been entirely appropriate. This report had been submitted by the Director of Roads and Transport in February 1997 to his committee which reviewed chauffeur services within the Council. As one of the proposals in the report affected the Lord Provost's chauffeurs, I was unhappy that the issue hadn't been raised with myself. The proposal would have increased the number of the Lord Provost's chauffeurs from two to three and altered the shift patterns of these personnel. So I inquired why the report had been prepared and this alteration proposed. I was told that the instruction to the Director to make the proposal in the report had come from the Chief Executive at the instigation of senior councillors. I then wrote to the Labour Group Secretary to ask that the matter be raised at the Executive, pointing out that it would have been normal procedure to consult with all the parties affected, including my own office. My letter was discussed at the Labour Group meeting on 3 March. The recommendations in the Director's report were agreed, with the caveat that the third post would be re-examined, as would the operations of the service. The outcome of these discussions was that the changes to the Lord Provost's chauffeur service, which I considered to be inappropriate and unnecessary, didn't proceed. It was proposed that there would be a

six-monthly review of the situation, but up until the date of writing, no such review had been carried out.

(2) I had to ask Mrs Murfin for substantiation of the allegation that I had supported a councillor who'd assaulted a senior local government officer, as I could recall no such incident. But Mrs Murfin failed to identify the councillor concerned. In the same position I would, in the case of any such allegation, have provided the name and insisted upon a fair and proper examination of the case, but that would only have been observing due process or natural justice, call it what you will.

(3) On the operation of the Common Good Fund, I presented a copy of a note from the Chief Executive that explained the Lord Provost's responsibilities concerning budgets and hospitality. I also presented the written response of the Council's Director of Finance, James Andrews, to three questions I had raised concerning the conduct of the Lord Provost's office. Had there been anything inappropriate, irregular or illegal in the way its activities had been conducted? Had the finance department any reason to be concerned about those activities? Did the finance department's monitoring of funds indicate any actions contrary to the rules and regulations of the Council? In a preamble to his answers, Mr Andrews indicated that any suspicion of a procedural irregularity would lead to an immediate investigation by the Chief Internal Auditor. His report would go to the department being investigated, to the Chief Executive and the external auditor. Any fraud or other suspicious loss of money would be immediately reported to the police. 'Turning to your three questions, and bearing in mind the above comments, the answer is no in each case.' His response could not have been more succinct or clear.

At the conclusion of our meeting, Peter McCann and I agreed that our verbal responses and written submissions made it quite clear that I was innocent of any wrong-doing or even of any minor misdemeanour. They should also have confirmed that I was both fully cognisant of the Labour Group rules and concerned that they should be observed by all members of the Group. It was equally clear that in its actions the Party had not shown such respect for the Council's Group rules. Had our well-established internal procedures been followed, Bob Gould's accusations might have been swiftly dealt with in a manner that limited the damage to the Labour Party and, more importantly, to the city of Glasgow.

Through the whole course of the interview Noel Foy said nothing and appeared to concentrate on taking notes. Mrs Murfin appeared to be listening, but I wondered whether she really could have been given the report she presented to the National Executive of the Labour Party.

As we left Keir Hardie House, Peter McCann and I felt that once the material we had submitted was passed on to the Labour Party's National Executive Committee, that body would overrule the accusations which had been made against me. However, we were unaware that our evidence would not be submitted in a manner which would allow the National Executive Committee the opportunity to give it proper consideration.

CHAPTER EIGHTEEN

Political inquiries at local level can all too easily be based on petty prejudice. There are always those who have scores to settle with individuals in influential positions and others wishing to establish their reputations. Any backdown in the inquiry would have been hugely embarrassing for the Labour Party in Scotland. But proceedings had now moved away from Glasgow and were in the hands of people who had influence within the National Labour Party machine.

Such was the volume of publicity that had accompanied every stage of the proceedings over eight months that great courage was required to recommend to the National Executive Committee that the evidence was what the legal profession would describe as 'unsafe'. The time had come when the views of the individual had to be very seriously considered and carefully balanced against the substance of any allegations. After my meeting with Mrs Murfin at Keir Hardie House I did indicate to the press that I had dealt with all matters raised, and I had been doing a lot of talking. Asked if I had managed to convince Mrs Murfin of my innocence, I commented, tacitly acknowledging the pressure which I knew was upon her, 'We shall have to wait and see.'

Mrs Murfin had originally indicated that I would have the opportunity to respond to the 'evidence' against me before the National Executive Committee decided whether any charges would be referred to the National Constitutional Committee. She had also made it clear, in her letter of 15 October, that our interview on 22 October would not be 'a "trial" or hearing of any issue or allegation'.

But my responses to the allegations were never considered by the National Executive Committee. In my view this was a total dereliction of duty by the members of the NEC. With the honourable exception of three members the Labour Party's ruling body blatantly failed properly to exercise the responsibility and duties entrusted to them by the Party membership. In so doing, they displayed a total disregard for the consequences for me as an individual member of the Party who held a very responsible public position.

On 29 October, Eileen Murfin submitted her report to the NEC. She recommended not that the case be dropped but that the matter be referred to the National Constitutional Committee. My views had not been taken into account by the NEC, and I also understood that the submissions which Peter McCann and I had carefully collected, and which had formed the substance of our meeting with Mrs Murfin, had not been passed to the NEC for consideration, although I had specifically asked that they should be. Had the material been copied to the NEC, with appropriate time for consideration, the members of that body might have been able to make up their own minds.

As it was, it seemed that the members of the National Executive Committee were purely steered by the recommendation of the officers who had conducted the inquiry. Given the strength of my refutation of their initial case, it was deeply upsetting that the National Executive Committee appeared not to want to be confused by facts in merely nodding the matter through to the National Constitutional Committee.

So I decided to write to every member of the National Executive Committee. On 30 October 1997 I sent thirty letters to that august committee, whose better known members included the Right Honourable Tony Blair MP, the Right Honourable John Prescott MP, the Right Honourable Robin Cook MP, Diane Abbott MP, Ken Livingstone MP and Dennis Skinner MP. As it turned out, all the right honourables demonstrated that perhaps they weren't quite as honourable as I might have imagined. However, the last three – all members of the Campaign group – demonstrated that one thing that they were prepared to campaign for was justice.

In my letter I expressed my astonishment that recommendations against me were being made to the National Constitutional Committee. I explained that in my two and a half hour interview with Mrs Murfin, I had presented eleven productions refuting the allegations against me. I complained strongly that this defence had not been considered by the NEC's members:

> I find it hard to believe that you were asked to make a decision on the allegations made against me without being made aware of my side of the case. I believe that NEC members have an obligation to ask for copies of the eleven productions I placed before Mrs Murfin in my defence, and indeed I am prepared to provide you with copies of the documents if necessary.

> I consider that with forty-seven years' membership of the Labour Party, it's not too much to ask that my case be fairly considered by the NEC.

I concluded that I looked forward to hearing from them in due course.

My point was that if the evidence I submitted had been properly considered, the matter would never have been referred to the National Constitutional Committee. The Labour Party rules required them to consider it, so why had they seen fit not to?

Of the thirty members of the Committee to whom I wrote only eight replied. Of these, only three were constructive. The other five were dismissive – politely dismissive maybe, but dismissive none the less.

It turned out that three Members of Parliament had voted against the NEC decision. Dennis Skinner took the trouble to phone my office to let me know that they were Ken Livingstone, Diane Abbott and himself. In his reply to my letter, Ken Livingstone, who of course had famously defeated Tony Blair's pal Peter Mandelson in the autumn of 1997 for his place on the National Executive, stated:

> I agree with your comments about the way your case was handled, and I voted against proceeding on that basis.
>
> The document was handed around the NEC meeting at the start, along with several others, which by anyone's standards is an offence against natural justice. Furthermore, the NEC was not allowed an adjournment in order to read the documentation.

He asked me to keep him informed of developments. Diane Abbott requested copies of the documents which I had referred to in my letter. She also asked for a copy of my response to the allegations which I forwarded to her. Here were three people, in London, who had never met me in their lives but who nevertheless were not prepared to support charges against me without having the necessary information. Sadly their fellow NEC members chose simply to do as the Party officials advised.

The reply from the Right Honourable Margaret Beckett MP, the President of the Board of Trade, avoided the issue entirely:

> As I am sure you will understand, NEC members are placed in a somewhat delicate position when questions are asked about how particular cases are handled. This is particularly the case when, as sometimes happens, there are queries about potential legal action in the future.

In consequence, it has always been my practice not to engage in correspondence about matters which have to be dealt with by the NEC as such. I hope that you will understand this approach to what is, as I say, a rather difficult and delicate position.

Quite honestly, I did not understand Ms Beckett's position. If she'd ensured that she considered all the facts from both sides before agreeing that the matter should be referred to the National Constitutional Committee, there might have been no need for the legal wrangles which were to follow or, indeed, for further embarrassment for the Labour Party or the city of Glasgow. My wife Peggy, whose forenames are Margaret Beckett, was particularly upset by this response.

The Right Honourable Clare Short MP replied that she had not been at the NEC meeting as she had been out of the country on Government business. She had, however, passed my letter to the General Secretary of the Party, Tom Sawyer, and asked him to reply directly on her behalf. Tom Sawyer chose not to trouble himself, showing scant regard for Ms Short's request. After all, she was only a Government minister.

Steve Pickering, Deputy General Secretary of the GMB union, responded that he wouldn't respond. 'I would not respond on this matter as it is going through procedural channels which are well established and understood within the Labour Party.' Mr Pickering is doubtless a very busy man, confident in the knowledge that everything will go very well through well established channels. However, as the representative of a union with the slogan 'Working Together', Mr Pickering's attitude is lamentable. If he is not prepared to consider the real facts and prefers instead to rely on 'procedural channels', he is rendering poor service to the Labour Party and to his union's members.

I had expected a constructive response from the Right Honourable John Prescott MP, the Deputy Prime Minister. Nodding the matter through the NEC was quite unacceptable, but on receipt of my letter he, above all others, must surely have seen the error of his ways. This, after all, was the Government's representative of the ordinary folk, the left-winger and champion of the 'little man'. As Deputy Prime Minister Mr Prescott would surely be expected to keep to the fore the interests of the working people who had founded the Labour Party and sustained it through the decades.

Sadly, it was not to be. Mr Prescott's response consisted of two lines. 'I have read your letter carefully and have passed it on to the General Secretary of the Labour Party for his attention.' Why had he bothered reading my letter carefully? Was his careful reading in order to check whether this was something which required his personal attention? If so, then he'd clearly concluded, in my view quite wrongly, that it was not. Or did he read it carefully in order to make specific recommendations prior to passing it on? There was no evidence that he had done.

Perhaps Mr Prescott was in the habit of carefully reading everything prior to passing the buck. If he made no recommendation whatsoever, then he might as well not have read the letter in the first place. Even if he did not have any recommendations to make, none the less he had no more effect on the General Secretary than Clare Short had done. I subsequently heard nothing from Tom Sawyer.

The reply to my letter from Ten Downing Street ran to four paragraphs – the longest letter I had in response. It went as follows:

> Thank you for advising me of your concerns regarding the progress of the National Executive Committee's inquiry into Glasgow Labour Group.
>
> In late October, a very considerable amount of evidence was presented to the Inquiry Team including your own submission and this is in the process of analysis and assessment.
>
> The National Executive Committee is always mindful that such matters must be dealt with expeditiously. It's my understanding that dates in January have now been set for the National Constitutional Committee to finally resolve outstanding matters which may be referred to it.
>
> This has been a complex situation with a number of members involved, all of whom are entitled to expect detailed and objective attention to those aspects of the inquiry which concern them individually. Given that this has been the approach to the work, I nevertheless look forward to learning that the promised early conclusion has been achieved.

Tony Blair is on record as saying 'we should say what we mean and mean what we say'. If that's the case, then this bit of gobbledegook is shocking. The Prime Minister's letter gave the impression that I was pressing him for an early meeting of the National Constitutional Committee. Bearing in mind that proceedings up to the date of his letter had taken eleven months, this would certainly have been appropriate. I fully understood his feeling that the whole process was taking an unacceptably long time, but his response suggested that he hadn't read my letter at all. Or if he had read it, he hadn't understood it. Or perhaps he simply chose to ignore its import.

Mr Blair's 'detailed and objective attention' would certainly have been welcome. It had been sadly lacking hitherto. It was deeply disappointing that someone who was a lawyer and presumably familiar with the concept and practice of natural justice had condoned the operation of the NEC meeting. This, after all, was a situation which raised fundamental issues of justice. The reputation of somebody who had dedicated nearly five decades of his life to working for the Labour Party and for the people of his native city was at stake. Yet the NEC meeting had dealt with matters in a thoroughly inappropriate, indeed peremptory manner.

Tabling papers at any meeting is not helpful. It simply doesn't give individuals the opportunity to consider matters or apply the appropriate consideration or, as the Prime Minister might put it, 'objective attention'. The National Executive Committee's members should have had time to consider the papers in advance of the meeting. If the papers in support of my case were tabled, and I have reason to believe they weren't, committee members should have requested an adjournment to give themselves time to review the papers in advance of making a decision.

It was quite wrong and contrary to natural justice for the National Executive Committee not to consider in detail both the allegations and the evidence offered in rebuttal. Why above all others did Tony Blair go along with this? He is, of course, very busy with important matters of state to deal with, and doubtless subjected to unbelievable pressures. In this situation, he put his faith in the advice of those who were prosecuting the case. Rather than asking any third party for independent advice, he accepted their conclusions without demur.

Although it might be inconvenient, even irritating to ensure that proper procedures are justly operated, that was the duty of the Leader of the Labour Party. I have to admit that I do have considerable admiration for the Prime Minister. I admire his energy, his dynamism, his commitment and his reforming zeal. I don't necessarily always agree with him, but I do respect him. The trouble with Mr Blair was, of course, that, like most of those who replied to my letter, he ignored my main point. I had demonstrated that they had failed to do their duty and asked what they were going to do about it. But at least Tony Blair and the others had taken the trouble to reply in some form or another. The other members of the NEC completely ignored my plea. I was shocked and saddened by this apparent indifference.

On 31 October, the day after my letter to the members of the National Executive Committee, Mike Penn, the National Constitutional Officer at Labour Party headquarters, wrote to thank me for meeting with his colleagues the previous week, and for my continuing co-operation. He confirmed that the NEC had referred matters to the National Constitutional Committee. He continued: 'I am now writing to confirm that we shall try to progress matters towards a conclusion, as quickly as resources permit.' I have to admit I had little sympathy for his resources problem – the whole affair was certainly stretching mine. The conclusion to his short note was, in the circumstances, ironic: 'We shall keep you informed of developments, of course.' I was, of course, duly grateful that the Labour Party intended to keep in touch. It was, after all, only my reputation and my future that they were dealing with.

The concert hall murals – joining in with the Adrian Wiszniewski Quartet (1995)

A moment for reflection – the opening of the restored Tobacco Merchants House (1995).

Celebrating the great council victory – Tony Blair, George Robertson and me (1995).

With Julian Spalding at the launch of the Gallery of Modern Art in front of 'Punjab' by Bridget Riley (1996).

Press interview (1996).

Arriving at the Labour HQ for the NEC inquiry (1997).

Light relief – me and Sir Jimmy Saville (February 1998).

Close-up (1998).

The Party abandons its defence (1998).

Celebrating with the Toon Council – opening of the MGM Store, Buchanan Street (1998).

Glasgow, a real City of Culture. The poet Edwin Morgan, jazz saxophonist Tommy Smith and me launching the new Glasgow song in the Glasgow Royal Concert Hall (November 1998).

The launch of 'Winning – the Design of Sport' – the first major exhibition of Glasgow's reign as UK City of Architecture and Design 1999.

Presenting the Glasgow Loving Cup to the Princess Royal (1999).

Receiving the Order of St Lazarus (1999).

Peggy, Carol Smillie, Nick Nairn and me at the Lady Provost's Fashion Show (1999).

CHAPTER NINETEEN

In mid-November I wrote to Tom Sawyer, the General Secretary of the Party. I indicated that I was bemused at the Party's seeming indifference to the smears on my name and damage to my reputation caused by its allegations and its inaction. I indicated that it was having a considerable effect on my wife and family and, of course, on the city of Glasgow, whose reputation I and many others had worked hard over the years to enhance.

My letter continued:

> I am rapidly reaching the conclusion that my good name and my reputation will only be restored by seeking the protection of the courts where those seeking to damage me will require to be identified, with whatever allegations there are clearly stated, with all evidence given on oath.

I went on to say that there was a time when members facing unstated allegations could have anticipated the protection of the Party, and observed that sadly this appeared to be no longer the case. I put it on record that I would not allow the current impasse to continue indefinitely, and would be seeking the guidance of my solicitor as to how I should proceed 'for my own protection'. I concluded by indicating that I looked forward to an early response. However, looking forward to an early response in a letter to Mr Sawyer relied much more on hope than experience.

I was still Glasgow's Lord Provost and determined to undertake my civic duties. Despite the cloud that hung over my own festive season, the city was looking forward to Christmas. In mid-November, on a late Sunday afternoon, a crowd of well over ten thousand people thronged into George Square to watch the switch-on of the annual Christmas lights. This event has always been a major part of Glasgow's annual celebrations, the lights bringing cheer to a dark, northern city in winter. On this occasion, I was delighted that Charles Comiskey, a very brave little eight-year-old who was severely disabled, had won the competition to switch on the lights. He was absolutely thrilled to be joined on the platform by the Danish Celtic star, Mark Rieper.

The inexorable Labour Party machine steamrollered on. I received a letter from Eileen Murfin at the National Constitutional Office formally advising me of my 'hearing date'. As they were still pursuing cases against several members of the Labour Group, I was advised of two dates, 30 or 31 January 1998. I was also advised that details of the case would be given to me and my legal representative in the week commencing 15 December, 'in accordance with the Party's disciplinary rules'.

On 27 November 1997, the *Scotsman* published an article based on an 'unguarded remark' by the Labour Group Chairwoman, Jean McFadden, in a letter to the Scottish Socialist Alliance councillor, Tommy Sheridan. Mr Sheridan had contacted her requesting information on a Council audit report from 1995. In her reply, she wrote: 'I was not the Leader of the Council in 1995 when the investigation was instigated. Councillor Lally took over as Leader in May 1994 and I was on the back-benches. Had I been Leader at the time, the matter might have been handled differently.' As Mr Sheridan pointed out in the *Scotsman*'s article, the import of her response was very clear. She was accusing me of not handling the matter appropriately.

The *Scotsman*'s article was less about the minutiae of an historic inquiry into financial irregularities than about the relationship between me and Mrs McFadden. (The inquiry's report was passed to the Procurator Fiscal who agreed with its findings that no action was justified.) In making derogatory comments about my actions to a member of another party, particularly to Tommy Sheridan, she was doubtless well aware that he would scurry off to one or other of the Council correspondents. She must also have known that her comments would be taken as evidence of factionalism.

One of the most irritating aspects of my character, as far as my political opponents are concerned, is the fact that I tend not to rise to the bait. Throughout my political career, I have prided myself on my knowledge of the rules and my care in adhering to them. Rather than start a public slanging match with Mrs McFadden as some others might have done, I decided to write to Bailie Marshall, the Chief Whip of the Glasgow Labour Group.

My letter, dated 27 November, enclosed a copy of the *Scotsman* article. I indicated that the piece was critical of my handling of a Council inquiry into allegations over the misuse of public funds in community projects. I went on to say that, ignoring the fact that the allegations were wholly inaccurate, I was angered that Mrs McFadden had chosen to make such a criticism to Councillor Sheridan, knowing that he would inevitably talk to the press. I asked that her actions and the purpose behind them should be looked into by the whips' office.

My letter went on to indicate that the investigation into the community project funds in question had been handled by internal audit and senior council officials. Mrs McFadden, I suggested, should either have directed Mr Sheridan to me for comment, or at least had the courtesy to discuss the matter with me. I concluded that such evidence of factionalism in the *Scotsman*'s report would be far from welcome at a time when Glasgow's new Leader, Councillor McAveety, was working hard to bring the Group together.

Bailie Marshall took three weeks to reply. The delay, he explained, was due to the need to take 'appropriate advice'. He observed that as 'a number of matters remain to be dealt with by the National Constitutional Committee', these matters would be beyond his own remit as Chief Whip, but he would undertake to remind members of the Labour Group that they should not be talking to the press 'on matters which are the subject of party discipline'. He also undertook to speak to members individually where necessary.

I replied that I was puzzled that he considered the issues I'd raised to be beyond his remit as Chief Whip, as none had anything to do with the matters before the National Constitutional Committee. I couldn't see why he was unable to give me a satisfactory response, and I suggested that his unwillingness to deal with the matter implied that I was no longer subject to the Labour Group Whip.

I then wrote to the General Secretary of the Labour Party, Tom Sawyer. I told him about the Jean McFadden case and my request that it should be investigated by Bailie Marshall. With surprising speed he replied that my understanding had been correct and such a matter did fall within the remit of the Glasgow Labour Group Whip. Mr Sawyer indicated that he would copy my letter to Lesley Quinn who would ensure that my concerns would be 'property addressed by the Group Whip'. I heard nothing further.

I felt that this little episode highlighted a general presumption within the Council that the whole affair was all over bar the shouting. It seemed odd that these people, many of whom had known me for a great number of years, imagined that at some stage I would simply accept the Labour Party's edicts.

It also struck me that, irrespective of my fellow councillors' feelings towards me, they should all have been aware that the process which was underway was unjust. If so their passive acceptance of the injustice which was being meted out to their friends and colleagues testified to the might of the machine.

One short episode in early December which gave me some amusement was the response of my political opponents – in this case I mean members of other political parties – to my short civic visit to Glasgow's twin city Nuremberg. As I was the guest of the Oberburgermeister of Nuremberg, the Council provided only travel expenses. The visit was extremely constructive and helped prepare the ground for further exchanges of trade with Glasgow's German twin city. Predictably, Councillor Sheridan questioned the value of my trip, doubting how it might benefit 'ordinary citizens'. John Young, the Leader of the Conservative opposition on the Council, suggested that modern communications would enable the development of our twinning link without any travel being necessary. This cannot have been a heartfelt comment from a man who had, in the past, proven himself a very good ambassador for Glasgow on other international visits when, benefiting from the magnanimity for which the Glasgow Labour Group had, under my leadership, been notable, he had travelled with Council trade delegations. It was, however, our sole Liberal Democrat, Doctor Christopher Mason, a man well known for his elegant turn of phrase, who gave the best response to the *Herald*'s inquiry about the trip. He suggested that I was making the trip in order to 'hire a hoard of Valkyries to sort out the National Executive'.

Valkyries being somewhat impractical, I sought alternative means to protect myself. In the middle of December, Euan McColm wrote in the *Scotsman* that while I had been 'one of the least vocal amongst those suspended' I had been in discussion with my lawyer, the unfailingly wise Mr McCann, with regard to pursuing a judicial review of my case. The Party had, after all, promised full details of its charges against me and these were still not forthcoming. As one of the other councillors who still stood accused, Jimmy Mutter, commented, 'we were suspended in September, surely then the Party knew why it was taking that action'. Given the pace of its actions, the Party was either endeavouring to ensure it had a watertight case or working feverishly to build any sort of case at all.

In his *Scotsman* article Euan McColm also wrote that the new Council Leader had formed a commission on standards which would draw up guidelines on the behaviour of councillors. This commission would consist of Mr McAveety, his Depute Charlie Gordon, and their fellow

Labour councillors Louise Fyfe, Susan Baird and Bill Timoney. The leaders of the four opposition parties would also serve on the commission. In addition, members representing the trade unions, the media and the academic world were to be confirmed in the new year.

This endeavour was a good example of the New Labourite predilection for inclusiveness, consultation and lots of words on paper. It was clear that Mr McAveety would go far.

On 19 December the Labour Party issued the list of accusations which would form the basis of the National Constitutional Committee's hearing at the end of January. A couple of days later, they announced their list of witnesses against me. These included two former Lord Provosts – Councillor Tommy Dingwall and Councillor Robert Gray – and the former Group Leader, Councillor Jean McFadden. Writing in the *Herald* on 23 December, John MacCalman reported that, along with my colleagues Bailie Mutter and Bailie Mossan, I would now face expulsion from the Labour Party, the ultimate sanction in response to their charge that I had brought the Party into disrepute.

The specific allegations against me focused on the now familiar refrain that I had undermined Bob Gould's leadership, that I hadn't acknowledged the authority of the Labour Group Whip or the National Executive Committee, that I hadn't recognised the potential conflicts of interest in being both Lord Provost and Chairman of the Hospitality Subcommittee, that I had abused my position with regard to hospitality and Council cars. These allegations were joined by a new humdinger – that I had exercised undue influence over Council staff in the procurement of testimonials in defence of my position. It was further claimed that I had used the press to promote my defence.

My detailed defence would be included in my submission to the National Constitutional Committee at the end of January, but in the interim my lawyer, Peter McCann, indicated that I would be contesting the charge, that he would be representing me and that we would be submitting a witnesses list. We had yet formally to receive the Labour Party's witness list.

My co-accused were, for the most part, vigorous in their response to the Party, although Gordon Macdiarmid had become seriously ill in the interim. According to his doctor, his illness was solely attributable to stress. In my view, and his, that stress was in turn solely attributable to the machinations of the Labour Party.

Gordon's case differed from the rest of us. In the early days of the affair, while each of us was being named and condemned in the press, he had consulted on several occasions with Lesley Quinn. Each time

Lesley had assured him that the accusations did not affect him and that ultimately he would not be examined by the National Executive Committee and thereafter by the National Constitutional Committee and so on as the Labour Party's inexorable machine rolled on. Of course, if action had not been taken against Gordon, he would automatically have succeeded Bob Gould as Leader of the Council. It was, I believe, the shock of finding himself in the full glare of negative publicity and accusations, after all the promises of the Scottish Labour Party, which precipitated Gordon's illness.

Of the others originally accused, Deirdre Gaughan awaited details of the charges against her and Heather Ritchie was suspended pending a court appeal against a conviction for assault. Two others, David Stevenson and Steven Purcell, had been cleared of any accusations.

Christmas 1997 was destined to be a relatively quiet, family affair. We had Christmas dinner with the prospective in-laws of my younger son, Derek. Peggy and Derek's future mother-in-law, Anne Fitzpatrick, shared the preparation of a superb festive meal. It was an enjoyable and relaxing occasion which diverted us all too briefly from the prospect of events to come.

As the year proceeded towards its conclusion, and I reflected on what had certainly been one of the more memorable periods of my political career, there remained one important decision to make. For virtually all of 1997, I had been the focus of an unprecedented media campaign, which, on the flimsiest of evidence whipped up by the Labour Party, had attempted to destroy my reputation. While I had long since learned not to believe anything in the papers, unquestionably the intensity and harshness of press criticism had created an atmosphere of distrust and damaged the good standing of Glasgow City Council.

For many years, the traditional Hogmanay celebrations in George Square had been accompanied by a reception in the City Chambers for many of those who had worked hard within the city to improve its image, its economy and the quality of life for its citizens. Invitations to this event had traditionally been issued by the Lord Provost's office. Unfortunately in recent years members of the Council had not taken this opportunity to get together socially, choosing instead to pass the invitations to others who had little connection with the Council. This seemed to defeat the whole purpose of the reception. We contacted members and advised them that invitations were not transferable and asked if they were still interested in receiving invitations. There was a fairly lukewarm response and I decided in late December, with some regret, to cancel the event. Predictably the *Evening Times* ran the story under the headline 'Lally Scraps New Year Bash: Sleaze Council's Party Snubbed'. It was a pity but even if there was no event in the Chambers, the year did end with the traditional party in George Square. As the bells, whistles and cheers of midnight on that particular, chill New Year's Eve died away, I was all too aware that in the year that was to come I would be facing the greatest challenge of my life.

CHAPTER TWENTY

I was touched to receive, albeit on my return to the Chambers early in the new year, a Christmas card with the simple message 'Best Wishes from Tony and Cherie'. This was either a bureaucratic gaff or the Prime Minister's way of telling me that he was really rooting for me. Maybe I was naïve, but I chose to believe the latter. It certainly brought a smile to my face. I was confident that when we took our case before the Labour Party's National Constitutional Committee, if that body had any objectivity at all, I would be vindicated. Given what had occurred to date it seemed that neither the Scottish Labour Party nor the officers from Party Headquarters in London had demonstrated objectivity.

On the first Sunday of the new year, both *Scotland on Sunday* and the *Sunday Times Scotland* revealed what the Scottish Labour Party was planning. Both papers announced that I would be expelled from the Labour Party for life unless I managed to disprove my guilt on the charges the Party had raised. This was somewhat contrary to the normal process of justice whereby the assumption is 'innocent until proven guilty'.

Through my lawyer, the redoubtable Peter McCann, I enquired of the NEC if they were aware that reliable Labour Party sources were in effect suggesting that the National Constitutional Committee's hearing was little more than a rubber stamp. I made it clear that although I was upset by the conduct of these sources I was confident that the allegations against me would fall since they were without substance.

In early January 1998 the *Express* confidently predicted that I would not be beaten. My real crime against New Labour, it argued, was my belief in political collectivism and visible local government. It declared some of the allegations against me to be 'plain ludicrous', and predicted that this Lazarus, 'like his Biblical counterpart . . . will surely rise and walk again'.

In a vain attempt to escape the spotlight, Peggy and I took a cheap package deal and headed for Gran Canaria. We certainly weren't going to get away from it all, but we hoped we might get away from some of it.

Puerto Rico is one of the smaller resorts in Gran Canaria. What must originally have been a small port on a wide bay has gradually expanded, and now there are developments high up the hillsides overlooking the commercial centre of the town. Despite the fact that tourism must now be almost its only source of income, Puerto Rico's natural setting has, I suppose, restricted its development and contained its scale, so while the commercial centre leaves a lot to be desired in architectural terms and the discos blare until the early hours of the morning, it's still quite possible to relax there, enjoy the beach, walk among the parklands and enjoy good food. But we were deprived of true relaxation through the constant nagging awareness that in just a few weeks' time my political future would be threatened by the vicissitudes of the Labour Party's far from perfect disciplinary process. And then there was the fact that on various occasions we caught sight of day-old newspapers for sale in the town centre with my face accompanied by the, by now rather hackneyed, sleaze allegations.

Throughout our week in Gran Canaria the fax machine in the general office of the Castilla Del Sol apartment building was kept busy as press cuttings and correspondence relating to the case were transmitted to me from Glasgow.

The tireless Peter McCann wrote a brisk letter of complaint to the Labour Party's General Secretary in London concerning the *Sunday Times Scotland* and *Scotland on Sunday* articles. He highlighted the impropriety of the publication and complained that it prejudiced both my position as Lord Provost and the impending hearing. He also recorded his unease that an eminent Arab client had contacted him in some distress at my reported exclusion from office. Peter McCann has worked for a number of Arab causes for many years and is held in high esteem for these good works. He was able to reassure his client that the case had not even been heard, but the incident served to highlight the damaging effect that the Labour Party's action was having well beyond Glasgow.

My old adversary John Young launched a particularly strong attack on the machinations of the Labour Party. He had recently been appointed by Glasgow City Council's new Leader, Frank McAveety, to the Council's Standards Commission.

On more occasions than either of us could recall, John and I had crossed swords on innumerable issues. But although John is a Tory and

I disagree with his politics, I have come over the years to respect him as a fine individual who has always worked hard on the Council for his constituents and fought, usually against the odds, for his beliefs. John is not one of those people who, having been born into a certain level of privilege, sees it as his duty to work for only those with similar advantages. In fact, the first Council seat he ever fought for was in the land of my childhood, the Gorbals, more precisely Hutchesontown.

John has often told the story against himself that as a callow Council candidate, completely unaware of how folk lived in the Gorbals, he climbed the stairs of one tenement building and knocked firmly at a door. He was slightly taken aback to be greeted by a gruff enquiry, 'Who's that?' After he had stammered his response, he listened to the sounds of the door being unlocked and was met with the apparition of a large and very discontented gentleman. 'Look son,' said the man, 'a wee bit of advice. Ye'll no get very far banging at cludgie doors!' Not having had a Glasgow, working-class upbringing, John didn't realise that the half-landing door in a Gorbals tenement belonged not to a dwelling but a shared toilet.

After the departure of Dick Dynes and myself from the Council in 1977, Dick permanently, myself for a short sabbatical, John became Leader of the minority Tory administration, a position he managed to cling on to, rather admirably, for two and a half years.

By the early eighties, we were living quite close to each other in Simshill and, I think, developing a mutual, perhaps slightly begrudging, respect and affection. John was certainly good company on the various trade missions we undertook together and served the city admirably as a Bailie, a position which indicated the respect in which he was held within a Labour-controlled Council.

Here was John then, having carefully observed the way the Party was conducting its inquiry, speaking out publicly. He compared the machinations in Glasgow with the endeavours of Joseph Stalin in Russia. He was quoted in the *Herald*: 'If Stalin were still alive, he would be green with envy at how the Labour Party's National Executive appears to operate.' He continued: 'The implication is that they are guilty and there seems to have been a string of leaks to the media on this matter.' At the suggestion that the NEC's investigation might be written off as 'sheer ineptitude', John Young concluded that it seemed more likely to be an endeavour to root out elements which were considered 'anti-Blairite'.

I couldn't help reflect on how strange it was that my friends and supporters should turn out to be Labour Party left-wingers and a former Tory Leader of the City Council.

On 15 January I submitted my list of witnesses for the NCC hearing: they were the former Lord Provost Susan Baird CBE, Steven Hamilton CBE, the former Town Clerk of Glasgow, and Jim Clark from my own office. Susan would address the role of the Lord Provost over the last quarter century, specifically considering the Labour Party's complaint vis-à-vis the Tattoo; she would also give her views on my conduct both as Leader and Lord Provost and on my relationship with Group officers and colleagues. Steven Hamilton would talk about the formal roles of Lord Provost and Lord Lieutenant and the responsibilities arising from those posts. He would also describe, from his own experience, how the role and responsibilities of the Lord Provost developed and modified over the years he served as a Council officer. He would offer an expert view on the constitution and operations of Glasgow's Common Good Fund, the role of officers and the government of hospitality and expenditure by Lord Provosts. He would consider the Tattoo and the tradition which had grown up in Glasgow, over five decades, of attending the event. And finally he would comment on my performance as Leader during the period when he was Town Clerk.

As an officer within the Lord Provost's office, Jim Clark would address the current operation of the hospitality committee and the Common Good Fund and provide further information on matters relating to Roads and Transport, chauffeur services and my attitude to Council officers and employees. Jim would also address the day-to-day role and responsibilities of the Lord Provostship.

In the letter listing our witnesses, the ever precise Peter McCann noted that although the Labour Party had set a deadline of 16 January for our list of witnesses, it had yet to submit its own. He also enclosed a signed affidavit from the four officers who had kindly written in support of me and against the Labour Party's earlier accusation that I 'had adopted an inappropriate attitude towards staff'. This affidavit was required because the Party's position had changed to their new accusation that 'Councillor Lally has inappropriately secured character references from officers of the Council'.

The four officers concerned each signed a legal statement carefully framed by the always meticulous Mr McCann: 'We hereby affirm and attest that no approach was made by or on behalf of Councillor Lally to secure such letters, these having been written by us spontaneously following articles which appeared in the press.' The Justice of the Peace who witnessed this statement was a senior Glasgow Tory councillor, John Young's colleague Bill Aitken.

It was the best part of a week later that we were informed by the

Secretary of the National Constitutional Committee that the Labour Party's witnesses would be Councillor Tommy Dingwall, Councillor Walter MacLellan and Councillor Jean McFadden. Unlike our letter to Eric Wilson, the Secretary of the National Constitutional Committee, the Party's list of witnesses gave no indication of what each of these individuals would be contributing to the process. While we were open about the case we intended to present, the Labour Party were characteristically reluctant to release any information that might help our defence. We had yet to see a copy of Eileen Murfin's report on her interview with me, which would have helped us to identify areas of confusion and issues to raise in the battle to clear my name.

As the date for the National Constitutional Committee's hearing approached, press comment on the whole affair increased. On the preceding Sunday both the *Sunday Times* and the *Observer* ran long and reasoned articles.

The *Observer* followed the predictable and by this stage rather hackneyed Lazarus line. But they also added a new nickname, 'Methuselah'. It was not one that I wanted to encourage. The piece noted that the charges against me had been brought under the Labour Party's Rule 2A.8 which forbids conduct 'prejudicial or grossly detrimental' to the Party, and pointed out that I was not accused of anything corrupt or illegal. It quoted the statement I had made several times that as I had done nothing wrong I had no intention of resigning.

To substantiate their Methuselah claim, they referred to what they called my 'exceptional coyness' about my age, and kindly noted that I had 'the wiry build and lively step of a younger man'. They also, for the first and I think perhaps the only time in any newspaper article, noted that in the past I had not been entirely consistent when requested to give my age. I have to confess that over many years I have continuously misled just about everybody who has ever asked me. My inaccurate claims with regard to my age did not arise, as seems to be the case with many women and egotists, because I wanted to pretend to be younger. It is just that I have never been particularly preoccupied about my age, so I have tended, when asked, to give the first age approximating my own which comes to mind. Consequently, my reported age has gone up and down like the proverbial yo-yo, a process which I've never done anything to correct until now. The date of birth given in this book is wholly accurate.

The *Observer* also commented, astutely, that because my fame was local to Glasgow, I could be discarded 'without much pain to the Party's central nervous system', although it noted, I would be seeking a judicial review if I was found guilty and expelled. The article then reviewed what would happen to my position as Lord Provost if the Party chose to expel me. It predicted a tortuous debate, pointing out that the Standing Orders would make it difficult to remove me. It was too early to write off Lazarus yet:

> A friend recently asked Lally what he planned to do next. He gave that pawky twinkle and said 'What about the Group Leadership?' and he wasn't entirely joking.

You know you've really hit the big time when you're the subject of one of those lengthy, small print pieces in the *Sunday Times* magazine. The journalist, Brian Deer, had certainly done his homework and although some of the assumptions were wrong, his analysis of the Party rationale made sense:

> Clydeside is not only a Labour stronghold: it is also more than anywhere else in Britain, the heartland of its traditional philosophy. Rooted in heavy industry and trade unionism, and with the birthplace of the Party's first ever MP, Keir Hardie, just down the road in Lanarkshire, here is the United Kingdom's greatest socialist fortress. It is what Blair and his modernising New Labour colleagues had decided that they must dismantle.

The article examined the by now familiar case history of events following Bob Gould's 'votes for trips' claims. It also gave a deeper, historical context to the circumstances of Labour in Glasgow. Brian Deer described the City Chambers, which from its Royal opening in 1888 had served as the seat of local government in Glasgow:

> Designed in the style of an Italian palace, with grandiose pinnacles and balustrades. Inside, there are extravagant marble staircases, mosaic floors and glazed-pottery ceilings. There are great glass domes and chandeliers, rich carpets and finely carved woodwork. Gould's and Lally's offices resemble the sanctuaries of Borgia princes.

Although 'sanctuaries of Borgia princes' was a bit exaggerated, the offices of the Leader and Lord Provost in the City Chambers are certainly handsome, richly decorated, Victorian rooms. But in his consideration of factionalism within the City Chambers, Brian Deer went right off the mark. There were two factions within the City Council, he explained, one led by Bob Gould and the other, larger faction, by myself. Although it is true that there had long been two distinctly separate Labour groupings within the Council, one led by myself, the other by Jean McFadden, in more recent years there have been anything up to four separate groups. Historically, these arrangements have never been formal. I remember the former Labour Group Secretary, Pat Chalmers, once telling me that it was impossible to find within the City Council even a dozen councillors who had consistently voted in support of either myself or Jean McFadden on the various occasions we had stood against each other in leadership elections. What the apparatchiks of New Labour would describe as my faction was just the sort of loose association that had been in existence for many years in Party organisations the length and breadth of the country, indeed even in Parliament.

The Glasgow Tribune Group was formed as a result of informal discussions between members of the Labour Group, often in the less than glamorous surroundings of the Council buffet. What must be clear is that this was not a party within a party but, effectively, a discussion forum which convened to consider the development of policy. The shared perspective of those who came together in the Tribune Group might, I suppose, be described as 'soft left'. We were certainly far removed from Militant.

From the formation of the Tribune Group more years ago than I can remember, people would come along, sometimes inviting other colleagues to join us, in effect to test the water. There was never any whipping system, people gathered in advance of Council meetings to look at the propositions that were coming up before the Group and establish if a common view could be developed. Usually there was a consensus of agreement or disagreement with what was proposed, but when the proposition was put in the Labour Group, members of Tribune would support it or not according to their own consciences. So the Glasgow Tribune Group was not an organisation operating on the basis of any whip, but simply a loose-knit grouping with a shared viewpoint on a variety of issues.

Inevitably budget time was the occasion for most disagreement, both within the Tribune Group and within the Labour Group itself. Attitudes to the allocation of resources could never be entirely divorced from the differing effects on individual wards. So proposed expansions of service in one area or reductions in another would lead to heated debates with local councillors who, quite rightly, sought to protect their own patch. Within the Glasgow Tribune Group there was never any enforcement of discipline. It was never that sort of organisation.

Tribune meetings used to take place around once a month, although they could often be very irregular and membership too has fluctuated immensely. When appropriate, Tribune meetings would consider the list of candidates for positions within the Labour Group itself. We often came to a conclusion about who might receive our collective support, although there were inevitable disagreements and each member of Tribune had autonomy in the Group meetings.

Over the years, in advance of the Scottish Conference of the Labour Party, Tribune Group meetings have examined the motions and amendments on the agenda and considered slates for the Labour Party Executive. The same thing has applied at the National Party Conference. To this day the Tribune Group meeting is still one of the largest during the conference season.

Historically, of course, Tribune was founded by Nye Bevan and Michael Foot, to give a voice to the left of the Labour Party and to encourage and promote the development of policies to improve the lives of ordinary people. It was ironic that as simply the local leader of a Tribune Group I was being singled out as some sort of criminal. If factions are unacceptable to Tony Blair's New Labour, surely that should apply equally to right- and left-wing groupings. Of course, the best known former member of Tribune in the current cabinet is Tony Blair himself.

It would be less easy to describe the other grouping that had been such a regular feature of Glasgow's Labour Group. It could perhaps be best characterised by its consistent opposition to Tribune or by its allegiance to Jean McFadden. It certainly did not conform to any established pattern within the Labour movement.

The following example will serve to give some insight into the nature of Mrs McFadden's group. In the run-up to the Glasgow City Council elections in 1995 and up until the first meeting of the Shadow Labour Group, its members held five or six meetings, usually chaired by Councillor McFadden, in the offices of the Transport and General Workers Union in Bath Street or at Strathclyde University, where Mrs McFadden lectures. The purpose of these meetings was to agree a strategy for obtaining positions of influence within the new Council and, at the final meeting, to choose a slate for positions within the Group. Notable among the thirty-odd councillors who regularly attended were Alex Mosson, Frank McAveety, Walter MacLellan, Charles McCafferty, Steven Purcell and Dierdre Gaughan. Among others who attended occasionally was Des McNulty.

These meetings authorised Jean McFadden to negotiate with Bob

Gould to reach a slate on positions. It had been hoped that Jean McFadden would stand as Group Leader but at the last but one meeting she announced that her employer could not grant her enough time to undertake this role but she could manage the post of Convenor (the shadow Provostship). The final meeting before the Group elections agreed not only a slate but the proposers and seconders for each position.

Bob Gould did not lead any group in this way. Some former Strathclyde Region councillors gathered behind him, but soon discovered that he was not suited to leadership and began to look elsewhere, even on occasion into their consciences, for how best to vote on particular issues.

A further alliance of members emerged when Mrs McFadden's group started to fall apart. This disaffection manifested itself after the group's first AGM in 1996. Individuals drifted away because they were unhappy about the manoeuvring and machinations within the group. A few did collectively decide that they had had enough, and left. McFaddenites from working-class backgrounds felt that their views were not valued among Jean McFadden's closer associates.

While they never formally became a group or faction, Alex Mosson was generally agreed to be the leading light in an influential block within the Council that amounted to about nine people. While they didn't want to join Tribune, and most members of Tribune would have been quite uneasy about having them, their influence was apparent in the substantial vote that brought me the Lord Provostship and made Alex Mosson my Depute. Curiously, most of the McFaddenite dissidents were targeted by the Scottish Labour Party in the inquiry.

That then was the basis of the so-called 'factions' in the Glasgow Labour Group. Poor Brian Deer had effectively bought the Labour Party's revisionist line. In the *Sunday Times* he was rewriting history by inventing Bob Gould as the leader of a faction. This would have been much more acceptable to the Labour Party, which could then argue that it was rooting out both of the factions.

On balance, Mr Deer's analysis was pretty sound, and his consideration of New Labour's motives profoundly so:

> As today the area recovers from a quarter-century of collapse, some people think that, with varying motivations, Blair, Brown and Dewar are exploiting this traditional vulnerability. In short, they are doing what the bosses used to do: dividing in order to rule. 'New Labour(?)' said Alex Mosson, Lally's Depute, and a

former shipyard worker in a newspaper interview last year, before being banned by officials from further comment. 'There is nothing new about New Labour. It is only new capitalism dressed up.'

Brian Deer considered the Labour Party's prejudgement of the case, suggesting that, by comparison with parliamentary travel patterns, those of Glasgow City Council were modest. He quoted Bill Robertson, a well-known municipal correspondent, on his reading of the Party's ultimate purpose:

> It's to create sufficient casualties to destabilise the ruling clique and demolish the biggest power base of old Labour in Scotland. With Glasgow sorted out, the hearts and minds of Party activists elsewhere will quickly fall into line.

This was a frightening scenario that Brian Deer accurately described as 'less of an assault on abuses of power than an abuse of power by Downing Street'.

In the few days leading up to the National Constitutional Committee's hearing, press coverage revealed that there was still strong support for me in the City Council in spite of six months of sustained vilification by the Party and the press. In the *Sun* Jim Sillars argued that the process was not justice but a 'show trial'. He argued, rather profoundly I felt, that as I was not guilty of any crime and had been a good Lord Provost, I was quite the wrong scalp. There were, he said, government ministers whose actions should be looked at instead.

Three days before the hearing, we received a letter from Eric Wilson to the effect that the panel of the National Constitutional Committee had revised its witness list: now Councillors Gould, O'Rourke, Carroll, Dingwall and MacLellan would be speaking against me. The addition of Messrs Gould, O'Rourke and Carroll was presumably in order to provide their particular insight into items of 'evidence' that the Party had gathered in support of its accusations. Perhaps Councillor McFadden had decided that keeping her head below the parapet was the wisest course.

A slightly odd addition to the Party's witness list was Noel Foy, the minor Party bureaucrat who had acted as secretary to the earlier inquiry. It was difficult to imagine what he could add to the proceedings. He'd never been involved with the Council and didn't even know me.

I had written to the Party requesting that my case be heard first. Two days before the hearing, I read in the *Herald* that the NCC had decided that, rather than rush through its deliberations on the cases of all those councillors who'd had charges laid against them by the Party, I was going to be given the privilege of a whole day's hearing on the Friday with my Depute Alex Mosson getting the whole of Saturday. Messrs Mutter, Macdiarmid, Gould and Dierdre Gaughan would simply have to wait.

CHAPTER TWENTY-ONE

The charges I was to address on 30 January differed from those which had been raised in my meeting with Mrs Murfin. While that meeting was 'not a "trial" or hearing of any issue or allegation', nevertheless a number of issues contained in the original list of allegations against me were subsequently dropped by the Party. Either their own investigations had led them to conclude that these matters did not stand up to any scrutiny, or, as seems more likely, my meeting with Mrs Murfin had in fact been a 'fishing expedition' to ascertain how I might defend each allegation.

In the three months between my meeting with Mrs Murfin and my hearing before the National Constitutional Committee three of the four items which had been raised in support of the contention that I had undermined the Group leadership had been dropped. My receipt of a letter from the Chief Constable was, it seems, no longer a cause for complaint, nor was my meeting with a developer or any involvement I might have had in Group meetings. Similarly, the suggestion that I had supported a councillor who had assaulted a senior local government officer was withdrawn.

However, the Party's claims of impropriety in my communications concerning bus shelter contracts, chauffeur services and the Common Good Fund were reworded and additional charges were brought forward. I was now charged with exercising inappropriate influence in the function of the office of the Leader of the Labour Group and the work of the budget working group; failure to acknowledge the authority of the Labour Whip and the NEC; and also failure to recognise conflicts of interest in my holding office as Lord Provost and as Chair of the Hospitality Subcommittee simultaneously. Two further charges were levelled. I was accused of exercising undue influence over Council staff in procuring testimonials. And despite the fact that I had stalwartly refused to give statements to the press, indeed had notified the Party every time members of the press had sought clarification from me on information they had received from 'reliable sources' within the Party, I was accused of using the press to promote my defence to the detriment of the Labour Party.

The other significant change between the case I was answering in October and the one that I came to address at the end of January was that in the October inquiry I was accused of a *'prima facie* case of breach of Labour Group rules'. I was now up on a charge of a *'prima facie* case of breach of Labour Party membership rule 2A.8'. Not only was there a huge discrepancy between the original allegations and the ones which I was now required to answer, but within a very short space of time the charges against me were with regard to two quite different organisations. The Glasgow Labour Group was one thing, but now we were answering a charge of offences against the Party.

Cynics might suggest that the nature of the organisation against which I had supposedly caused offence had been changed because the potential sanction was greater. Also, perhaps this particular change was made because rule 2A.8 is such a broad catch-all that it would be much more difficult for me to refute even if I demolished every specific accusation against me. Which was exactly what I intended to do.

When we arrived at Keir Hardie House, the press posse was waiting on the doorstep. As we arrived one of the journalists challenged me: 'What will be your defence'. My riposte was wholly accurate: 'My innocence!' The day was dry but cold, and, by its end, the poor souls who'd spent the whole day camped on the doorstep waiting for the big story were thoroughly chilled. We learned later that we had been preceded by all of the National Constitutional Committee's witnesses and by our own, Susan Baird, Jim Clark and Steven Hamilton. Our witnesses were asked to leave with instructions to return in the early afternoon.

The hearing took place in a ground floor committee room. The members of the National Constitutional Committee itself were Anne Gibson, Dianne Hayter and their chairman Derek Install, Industrial Officer of the Graphical, Paper and Media Union. Mike Penn, the National Constitutional Officer, served as Presenter, the National Constitutional Committee's equivalent of the Scottish Procurator Fiscal, assisted by Lesley Quinn. On our side were the doughty Peter McCann, his assistant Mr Jain and myself.

From the tone of the National Constitutional Committee's introductions, it was apparent that they wished proceedings to be conducted in an informal manner. Their mood seemed light-hearted, almost chummy. While I regarded forty-eight years of membership of the Labour Party as something of great value, I felt that these people didn't see it that way. The meticulous Mr McCann very rapidly made it clear that we did not consider chatty informality as an appropriate tone for the proceedings. This was a matter of the utmost seriousness.

The first witness for the Party was Councillor Gerry Carroll. Gerry has been a constituency colleague of mine in the Cathcart Constituency Labour Party for a number of years, but he wasn't really an active member. An intermittent participant at constituency level, when he attended meetings he would leave early, often very early, usually having made a point of asking a question at the start of the meeting. He would always sit close to the door ready for the proverbial sharp exit.

In 1995 Gerry Carroll was elected as Vice-Convenor of the Shadow Council with Jean McFadden as the Convenor. They were in effect the Shadow Lord Provost and Shadow Depute Lord Provost, who would take over when the new council assumed power, subject to being selected for those offices at the next AGM. During that shadow year, Gerry Carroll was very close to Jean McFadden, never missing an opportunity to extol her virtues. He clearly believed she was in the ascendancy.

Not so long ago, the salary levels of a number of Scottish advocates were quoted in the press. Gerry Carroll was earning comfortably over £100,000 – clearly a man with a very busy legal practice. It begs the question of whether it is possible to earn so much in the courts and at the same time attend to the interests of one's constituents. Councillor Carroll's attendance record at Council meetings suggests an answer. Between April 1996 and March 1997 he attended only twenty-seven out of ninety-four meetings, fairly typical of a very poor overall attendance record. Yet the Labour Party seemed to favour this individual. When the City Council was asked to nominate a member to serve on the West of Scotland Water Board, we nominated a well respected member of the Council, Denis Murphy, Chairman of the Commercial Operations Committee. The Secretary of State, Donald Dewar, rejected that nomination and chose Councillor Carroll instead. Councillor Carroll had, in the process, gained another fee-paying responsibility to add to what already looked like a pretty extraordinary workload.

What then was the damning evidence that the eminent lawyer Gerry Carroll had to offer the National Constitutional Committee? He had nothing specific to say about any of the charges, but spoke instead of the general 'bad atmosphere' within the Council. He claimed that no significant decision was taken without my involvement, but under questioning had to admit that his assertion was based on hearsay from other councillors. Well, it would have to be, because he was hardly ever around to hear anything himself. In spite of his poor attendance record, he could still express the view that the Council whips were ineffective. Perhaps he thought this because they took so little action over his own absences. Whatever, the performance of the whips was not a matter for which I could in any way be responsible, so its relevance was questionable.

Councillor Carroll confirmed that he had arranged with Councillor McFadden and her group that when she stood for Provost in 1996 he would stand for Depute Lord Provost. He agreed that there were a number of factions within the City Council and named councillors Gould, McFadden, Mosson and Lally as being the respective leaders.

Despite the fact that at the time of the most recent leadership election, I had been suspended from the Group, Councillor Carroll was convinced that I was somehow in control. He offered two pieces of evidence in support of this contention. After the Group meeting at which Frank McAveety had defeated Jean McFadden for the leadership, he saw me shaking hands with one of my colleagues, Councillor Shaukat Butt. Perhaps because Councillor Carroll was so often absent he had not observed that Councillor Butt and I are good friends and tend to shake hands every time we meet. Sometime later I told Shaukat about the hand-shaking allegation. He couldn't help laughing, finding it impossible to believe. Henceforward he always checked before shaking my hand, just to make sure that Councillor Carroll wasn't watching.

Gerry Carroll's other piece of evidence in support of my supposed control of the Labour Group was that when he was canvassing Councillor Matt Adam's support for Jean McFadden, Councillor Adam had replied, 'I couldn't do that, Pat wouldn't let me.' Matt Adam later confirmed to me that he had been canvassed by Gerry Carroll, but his response had been, 'I couldn't do that, I could never vote for that woman.' It's exactly the kind of response I would have expected from Matt.

Frankly, after Councillor Carroll's evidence had been heard, I was left wondering if this was the quality of evidence which this high-earning lawyer would offer in a court of law. All I can say is that, having sat as a judge in the magistrates court, this kind of drivel would not have washed with me or, I believe, with any other magistrate.

The next witness was the Party apparatchik Noel Foy.

Noel Foy had been secretary to the inquiry panel of the Scottish Labour Party, but his report of my interview with that panel failed to record that only two members of the panel were present when there should have been three. It was also riddled with inaccuracies. At my subsequent meeting with Mrs Murfin I spent a considerable time detailing these so that they could be corrected. I was assured that this would be done, but I have never seen a copy of the corrected report. In his role as secretary during my interview with Eileen Murfin, Noel Foy was present when she assured me that my side of the case would be presented to the National Executive Committee.

The very fact that Noel Foy was giving 'evidence' against me at the National Constitutional Committee's inquiry was bizarre, since he could indicate only what others had alleged to him. The Scottish Labour Party was obviously desperate to find anyone to pad out its allegations.

Noel Foy spoke about the general conduct of the National Executive Committee's inquiry. He referred to an 'administration at war with itself' and indicated that there were written statements which identified me as being instrumental in this. He reported that all the thirty-seven witnesses the Party had interviewed had stated that the appointment of Bailies was an unnecessary and anachronistic practice, but these appointments have always been made by the Labour Group, and in all my thirty years' service no member ever complained or objected to this selection process.

These written statements were not, however, produced and upon questioning Foy conceded that the statements hadn't been shown to their supposed authors to verify the accuracy of their contents. I was particularly puzzled because I had been one of the thirty-seven witnesses and hadn't made any negative comments about the appointment of Bailies. Noel Foy expressed the personal view that it was inappropriate for me to have included a number of Bailies among my guests at the Edinburgh Tattoo. He affirmed that the NEC had thought such invitations inappropriate, but admitted that a number of those interviewed had indicated that they were a tradition.

We asked Noel Foy why there had been no inquiry into the activities of Mrs McFadden's group. He replied that he didn't know. If factionalism was the charge, then surely all the factions were equal in their guilt. But within the hierarchy of the Scottish Labour Party, it seemed that some factions were more equal than others.

The next witness for the 'prosecution' was something of a surprise. She'd been on the list, then taken off, but now here she was in the flesh – Jean McFadden. She walked calmly into the room. I detected a hint of a smile at Lesley Quinn and the representatives of the National Constitutional Committee. We had no doubts – this was the lady thwarted over the 'knife and fork job' of Lord Provost – this time there was no fork.

I have known Jean McFadden since our time together on Glasgow Corporation. I had known her late husband John better, because he was an active member of the labour Party and a very likeable person. I don't think I've ever heard anyone saying a harsh word about John McFadden.

When I first met Jean McFadden, I had liked her, although I can't say that I've ever been able to understand her. It was unfortunate that the outcome of the 1977 elections prematurely catapulted her into the leadership of the Labour Group. Until that time, her only experience of office had been as Chairwoman of the Manpower Committee, not the best preparation for leadership. As I have previously mentioned, she made the mistake of accepting the advice that the Group go into opposition in the Council, even though it was the largest party.

In the years that followed, Jean McFadden became dependent on three fellow councillors, and this group came to be known as 'the gang of four'. In time, her colleagues moved on and she became more isolated. You could develop a good working relationship with Jean McFadden as long as you were supporting her. You could also discuss the outcome of group elections for the leadership, but only as long as she won and you lost.

She never seemed to be truly at ease with most members of the Labour Group. I think she probably has great difficulty in letting down her guard. But members regularly commented upon her conspicuous efforts to be friendly around the time of Group elections.

She can be pretty bloody-minded when things don't go her way. One example was the campaign of two Govan councillors, Stephen Dornan and Dierdre Gaughan, to keep St Leonard's school open. Just before the 1996 Provostship election, Stephen got a surprise phone call from Jean McFadden. He was slow in picking up his phone and the answering machine began to record the conversation. Jean told him that she'd been speaking to the Leader, Bob Gould, about St Leonard's. She said that it might be possible to keep the school open and she had been trying to contact Dierdre to tell her. Stephen offered this tape to the Labour Party inquiry but they declined to accept it.

In the Provostship vote both Stephen and Dierdre supported me. Afterwards they had a very difficult time securing funds for a local community hall. Despite a clear decision by the Labour Group to support this endeavour, it had to go back to the Labour Executive on more than one occasion as Jean's social strategy committee seemed to be unable to make the funds available. This sort of petty political game-playing might be irritating for the councillors concerned, but much worse is the effect it has on the community.

Jean McFadden has great difficulty in making decisions. Like many academics, she tends to consider the pros and cons of any decision very carefully. She invariably needs more information and further consultation with the various groups and organisations that might be affected. Then, before anything can be done, the priorities change and the focus moves on to something else.

Councillor McFadden was always a bit prone to what I've heard described as the 'Scarlett O'Hara syndrome'. You know the scene at the end of *Gone With the Wind* where Vivien Leigh puts her hands up to her head and says 'I can't think of that just now! Tomorrow is another day.'

Jean McFadden's evidence against me had two major defects. First, it was inaccurate. Second, it bore no relationship to the written allegations. The rules governing the hearing made it quite clear that evidence must be on the basis of the so-called charges outlined in the report, but the gist of Mrs McFadden's evidence was simply that I was a disruptive influence. This should have been ruled to be inadmissible.

As evidence of my disruptiveness she cited the public row between me and the then Group Leader Dick Dynes which led to Labour's loss of its majority in the municipal elections of 1977. This was really dredging up ancient history. Perhaps because the incident was so long ago she may well have forgotten the facts.

She omitted to mention that I had instituted an inquiry by officers of the Council to investigate prima facie evidence that a number of my colleagues were in breach of Council rules, and that the Group Leader of the time, Dick Dynes, launched a public attack on me in the media. This publicised the allegations before they had been properly investigated. Eventually, when the investigation did happen Dynes' allegations against me were found not to be justified. Nor did she mention that when I appealed to the Labour Party National Executive Committee against my suspension, they found in my favour, or that the Cathcart Constituency Party also found in my favour, that I was restored to the panel of candidates by Glasgow City Labour Party and that Dick Dynes never played any further active part in public politics. In fact she became the major beneficiary of this situation, assuming the leadership of the Labour Group. The press at the time quoted her as saying she was pleased that my case had been upheld but then this was all a long time ago.

As Noel Foy had done before her, Jean McFadden also disapproved of the notion, or perhaps the number, of Bailies within the Council. Questioned as to why she had not tried to abolish their appointment when she was Party Leader, she responded that at that time the appointment of Bailies was not a form of patronage, simply a recognition of seniority. She said that the Party whips were not strong and she felt I didn't pay any attention to them, but she offered no evidence in support of this claim.

Councillor McFadden's most extraordinary piece of evidence was that she was never a member nor a leader of any informal grouping. Yet her close friend and confidant Councillor Carroll had previously spent some time elucidating the role of factions within the Labour Group and explaining the deals which had been done within Mrs McFadden's group concerning the Provostship. Over the years, the press had expended innumerable column inches analysing the support for the two acknowledged groupings: Tribune and the McFaddenites. Yet all of a sudden history was obliterated and it seemed that Tribune was the only faction in town.

The regular attendees at Mrs McFadden's meetings were Janet Andrews, Gordon Archer, Bill Butler, Elizabeth Cameron (who had once been taught by Jean McFadden although their relationship later seemed strained), Gerry Carroll, Josephine Dodds (an employee of Mohammed Sarwar), Eamon Fitzgerald, Louise Fyfe, Patricia Godman, Archie Graham, Irene Graham, Douglas Hay, Frank McAveety (who acknowledged that Jean McFadden was 'at the heart of factionalism') Charles McCafferty (who had been Jean McFadden's 'stalking horse' for the leadership), Margaret McCafferty (Chic McCafferty's wife), Alan McGarrity, Walter MacLellan, Mohammed Sarwar, Archie Simpson, Ruth Simpson and Audrey Strain.

Others who defected from Jean's group along with Alex Mosson were Ron Davey, Stephen Dornan, Dierdre Gaughan, Charles McDonagh, David Moxam, Steven Purcell, Heather Ritchie, George Ryan, Jim Sharkey, Elaine Smith, David Stevenson and Alister Watson. A number of these individuals were, like myself and other members of the Tribune Group, targeted in the Labour Party's attempted rout of 'sleaze' in Glasgow. Some councillors were occasional visitors at Jean's meetings, namely Hanzala Malik, Bob Marshall and Des McNulty. Others present included Jim McKechnie (former Chair of the City Labour Party), Mary Picken (Chair of the City Labour Party) and David Stark (an officer of the Transport and General Workers Union).

After Jean McFadden's revelation that what all of these people had been attending was not, after all, any sort of group or faction, I found myself recalling the convoluted logic of George Orwell's *1984*, where words did not mean what you thought they did. I briefly pondered the irony of the situation and reviewed my life and the circumstances which had brought us to this state of affairs.

Jean McFadden was rattled by Peter McCann's cross-examination. She became irritated and lost her previous composure. At various stages she seemed angered by his effrontery and looked towards the panel for help. She eventually left the room looking thoroughly perturbed. It had not been as easy as she must have imagined.

The Party's final witnesses were to be Messrs Dingwall and Gould. We'd had their 'expert' witnesses, two lawyers and a bureaucrat, and none of them had provided any real evidence of anything. Now we would find out whether either my former supporter or the whistle-blower had anything to add.

CHAPTER TWENTY-TWO

Coming from Tommy Dingwall, any criticism of my actions as Lord Provost was pretty rich. This former supporter of mine and long-time member of the Tribune Group had a very individual view of his rights as Lord Provost and didn't like being reminded of past indiscretions. Yet ironically, had the Labour Party really been in the business of rooting out impropriety and abuses of position, they would have found, in Tommy Dingwall, a fascinating subject for scrutiny. This was the man who had head-butted his colleague Larry Flanagan and who in his short term as Lord Provost had used a Council car to transport him to do a little house cleaning – in Rothesay!

Tommy's state of mind might be gauged from a little incident at one of the Group meetings in the months leading up to the National Constitutional Committee's hearing. One of the councillors made a contribution to the meeting which irritated him. He turned to me and commented that what the man needed was some of what Larry Flanagan had got.

Tommy had recently developed another habit which was clearly designed to irritate the councillors, including myself, against whom the Party was pursuing its action. He would carry a briefcase around the Chambers, and whenever any of the accused councillors was within earshot, he would tap on the case and comment, 'It's all in here, you know – it's all in here.' What he didn't realise was that most people treated this behaviour with complete disdain. We all knew that Tommy was much more likely to carry a cheese sandwich in his briefcase than any reading matter.

In the weeks before the hearing, I'd been getting reports that Tommy was determined to give evidence. As he had often attended Tribune meetings, I felt I might be able to convince him that his behaviour would do him no credit and might damage the Party. I reminded him that the Larry Flanagan incident had been a very serious misdemeanour, but his colleagues had decided to give him a second chance. He insisted that all he intended to do was to 'tell the truth'. Fine, I said, but he should remember that the truth was many-faceted. I reminded him of Nye Bevan's comment, 'I will tell you my truth and you can tell me yours.'

Tommy continued to tap his briefcase in the Council corridors in a manner that reminded me of those poor souls you sometimes see out on the streets in animated conversation with a non-existent friend. But now he was also complaining that I had tried to stop him giving evidence. He asserted that I had threatened him.

At the hearing Tommy confirmed that he had regularly attended Tribune Group meetings, or, as the Party preferred to put it, that he was a member of my faction within the Council. He also told the hearing that I had tried to persuade him to reconsider his decision to give evidence to the inquiry. However, his further assertion, that I had used threats, was utter nonsense.

Peter McCann questioned him about his conduct as a former Lord Provost when he had attended the Edinburgh Tattoo on behalf of the City of Glasgow. Tommy confirmed that he had attended the Tattoo three times, once as Lord Provost and twice as a guest of the Lord Provost. While he forgot to mention his very individual guest list he confirmed that the general practice was that the Glasgow party would attend the Tattoo and after the Lord Provost had taken the salute, the Glasgow delegation would go on for a meal, usually rather later than was good for the digestion, before returning to Glasgow. None of this was news to anyone. I still failed to see how a process which had been going on year after year for the best part of five decades was suddenly improper when it was me who was following in the tradition.

The Labour Party's final witness was Bob Gould: Bob, whose comments to the *Evening Times* had set this whole horrendous process in motion; Bob whose poor political judgement on budget cuts had forced him into a corner; Bob whose ridiculous statements had brought the city, his colleagues and the Labour Party into disrepute. And now here was the same Bob acting, on behalf of the Labour Party, as a witness against me.

The Party had long since dropped any reference to 'votes for trips' from its list of allegations. There had been no tangible evidence to support it. Instead, I and a few of my colleagues now faced the absurd charge of undermining a man who treated the leadership of the City of Glasgow as an undemanding job that required little of his attention.

This was after all a man who had lost his last major vote on the Council by sixty-four to three. If Bob Gould had been competent as a Leader, he would have seen that vote coming, indeed would never have sustained such a defeat in the first place. Irrespective of how many groups or factions there might have been in the Council, that margin amounted to a genuine vote of no confidence on a quite unprecedented scale.

When he was Leader, Bob Gould complained to me on a number of occasions that people were undermining him, but he never made it clear what he meant by 'undermining'. I suggested that maybe he meant that people were disagreeing with him. I pointed out that, having been Leader for a total of eight years, I had become quite used to people disagreeing with me, but never regarded it as undermining. It was simply part of the normal and proper democratic process.

When Bob Gould was asked about his comment to the *Evening Times* which had sparked off the whole series of inquiries, he said it was an accident. His interview with the *Times* had been about the budget, and he had just made some passing comment at its conclusion about 'votes for junkets'. But this was picked up and made the headline of the article. Bob maintained that he was surprised at this turn of events, but any journalist worth his salt would obviously see such a comment 'on the record' as a heaven-sent opportunity. If he really was surprised then he must have been very naïve.

Asked about the annual Tattoo visit, Bob Gould said that it was a long-standing tradition to which he had no objection. He had only criticised it after the Chief Executive, John Anderson, expressed his concerns about the number of people who were taken along.

Gould was actually quite complimentary about the working relationship he and I had had as Leader and Lord Provost. We had got on well, he said, and our meetings had always been cordial.

But in spite of this he maintained that I had tried to undermine his leadership. He cited as examples my proposal for hosting the Olympic Games and my talking to the BBC about holding the Eurovision Song Contest in Glasgow. Under questioning he acknowledged that my comment on the Olympic Games had been part of an exchange between the Lord Provosts of Glasgow and Edinburgh and, given their civic roles, wasn't inappropriate.

Peter McCann suggested to Gould that, as he was to face charges himself at a later stage, his evidence to the hearing might be construed as the equivalent of turning 'Queen's Evidence'. But he made no reply.

So that was it. The fatuous five had presented their evidence. A high-earning Solicitor Advocate had regurgitated hearsay; a Party bureaucrat had parroted other people's accusations; a failed candidate for the Lord Provostship had rambled through ancient history; a former Provost had undermined the prosecution case. And finally, the man who had caused all the commotion, and whose foolish accusations had caused so much damage to the city's reputation, revealed to a waiting world that his authority had been utterly compromised by my having a chat about the Eurovision Song Contest without talking to him first.

As Bob Gould would emerge from the inquiry without any sanction from the Party, Peter McCann's allusion to 'Queen's Evidence' does not, in retrospect, seem to have been too far off the mark. However, although the Audit Commission cleared him of any wrongdoing over one or two property agreements in which the former Leader had taken a personal interest, it was suggested that procedures for meetings with developers should be tightened up.

The presentation of evidence by the Party's witnesses and Mr McCann's cross-questioning took until late afternoon. After that we had a short break for coffee and sandwiches while the National Constitutional Committee considered its verdict.

When we reconvened, the Committee announced that while they considered that there was still a case to answer, there was no question of corruption and I would not be expelled from the Labour Party. My initial reaction was relief that, at long last, the Party was beginning to see sense. The examination of the witnesses had exposed the party's case as a farrago of surmise, hearsay and sour grapes.

Some time later, I learned from a journalist that the source of the press speculation about my possible expulsion was the Scottish General Secretary, Jack McConnell. It only confirmed what I had always suspected. The authoritative tone adopted in the papers made it clear that they were depending on a source they imagined to be wholly reliable, someone very senior, with real authority. The list of suspects led to just one name. In the circumstances and knowing, as he must have done, the flimsy nature of the allegations and evidence against me, this was extremely foolish of Mr McConnell.

Even though he was the source of the leaks that had been pouring out of the Scottish Labour Party for months, Mr McConnell very rarely gave briefings directly, preferring instead to leave that task to his hapless press officer, Angus Macleod. Macleod is the brother of a respected journalist and the son of a very well known Free Church of Scotland minister who had once famously been in the news as the victim of unjust allegations. Having witnessed his father's suffering, perhaps Angus Macleod should have been a little more circumspect before allowing himself to become McConnell's mouthpiece.

Until now things had gone entirely Jack's way. The Party had trusted its faithful servant and allowed him to pursue the Glasgow sleaze inquiry. However, now, alas, it seemed that the remote outpost in the north hadn't really been doing the effective job they'd hoped for. It was an embarrassing situation in which the Party had to try to save face somehow. So although the threat of expulsion was lifted, the committee still determined that there was a case to answer. The next task for Peter McCann and I was therefore to deliver my lengthy, detailed and comprehensive demolition of the Party's case.

CHAPTER TWENTY-THREE

There were six specific allegations to answer. The first was that I had exercised inappropriate influence in the function of the office of the Leader of the Labour Group; the Budget Working Group; and the Roads and Transportation Committee. None of the Party's evidence detailed in what way or on what occasions I had exercised any influence at all, let alone inappropriate influence. The NEC had relied chiefly on the verbal accounts of Labour Group members. Minutes of Executive or Group meetings had been produced which merely demonstrated that there had been debate among the members; but the NEC failed to show who had made any allegations; or against whom they were made; or how the Group was in any way divided or disloyal to the Leader.

I replied that in my years as a councillor there'd always been healthy political debate within Glasgow City Chambers. A leader of the administration – any leader – had often faced criticism over their position on a particular matter, but this was simply an inevitable part of good, democratic government. I certainly didn't deny that I had on occasion disagreed with Councillor Gould, but I had done so only within the confines of Labour Group meetings and had always, without exception, accepted the final decision of the Group. I couldn't see that this disagreement was evidence of an ongoing campaign to undermine Bob Gould's authority.

The NEC submitted as evidence the letter I had written to the Group Secretary, Councillor McNulty, complaining about rumours circulating before the 1996 Labour Group AGM. These rumours were to the effect that I intended to remove certain convenors. In the same letter I had also mentioned that councillors had been promised support for local facilities just before an important Group election. According to the NEC my letter to the Group Secretary 'appears to confirm Councillor Lally's position of influence within the Group and that he for one did hear that votes were being traded for favours'.

This was an extraordinarily perverse and distorted interpretation of my letter. I had written in general terms to complain about members trying to influence the outcome of the AGM elections by methods that I didn't believe were consistent with the standards expected from elected members of the Labour Party. The NEC's interpretation inferred that somehow my denial of the malicious rumours which suggested that I intended to manipulate convenorships was a confirmation that, had I wanted to, I could. This was more arrant nonsense, as only the Labour Group can determine who holds convenorships. The letter didn't seem to me to confirm that I had influence or otherwise within the Group. In addition, I had not, up until this point, been aware that being influential was somehow against either the Group constitution or Labour Party rules. Indeed, I would have thought it would be in the Party's interest for every member of the Group to be influential.

In seeking to suggest my 'undue influence on the workings of the Budget Working Group', the NEC inquiry team behaved as if my role as Lord Provost meant that I was politically neutered. I had confirmed both in July and October that the position of Lord Provost required that my main role revolved around the civic life of Glasgow. The Provostship is an ambassadorial role which involves developing relationships with bodies and organisations outside the Council, but also acting as the Chairman of all Council meetings. It is specifically in this role as Chairman that the Provost must remain neutral, but in its interpretation the NEC extended this obligation to all matters of Council business. To expect any elected member representing a constituency to be politically neutral at *all* times is plainly ludicrous.

Applying this completely inappropriate standard of political neutrality, the NEC took me to task over comments I'd made during a meeting of the Labour Group in February 1996 when it was discussing the Council budget for 1996/7. In my defence to the National Constitutional Committee I pointed out that I had informed the NEC that even when I was Lord Provost my obligations as a Group member required me to be involved politically in the work of the Council. Under the Council's Standing Orders, I was a member of all standing committees, received all papers and, until September 1997, when I was suspended, had been a member of the Group and received all relevant papers. As the elected member for Castlemilk, I had a duty to represent my constituents to the best of my ability so I was in no way at all times politically neutral except on those specific occasions when I was undertaking duties in my role as Lord Provost.

Given the financial position the Council was facing as a result of

Government spending restrictions, the 1996/97 Budget was always going to be of major importance to the city. The Budget Working Group, of which I was not a member, had done its usual comprehensive and difficult job in bringing recommendations to the Group. At the meeting on 12 February Councillors Irene Graham and Bill Butler put forward a resolution that the Group should postpone making decisions on the budget. In the subsequent debate, I made a contribution in support and stated that I felt the Council should seek a judicial review on whether the Government had acted properly in setting its spending target. Bob Gould then advised that the Convention of Scottish Local Authorities had been warned that Glasgow City Council might not be in a position to set its budget within the timescale requested by CoSLA. I accepted that any judicial review would in this case be inappropriate.

I pointed out to the National Constitutional Committee that the deadline set by CoSLA of 5 March was not the legal due date and that I would never support not setting the Council budget by the date required in law. As a member of the administration, I defended my right to make my views on the Council budget known within the Labour Group and stated that the people who elected me would expect me to do so.

The National Executive Committee's allegation that I had infringed my neutrality as Lord Provost was in any case groundless simply because at the time of the meeting in question, in February 1996, I was not yet Lord Provost. At that time I had actually been Shadow Convenor of Planning and wouldn't be elected as Lord Provost for a further two months. Thus this particular accusation was somewhat compromised by a small matter of chronology.

The NEC's accusation that I had improperly influenced the work of the Roads and Transportation Committee was one that I had already refuted in my meeting with Eileen Murfin. So I repeated to the National Constitutional Committee the explanation I had already given before: my intervention was only to point out an inconsistency between a Committee decision and the stated policy of the Labour Executive.

I had acted in what I believed was the best interests of the Labour Group and the purpose of my intervention was not to prevent any action being taken on the matter but simply to impress the import of the Labour Executive decision upon the Committee chairman. I had tried to make contact with Councillor MacLellan by telephone but it had been too early in the morning to reach him. I had then ensured, prior to leaving the Chambers for a meeting of the Greater Glasgow and Clyde Valley Tourist Board of which I was Chairman, that my note was delivered to his pigeonhole in the councillors' corridor. A letter was also sent to the members of his committee.

In support of my account of events, I had asked the member of staff who dealt with the matter to supply an account of his recollections. This report fully confirmed the accuracy of my statements. I also made the point to the National Constitutional Committee that, while the Chairman of the Roads and Transportation Committee was unhappy about being at odds with the Executive, his letter to the Group Secretary contained no criticism of me in any respect.

The NEC's next major allegation was that I had failed to acknowledge the authority of the Labour Group Whip and the National Executive Committee. They maintained that I 'chose to dismiss Labour Party rules in respect of whips' office as inconsequential and of no real relevance or importance in Glasgow'. This supposed dismissal occurred during my meeting with the NEC's Mrs Murfin in October 1997.

In my written submission, I stated that, having been Leader of Glasgow District Council for eight years, I was familiar with the role of the whip in the constitution of the Party. I offered in evidence my experience as Group Leader in expelling members of Militant from the Labour Group because of their activities within the Group, stressing the importance of the whips in that procedure. I also submitted two sworn affidavits from former whips of the District Council Labour Group. These stated that during my time as Leader I had given the fullest support to all their activities as whips and at no time had I failed to acknowledge their role, duties or their authority in terms of the Standing Orders of the Labour Group.

The evidence before the National Executive Committee's team included two letters I had written to the Labour Group Secretary in which I had complained about particular issues. The fact that in those letters I had not expressed the wish that the whips should take immediate action was taken to indicate that I had no faith in their office. This was another example where the inquiry team had misconstrued information supplied by myself in refutation of their previous accusations, taking it instead as evidence of quite a different improper proceeding on my part.

The inquiry team also revealed a remarkably rudimentary knowledge of the procedures of local government. It had always been the case in Glasgow that complaints would be put to the Secretary who would channel them to the Executive and the Group for determination. If those bodies agreed that it was a matter for the whips, they would then refer it. In the case of both my letters, the Executive and Group merely noted their contents.

The irony was that in the course of its investigation the inquiry team itself had been critical of the operation of the Glasgow Labour Group's whips office. They reported that it had been under-performing, particularly from the spring of 1996, due to the protracted illness of the Chief Whip. They also noted that my complaint of March 1996 had never been referred to the whips' attention. I could hardly be blamed for these genuine shortcomings that seemed to exist within the whips office.

Finally it should be said that at no point had I ever been asked by the Group Whip to explain any of my actions as a member of the City Council Labour Group. Nor had I ever received any verbal or written warning. So there was no single instance when my acknowledgement of the authority of the Labour whip was actually an issue.

I was also accused of not accepting the authority of the Party's National Executive Committee on the grounds that during my interviews with the inquiry team, I had said that the issues being investigated would have been more expeditiously dealt with by the Group Whip than the NEC.

What I had actually said was that the press coverage had caused horrendous damage to the reputation of the Party, the Group and the members of the Council, as well as to that of the city, and had had a terrible effect on the families of those involved. I further offered the view that such damage might have been avoided had the action under the Labour Group's disciplinary procedures been allowed to continue.

The NEC team itself had previously accepted this point. In its own inquiry report it acknowledged that in the press coverage 'these allegations were extrapolated by speculation to the point where the good reputation of Labour in local government throughout the whole of the former Strathclyde Regional area and beyond was in jeopardy'.

At no point did I question the right or the authority of the NEC to intervene on any matter. I had been a member of the Labour Party for long enough not to make such a daft suggestion.

As a further piece of evidence of my alleged failure to acknowledge the authority of the National Executive Committee, the NEC team produced a letter from Tommy Dingwall. It was proof, they claimed, that I'd sought to dissuade him from exercising his constitutional right to present evidence to the NEC. As has already been mentioned, I had verbally suggested to Councillor Dingwall that people in glass houses should think carefully before throwing stones, and this was the conversation to which his letter referred.

Intriguingly, his letter also asserted that a very high official of the Council told him that I had instructed a member of the Lord Provost's staff to go over the books during the time that he was the Lord Provost.

This statement shed no light on the contention that I was undermining the authority of the NEC, but it did show how in preparing my own defence I had been careful to review the activities of those individuals who were now ranged as witnesses against me.

The inquiry team's third accusation was that I had failed to recognise conflicts of interest in holding the Chair of the Hospitality Subcommittee while I was Lord Provost. With their assumption that the Lord Provost should in all matters be politically neutral, they questioned why I had chosen to occupy such a Group position. This was another instance where they misunderstood the history and the real facts before drawing their negative conclusions.

Previously, it had been the convention in Glasgow District Council that the Lord Provost did not chair a committee dealing with hospitality. But in the year before the new unitary authority came into being, the Labour Group had adopted the former Strathclyde Regional Council model, according to which the Regional Convenor was also Chairman of the Hospitality Subcommittee. I was not happy with it, but under the new procedure when I became Lord Provost I automatically also became Chairman of the Hospitality Subcommittee. I didn't seek the chairmanship, or choose to become Chairman. All I did was accept the decision of the Labour Group.

A meeting of the Policy and Resources Committee, at which I was not present, agreed that as Lord Provost I should replace the former Convenor as Chairman of the Hospitality Subcommittee. In support of my argument I presented evidence of this decision. I also submitted a report from the Chief Executive and various minutes of the Council which confirmed that, as Convenor of the Shadow authority – in effect the Shadow Lord Provost – Councillor McFadden had also been Chairman of the Hospitality Subcommittee. In real legal processes precedence is of the utmost importance, but in what the press were later to term a 'kangaroo court', precedence seemed to have little bearing.

The NEC team's fourth allegation was that I had failed to adopt the required standard in public life in the provision of hospitality, Council cars and transport for members.

In respect of hospitality the inquiry team raised their concern over my views on the number of Bailies in Glasgow. At its first meeting in April 1996, the City Council had appointed seventeen councillors as Bailies. At the interim inquiry I had indicated that this was not an excessive number, given the heavy workload which had to be undertaken on behalf of the city. All the members of the Labour Group shared my opinion, unanimously accepting the recommendation from the Labour

Executive on both the number of Bailies to be appointed and indeed their names.

My visit to the Edinburgh Tattoo in August 1996 was yet again raised as evidence of my failure to meet the Party's standards. So I reiterated for the umpteenth time that it had long been the tradition that Glasgow took the salute at the penultimate performance. The 1996 arrangements were no different from previous years, and my predecessors – including Bob Gray, Susan Baird and Tommy Dingwall, who were members of the current administration – had behaved in the same way. The only difference was the adverse publicity which the 1996 visit had drawn. Yet again, I was required to reiterate the history of how Councillor Gould had requested that the Chief Executive, John Anderson, should provide information on the Tattoo visit and how, rather than making any proper internal complaint, as he should have done if he had felt the matter was worthy of complaint, he had gone straight to the press. It had been an outrageous personal attack based on a misapprehension by Councillor Gould.

I had subsequently advised the Group Secretary of my anger at the matter, particularly at the damage the press coverage had caused to the Labour Party. My letter to Councillor McNulty had subsequently been leaked to the press, which simply aggravated matters – that leak had most certainly not come from myself. The main substance of the complaint seemed to be that, in attending the Tattoo, my judgement was at fault. I could only reiterate that I was following fifty years of tradition in Glasgow, and surely if the tradition was so far out of line somebody would have noticed before now.

As regards transport for Council members, the central issue was the Council chauffeur service. Various minutes and items of correspondence were submitted in evidence. I made it clear that my prime concerns were the efficiency and value for money of this particular Council service. But I had only intervened in this matter because as a user of the chauffeur service, the Lord Provost's office should have been consulted and hadn't been. All I was doing was exercising this right to be consulted.

The NEC inquiry team's penultimate allegation in their submission to the National Constitutional Committee, that I had exercised undue influence over Council staff in procuring testimonials in defence of my position, was shocking and particularly offensive. The letters in question had strongly refuted the NEC team's previous – and in many ways more serious – allegation, that I was guilty of improper conduct in my dealings with Council staff. So it was deeply regrettable that Mrs Murfin and her colleagues should then see these letters as evidence for an absurd new allegation. I was getting used to my own good name and reputation being dragged through the mud, but I was very angry that the probity of a group of hard-working and dedicated Council employees should be called into question in this way.

I refuted the allegation with my own written statement to the National Constitutional Committee, and the four members of staff concerned submitted a sworn legal affidavit confirming that I had not exercised any influence to obtain testimonials.

The final charge was that in the course of the inquiry I had used the press to promote my own defence to the detriment of the Labour Party. It was also alleged that I had 'already tried to conduct a vigorous campaign in [my] own defence by contacting members of the NEC'. I did not deny this. Indeed in the papers I submitted I included a copy of my letter to the Prime Minister. My purpose in writing was to draw attention to the fact that I had undergone a very lengthy interview with the inquiry team and had submitted substantial written evidence containing much factual detail refuting the allegations made against me in the interim report. I had believed that that evidence would be considered by the NEC prior to it taking a decision, but this was not done. My decision to write to the Prime Minister and the other members of the NEC was simply to plead that my side of the case be considered.

The charge stated that, in accordance with Labour Party rules, none of the members of the NEC could be involved in my case, as 'disciplinary matters are outwith the remit of the NEC'. This was yet another example of the labyrinthine logic of the Party's whole inquiry process. The NEC was presenting the case against me, and the NEC was seeking my expulsion from the Party. Yet somehow the NEC could not be drawn into the process of my defence as this was beyond their remit. Similarly, on one hand I was being accused of not recognising the authority of the NEC, and on the other I was accused of seeking to invoke the NEC's authority.

As far as the press was concerned, I had been under considerable pressure to speak publicly about my case, but had stalwartly refused to do so. I only spoke publicly at the outset of the attack on myself in September when the allegations were first made against me, in October when I was questioned by reporters on the steps of Keir Hardie House after my interview and on 15 December, in response to a question posed by the local government correspondent of the *Scotsman*, when I said that I was still awaiting the details of specific charges, as promised by the Party.

Any examination of the thousands of column inches of press coverage over the months of the whole tortuous process would indicate that I had consistently refused to comment to the press since being suspended. I was referred to and abused in many of the reports quite without justification. The irony that the press had consistently been fuelled by the Scottish Labour Party itself did not escape me. I wholly refuted the accusation that I had conducted a press campaign in my defence, and there is no evidence to suggest otherwise.

A final little accusation from the NEC team was that I had improperly used the facilities of my public office to distribute written material to the members of the NEC. I responded that I had written to the NEC members as Lord Provost because it was as Lord Provost that I was facing accusations. The Leader of the Opposition on Glasgow City Council, John Young, had publicly defended my right to use the facilities of the Lord Provost's office to conduct my defence. I also pointed out that those members of the NEC who had deigned to reply to my letter had all used their public offices, whether they were trade union officials, MPs or even the Prime Minister himself.

In summary, in answering the various accusations made against me, I had clearly shown that I had a legitimate reason for behaving in the way I did. The accusations did not stand up to the slightest of scrutiny. There was no justification for my continued suspension from the Labour Group and I asked that the National Constitutional Committee rule accordingly.

What was a very long day of hearing and presenting evidence was wearing on.

It was early evening by the time my witnesses – Susan Baird, Jim Clark and Steve Hamilton – were called to give their evidence. When they did, they adhered to the subject matter which we had previously indicated to the Party would be detailed in their statements. Both Susan and Steven Hamilton talked about the role and responsibilities of the Lord Provost. Steven, as a former Town Clerk and Chief Executive, gave detailed information on the checks and balances which are built into Glasgow City Council's procedures to ensure that the public interest is served. Jim Clark covered those aspects of my lengthy evidence upon which he had specific knowledge, including the operation of the Common Good Fund, my communication with the Chairman and members of the Roads and Transportation Committee, and my intervention to ensure that proper procedure was observed in connection with the proposed changes to the Council's chauffeur services.

Susan Baird spoke very supportively of my conduct as Leader and

Lord Provost. She also described how over the years there had been a gradual build-up of antagonism between me and Councillor McFadden. She explained that when I had first become Leader of the administration I had ensured that Councillor McFadden got a senior post. So it was clear that by not treating me with similar respect when she resumed leadership of the Council, she had determined the tenor of our relationship thereafter.

Susan Baird also commented that on the many occasions when Councillor McFadden or others had attempted to rile me, they had found it extremely frustrating that I refused to get angry with them, and were frequently bemused when I refused to reciprocate personal slights or nastiness. I think Susan Baird understands my attitude very well. Life is too short and there's too much to do to waste energy on being bitter and twisted.

The National Constitutional Committee hearing took twelve hours. The presentation of evidence did not conclude until ten o'clock at night, by which time we were all exhausted. In his summing-up Mike Penn acknowledged that the Party's case was largely circumstantial. The meeting adjourned and after an hour the NCC team returned with its verdict. I was to be suspended from the Labour Party for eighteen months. This was far short of expulsion, but the implications of this 'sentence' were quite clear. I would be unable to stand in the approaching municipal elections or possibly even in the Scottish Parliamentary elections in 1999.

The press pack outside had been waiting most of the day. Standing around, they had been chilled to the marrow, sustained only by cups of coffee kindly provided by the *Daily Express* which had its offices just across the road from Keir Hardie House. On the advice of the Scottish Labour Party, some of them had adjourned in the early evening to a local pub, but when we emerged late at night the cameras were once again trained on me. In the absence of anyone else willing to make the announcement, I told them what my sentence was to be, adding that the affair had damaged Glasgow and the Labour Party, and that I was not Mister Happy that night. Mike Penn, who said that he was speaking on behalf of the National Executive Committee, indicated that it welcomed the decision of the National Constitutional Committee after what he believed to have been a 'fair and thorough hearing'. Quite how he'd managed to consult with the National Executive Committee that late at night was a mystery to me. Asked if the verdict would affect my role as Lord Provost, Mike Penn replied cryptically: 'That's a matter for Glasgow City Council.'

Jack McConnell, General Secretary of the Scottish Labour Party, also spoke – a rare event. He commented: 'Party officials today presented detailed evidence and that evidence has convinced the NCC. We are pleased that our actions have been endorsed.'

CHAPTER TWENTY-FOUR

On 31 January, Alex Mosson endured a considerably shorter meeting with the National Constitutional Committee. After a hearing of only six hours he too received an eighteen-month suspension. On the Sunday, I broke my press silence. I had, after all, been suspended from the Party, and confidentiality had hitherto been a very one-sided affair, with the Party flagrantly breaking its own rules. Now it was time to start giving my side of the story in a public forum.

I told *Scotland on Sunday* that I was unhappy with the conduct of both the National Executive Committee and the Scottish Labour Party. I was quoted at some length:

> My view is that the charges were woolly, inconsequential and unsubstantiated. The defence offered to these was substantial, so I was astonished with the verdict. It didn't appear to relate to the reality of the hearing. And the person leading the National Executive said the evidence was largely circumstantial. Nevertheless, they reached their conclusion. I am, of course, happy about retaining my Party membership after forty-seven years.

I made it clear that meanwhile my lawyer Peter McCann would be looking at the whole matter with a view to legal action.

The newspaper's front page carried the report that senior Labour Party figures were supposedly 'furious' with the results of the inquiry. They had wanted an expulsion, but this had not been possible in view of the complete lack of substance to any of the accusations or evidence of any misdemeanour. But none the less although every accusation had been soundly refuted, I was still suspended. The paper quoted 'sources in the Scottish Party leadership' as saying 'we got what we wanted. They may not be life bans, but it finishes their political careers'. Yet a source 'close to Donald Dewar' was said to be 'deeply concerned'. These comments were construed by the paper as the first hints of criticism of Jack McConnell as 'architect of much of the inquiry'.

The members of the National Constitutional Committee had done their business and scuttled back south. They had not done what the Scottish Labour Party expected of them. Rather than expelling me, they had left the local team to finish what they had started.

Having, for the time being at least, exhausted the Labour Party's procedural mechanisms in their attempt to push me out, the Scottish Labour Party went back to its habitual ploy of running its campaign against me through the press. But now the only possible way to unseat me was through the Glasgow Labour Group, so Mr McConnell and his colleagues started a new campaign.

Immediately after the inquiry, Rosemary McKenna, the Labour MP for Cumbernauld and Kilsyth, declared that 'the Labour Group must look closely at the firm action taken by the Party and do whatever is appropriate'. Another Party source was reported as indicating that my position was untenable. The *Sunday Times* stated that it was expected that I would be dismissed within two weeks and a shortlist of candidates for the Lord Provostship was already being drawn up. In the same paper, Jack McConnell was quoted as saying 'the evidence presented by the Party to the independent NCC has been conclusive and the action taken is right'. His tone was not quite as ruthless as it had been in the past, but he still felt able to issue threats to councillors. According to the press, they had been warned that if they didn't unseat Alex Mosson and me they would in turn face scrutiny and perhaps de-selection.

Predictably, the Scottish Labour Party's habitual cronies Michael Kelly and the *Evening Times* rallied to the cause. In the *Scotsman*, Kelly wrote, 'The process was seen to be fair.' But he must have been looking at a different process from the one I had been part of. He also speculated on legal matters: 'It's doubtful he has a case. Certainly he's never going to get an interdict preventing the Council changing its standing orders.' He urged me to resign to save the city further embarrassment.

The *Evening Times* was much more strident. Its front page headline in huge print was: 'Time to go, Mr Lally'. The lengthy editorial argued that my suspension was 'a sad and shabby end to a colourful career'. It went on to describe the verdict of the National Constitutional Committee as 'damning'.

The most reprehensible feature of the paper's attack on me was the inclusion of a telephone poll. This was their cheapest tactic yet. In view of the negative content of the *Evening Times'* editorials over the past year it was hardly possible for their readership to take an objective view on whether I should remain in office or not. Oddly, although they published the interim results of their poll the following day with four votes to one indicating that I should resign, they didn't follow through by publishing the results at the end of the next day when the poll closed. It was tempting to assume that by the time the vote closed it had shifted substantially in my favour and they couldn't possibly publish that sort of result.

I received official notification from the Secretary of the National Constitutional Committee. The letter indicated that the charge that I was in breach of the Party's Constitutional Rule 2A.8 was proved and that my eighteen-month suspension meant that until 30 July 1999 I would 'not be able to represent the Labour Party at any level, hold office at any level, or be a delegate on behalf of the Party to any body'. Nor would I 'be eligible to be considered for the panel of candidates to be drawn up to contest the City of Glasgow District Council elections to be held in May 1999'. But while I was suspended from office and representation of the Party, my membership of the Party remained valid, so I would be able to attend branch meetings. This, of course, gave me great consolation.

I replied that I believed the NEC's evidence to be flawed. I further noted that as the NEC Constitutional Officer himself had stated that the case against me was largely circumstantial, I felt I had convincingly demonstrated that the accusations didn't stand up to the slightest scrutiny. I asked for clarification on what grounds the NCC found that I had broken Rule 2A.8 and what proof supported the decision.

I also wrote to the *Evening Times*. I commented on my bemusement that their reporting seemed so at odds with a considerable number of other people in the media who felt they'd been misled by 'unnamed Labour Party spokesmen'. I pointed out that although they had claimed in their massive headline that pressure was mounting for me to go, they had named only Rosemary McKenna MP in support of this, a lady with no connection with Glasgow whatsoever. I myself was not aware of any such pressure to resign. On the contrary I had received substantial support from both inside and outside the City Chambers, including from influential members of the business community.

But meanwhile my colleagues in the Chambers were being put under real pressure. Frank McAveety had met with the Council's Chief Executive, John Anderson, and instructed him to investigate mechanisms whereby I might be thrown out of office. An article in the *Evening Times* indicated that Donald Dewar, the Secretary of State for Scotland, had 'been following the matter closely', and that he was 'deeply interested in what happens next'. The *Herald*, on 6 February, reported that, according to sources in London, Dewar was driving the Labour Party moves to oust me: 'Mr Dewar has been detailed to oversee the civic crisis in Glasgow and support a modernising strategy aimed at restoring the city's tarnished image.'

On 6 February Peter McCann wrote to Donald Dewar on my behalf. Enclosing the cuttings from both the *Herald* and the *Evening Times*, he asked the Secretary of State to issue a statement dissociating himself from such suggestions that he was acting against me: 'It is no doubt beneath the dignity of Her Majesty's Government of which you are so significant a member that anyone should even suggest that your presence might be construed as a means of influence to achieve any result in this affair.' As the matter might be referred to Her Majesty's Court of Session, he requested the Secretary of State to give his response as soon as possible.

The response, when it came, was not from Mr Dewar himself but from his Private Secretary. The letter stated that Mr Dewar had 'no statutory powers over the term of the Office of Lord Provost' and went on to detail the legal position. This was the answer to a question which had not been asked. We hadn't inquired whether the Secretary of State had statutory powers or any locus to interfere in the affairs of Glasgow City Council. We had simply asked him to deny that he had been given the job of removing the Lord Provost from office. A simple denial would have cleared the air. Instead, we had to make do with a convoluted avoidance of the question, which only left people to draw their own conclusions.

A few days later I received a letter from the Secretary of the National Constitutional Committee in response to my request for clarification of its decision. Given the Labour Party's declared predilection for openness and transparency, his response was astonishing: 'It has always been the position of the NCC that no reason or explanation is given regarding their decisions.' Yet he himself, in the formal notification of the NCC decision, had indicated that if I wished any further clarification I should not hesitate to contact him!

For most of the previous year the press had seemed willing to accept the Scottish Labour Party line, but now there were dissenting voices. The *Herald*'s Scottish political editor, Murray Ritchie, reviewed a number of recent instances in which 'Mr Blair's justice is not blind, just selective'. He mentioned Robin Cook, whose amorous indiscretions had recently merited a great deal of press coverage; Geoffrey Robinson, the Paymaster

General with his offshore trust; Lord Simon, a BP shareholder who as Trade Minister had exercised his influence on the oil industry (unwisely); and Bernie Ecclestone, who had given New Labour one million pounds: 'But what of Lally? His name is mud everywhere now, but still no one has quite managed to say why.' He concluded his powerful refutation of the Labour Party's actions with a description of my 'trial'. It was indicative, he felt, of the shambles of the Labour Party in the west of Scotland: 'It was held in private (even Stalin liked show trials). He was "convicted" of unspecified crimes by contravening a catch-all rule which prohibits members acting in a "grossly detrimental" way towards the Party.' He concluded that unless the Party was prepared to admit what I had done wrong, they were 'truly the ones acting in a grossly detrimental way, and bringing the Party into disrepute'.

But poor Frank McAveety was in a difficult position. In the *Daily Record* he pleaded that his colleagues should put their loyalty to himself as Leader before loyalty to me. Nominations for the Scottish Parliament were due and his place in this future august chamber might depend upon his actions with regard to myself. Rather delightfully, confirmation of the shambolic management of the Scottish Labour Party appeared on my desk in the Chambers. Officials had very kindly sent me information about how I might apply to be considered as a Labour Party candidate for the Scottish Parliament.

As Lord Provost, I was still Chairman of the Council. In this role at the first Council meeting after the NCC hearing, I had to welcome newly elected SNP Councillor John Mason. I advised him that he should always watch his back, and that the people sitting opposite him were not his enemies: 'They are the opposition. Your enemies are elsewhere.' Despite the somewhat strained circumstances, many councillors managed to retain a sense of humour and my comments were greeted with a warm response.

Around the middle of February on two successive days, the *Scotsman* published the results of a public poll it had conducted on whether I should stay or resign. A total of 78 per cent of those polled felt I should go. Frankly, I was surprised I had any support, in view of the Scottish Labour Party's continuous war of attrition against me. And as the figure had been 80 per cent in the *Evening Times* poll a week earlier, at least I was gaining ground!

The *Herald* published a lengthy and detailed account of the NEC's allegations against me and my responses. Their editorial was the strongest commentary yet in my favour:

A pensioner of mature years and long service in the cause of what used to be called the Labour Party, the Lord Provost of Glasgow has been hung, drawn, and quartered by Party functionaries on grounds which were mysterious, and which we show this morning to be merely ridiculous.

The piece continued, referred to the 'energetic and visibly venomous briefing campaign which was conducted against him by one or two New Labour officials'. It continued:

What is clear about Mr Lally is that his remarkable face no longer fits. Has he been guilty of anything? He clearly has, but it is a guilt which could be shared by many Labour politicians, for he has undoubtedly entered into robust politicking with the various factions which have always been an integral part of Labour politics in Glasgow. This is not a matter of corruption or anything else approaching it, even remotely.

The editorial concluded, 'He has been accused unfairly, and it must stop.' Yet meanwhile, the *Herald*'s sister paper, the *Evening Times*, demanded that I should clear my desk and go. By their peculiar interpretation, the secretiveness of the Labour Party's proceedings somehow added justification to the Party's case: 'Outsiders cannot properly judge the detail of the charges. No one will ever know the machinations of power-broking in the councillors corridor.'

By the middle of February, I learned from Peter McCann that the opinion of senior counsel was that there might be some basis for raising a petition. I agreed with Peter that we should press on.

Meanwhile the newspapers were cheerfully considering who might step into my shoes. Four contenders for the Provostship had been named: Bill Timoney, Convenor of the Police Board; Patricia Godman, the Vice-Chairwoman of Social Work; and Bailie Bashir Maan. One other name was in the frame, that of Susan Baird. I was fairly contemptuous of the whole proceeding of naming possible successors in the press, but the suggestion that one of my staunchest allies (who had indeed been a witness in my favour at the National Constitutional Committee) might seek to replace me in the office of Lord Provost was nothing short of disgraceful.

There were a couple of respites from the continuous pressure of the Party's machinations. I spent a day in the company of Jimmy Savile, which included a visit to the Castlemilk Pensioners Action Group. I was delighted that evening to present him with a Lord Provost's Award, as he has always been an active supporter of numerous Glasgow causes. At the annual Junior Chamber of Commerce Colquhoun Dinner I replied to the toast to the city. The response when I stood up to speak was a massive and enthusiastic ovation. I commented that there were clearly very few Labour Party members present.

On 17 February, the Labour Party Executive and then the Group were due to meet to discuss whether Alex Mosson and I were to be dismissed from our respective offices. Predictably, given the pressure from the Party, the Executive voted for the motion by ten votes to two. Only Susan Baird and Ron Davey voted against. The Labour Group then followed the guidance of the Executive.

The day afterwards the *Herald* reported that, as I was Lord Lieutenant of Glasgow, only the Queen could remove me from this position. If the Labour Party pressed on, matters were likely to become very embarrassing. Councillors John Young, the Conservative Group Leader, and Bill Aitken were scornful of the way the Labour Party had proceeded. They were right to be scornful, as prior to the Executive and Labour Group meetings the whole affair had taken yet another Machiavellian twist.

At their meeting the day before the Labour Group had been given copies of a letter signed by Jack McConnell, the General Secretary of the Scottish Labour Party. At the conclusion of the meeting, all the copies of this letter were collected in.

On 18 February I wrote to Jack McConnell requesting a copy of the letter after Frank McAveety, to whom it had been addressed, indicated that he could not give me a copy. I commented that as copies had been collected back from the councillors the contents had to be very significant. The Labour Party was starting to act like the KGB. I for one believed that the public had a right to know the basis for action proposed by the Labour Group. Clearly the Party's case was so weak that it could not be open to public scrutiny.

I never received a copy of the letter, but I continued to press that I had the right to read it. Sometime later, the Group Secretary, Des McNulty, conceded that I had the right to read the letter but not to obtain a copy. I therefore read it in his office and made notes on it afterwards. Fortunately I have always had a good memory.

Mr McConnell's letter was dated 5 February. It contained the instruction that the Glasgow Labour Group Whip must act under his direct supervision and guidance on outstanding disciplinary matters. The Group was to commission an 'external review' of the role and duties of the Lord Provost, the Depute Lord Provost, the Bailies and the Common Good Fund. The Group was instructed to 'reconcile the disciplinary decision of the Party in respect of the Lord Provost and Depute'. This matter was expected to be dealt with as soon as possible.

'Reconcile the disciplinary decision', translated into plain English, meant that Alex Mosson and myself were to be pushed out of office. It was shortly after his receipt of this letter that Frank McAveety called a special meeting of the Council in order to carry out the Party's instructions.

The pressure upon me was immense. One consolation was that the SNP and Conservative opposition declined this golden opportunity to attack and condemn me. Instead, they were doing quite the opposite. Commenting in the press, Kenneth Gibson, leader of the SNP group, expressed the view that I was 'an arch manipulator' yet also 'one of the most charming, most disarming men' he had ever met. The Conservative, Bill Aitken, spoke of me as 'a rogue and a good guy', the sort of guy he'd 'have a pint with'. Chris Mason of the Liberal Democrats indicated that 'if one looks along the gallery of paintings of Provosts and asks who has done more for Glasgow, Pat Lally would be in the top four in the city's history'. This left me wondering who the other three were.

It was now very apparent that the only way I was ever going to get any sort of justice was by taking matters to law. But since, technically, it would be the Council which would remove me from the office of Lord Provost, I would have to take to court not the Labour Party but the Labour-controlled Council, a quite different legal entity. This was frustrating, because it was really the Scottish Labour Party which was at fault, and I did not wish to bring any costs upon the Council. I consequently requested a 'truce' while we waited for the Court of Session decision. Peter McCann wrote to the Chief Executive, arguing that as my quarrel was with the Labour Party, the Council itself should not proceed with the attempt to oust me. But the leadership was not in the mood to reconsider its entrenched position.

Meanwhile, this time writing in the *Sunday Post*, Michael Kelly continued to attack me from his position as a 'former Lord Provost of Glasgow'. He was disparaging of those who were rallying to my support, and particularly dismissive of me, who he claimed was 'never going to accept he is guilty of anything'.

How right Mr Kelly was. And strangely, when matters came to court, the proper place for examining legal issues, Lord Abernethy didn't accept I was guilty of anything either.

On 27 February at the Court of Session in Edinburgh, Lord Abernethy

– on the basis of the same evidence as I had put to the Labour Party's National Constitutional Committee – issued an interim order, pending judicial review, effectively suspending my suspension. The *Daily Record*'s headline the next morning was predictable but gratifying: 'Lazarus Lally Wins Round One of Fight'.

In his presentation to the Court of Session, my advocate, Robert McCreadie, described my suspension as 'unlawful, perverse and a breach of natural justice'. Lord Abernethy followed suit, indicating that his decision to grant the interim order was because 'there was no factual basis for establishing any part of the charge against the petitioner'. He had 'no hesitation, after having regard to the circumstances, in granting the suspension'.

Lord Abernethy's decision was issued on 27 February, a Friday, late in the afternoon. On the Monday morning when I arrived back in the office, I was greeted by my usual very large mug of tea and a plate of Abernethy biscuits. Even in the days, sixty years earlier, when I had been given them, fresh-baked from the Cop-op bakery on my way to school, Abernethy biscuits had never tasted quite so good.

CHAPTER TWENTY-FIVE

Unbowed by the minor setback of a defeat in the Court of Session, the Scottish Labour Party continued to push for my dismissal from office. One of the most disturbing aspects of this process was that following Jack McConnell's letter fifty-eight members of the Labour Group signed a petition to the Chief Executive, John Anderson, requesting a special meeting to debate the change to the Council's Standing Orders which would allow the removal of myself and Alex Mosson. Councillor Stephen Dornan signed the petition and then shortly after wrote to the Labour Group Secretary asking that his name be removed. In his letter, he indicated that while he had originally been prepared 'to accept collective responsibility' his views had changed.

Of the fifty-eight signatories to the petition, fifteen of them had previously voted against the proposal – presumably they viewed McConnell's letter as an instruction. If their names had not been included, there were only forty-three in favour. Considering that there were seventy-four members in the Labour Group including the suspended members, the actual majority for this proposition was actually twelve. The majority in Council, assuming, as seems reasonable, that the opposition would vote against, would have been four.

I was upset that at least six of the people who signed the petition in favour of the motion to remove me were close friends who had been pressured by the bullying of the Labour Party. I understand that they were subjected to enormous pressure, but I don't think they can feel very proud of themselves.

The question remains whether the fifteen who originally voted against the motion should have signed the petition. As it only needed twenty-one signatures to requisition a special meeting, there was actually no need for them to sign. They could have left the signing to those who actually agreed with the proposition. Doubtless the explanation is that like Stephen Dornan, they were accepting 'collective responsibility'. It's an odd sort of collective responsibility that connives with an ethically reprehensible process and whose legality by that stage was clearly in doubt.

A few days after he withdrew his signature from the petition, Stephen Dornan was contacted by a reporter who had received information that he was in arrears with his council tax payments. In fact, the two further payments Stephen had to make for the financial year 1997 were not yet due. Stephen inevitably concluded that this leaking of confidential Council information on his personal finances was yet more evidence of the depths the Labour Party was prepared to plumb in order to oust me and my supporters from the Council. It was certainly a very sad state of affairs.

At the Labour Group meeting on 2 March, the proposal that Glasgow City Council's Standing Orders be changed in order to strip the Lord Provost of his office was approved. The Party was keeping up the pressure. Their tactics were certainly not in the spirit of the comments made by Lord Abernethy, but then fairness and law had never been at the forefront of their concerns.

Lord Abernethy's ruling had, however, gained me two significant concessions from the Labour Group. The plan had been that the Group meeting would approve the motion proposing a change in Standing Orders to the Council and that nominations would be sought for replacements for me and Alex Mosson. But the Leader, Frank McAveety, now moved that the meeting would not take nominations for the Provostship. It was also decided that, contrary to what had been previously mooted, Alex Mosson and I would not be summarily dismissed once the change in Standing Orders had been achieved. But I recognised this as just a temporary sop. There was no question that once the change in Standing Orders had been achieved the machine would roll on fairly rapidly to my dismissal.

The next morning, I received a surprising and very welcome letter. The former Lord Provost of Edinburgh, Norman Irons, wrote to pledge his full support for me. As he had been Lord Provost when Edinburgh had lost the bid for UK City of Architecture and Design, his letter was all the more big-hearted and delightful.

In addition to offering his support, he made a number of specific points which related to his experience serving as an SNP Lord Provost alongside a Labour administration from 1992 to 1996. He explained that as Chairman of the Tattoo it was he who had been responsible for inviting the Lord Provost of Glasgow to take the salute. This, he stated, was a privilege and an honour bestowed by Edinburgh upon the senior civic office holder of its neighbour, Scotland's largest city. He indicated that he would have been surprised had Lord Provost Dingwall not arrived at the event in the civic Rolls Royce.

As a businessman, Norman Irons had met one of the senior business figures who had joined me on a trade mission to Dalian. The man had expressed 'unsolicited admiration for your hard work and for the fashion in which you represented both Glasgow and Scotland'. This brought to my mind another unsolicited testimonial I had received from the business world. One of the most senior representatives of the famous Glasgow brewer Tennents, who had also accompanied me on a trip to China, commented that I had 'worked tirelessly and professionally in support of our objectives'. He also recalled how I had worked together with the former Secretary of State for Trade and Industry, Iain Lang, on behalf of this major Glasgow employer and he offered his files in support of my case. This threw Bob Gould's nonsensical original claims, long since refuted, into very sharp relief. Not only had our international work been far from junketing, but it had created substantial new markets for Glasgow business and kept people in jobs.

Norman Irons's comments on the 1999 bid process were, in the circumstances, particularly kind and revealed a man of very great integrity:

> When we lost to Glasgow we attributed our defeat to a single cause – Pat Lally! The minutiae of the business is unimportant. What is important in the context of your present troubles, is that we knew that when you took over the management of the bid then we were always in danger because we knew that you would *work for Glasgow* in every way that you could; and that you would work effectively.

In my lifetime of public service, I have been the grateful recipient of many compliments and honours. Few people have been quite as selfless in their praise as Norman Irons. He concluded his letter by expressing his belief that my treatment was 'a public scandal' and wishing me all good fortune and success.

On 3 March I attended a crucial Council meeting. In the *Sun* that morning Jim Sillars, a well-known one-time defector from Labour, ultimately to the SNP, commented that 'anyone reading the case and the judge's comments could see that the Labour commission which sentenced Lord Provost Lally to perdition was a kangaroo court where the accused was going to be found guilty – however innocent'. To adopt another animal metaphor, the Council meeting I walked into early in the afternoon of Tuesday 3 March wasn't a kangaroo court – more like a nest of vipers.

At the opening of the meeting, the Leader of the Opposition (a role which had been assumed by the SNP), Councillor Kenny Gibson, rose to his feet and indicated that he wished to make a point of order. I allowed him to do so. Councillor Gibson indicated that Section 2 of the Council's Standing Orders indicated that the agenda should be made available to all councillors at least three days prior to the meeting taking place. As this had not happened, he asked that as Chairman I should rule the meeting incompetent. I suggested that we should wait until we'd heard from all other members before I reached a decision on the matter.

Dr Christopher Mason, the only Liberal Democrat on the Council, agreed with Councillor Gibson and added that he felt that consideration of the motion would also be in breach of Standing Order Number 4 of the Local Government (Access to Information) Act of 1995. This Act requires that the general public should have three days' notice of any business to be transacted at a meeting of the Council. As he had only received the proposed amendment from the Chief Executive at lunchtime that day – and he had not been made aware of what was being mooted before – he objected strongly.

The opposition was clearly of the view that, while the meeting might have been about amending Standing Orders, it was not itself properly constituted within our Standing Orders. After noting their comments, as Chairman of the meeting, I indicated that I considered that their points of order were not without merit . . . It was clear that I was about to utter the word 'but' or something similar. There were sighs of relief from a number of those on the Labour benches who saw my attitude as a capitulation.

The Conservative leader John Young, shouted out: 'Allow this meeting to continue, and you'll be pouring yourself a glass of hemlock, Lord Provost.'

I thanked him for his good advice, and proceeded. 'However,' I said, and paused. From the Labour benches there was a unified and audible sharp intake of breath. And then I continued:

> As custodian of the constitution, as provided for in Standing Order 7(i), I have to advise that the proposal before the house today is not competent, as the Standing Orders of the City Council make no provision for the alteration of the Standing Orders. The meeting therefore cannot proceed.
>
> This is something which should be addressed before any

consideration is given to changes of substance. No doubt the Chief Executive can address this issue and advise the Council at a future date.

With this statement, I ruled that the meeting was closed. Thus I declined to take a motion from Councillor McAveety for the suspension of Standing Order 7. The Depute Leader, Charlie Gordon, moved that Standing Orders be suspended, to which I responded politely, but firmly, 'without Standing Orders, there's no Council meeting'.

John Young, smiling in the direction of the Labour leadership, pronounced: 'You've cocked it up!' while I, with all appropriate dignity as the Lord Provost of Glasgow, stood up and motioned to leave. The mace bearer, an excellent Council officer who knew his responsibilities, lifted the mace and walked out in front of me. Alex Mosson followed. Within a very short time, the opposition councillors had mustered and followed us out. As Dr Mason departed, he turned towards Frank McAveety and commented: 'You're making this up as you go along. I'm leaving this rabble.'

After I had closed the meeting, Councillors McAveety and Gordon each asked John Anderson, the Chief Executive, if the meeting could proceed. John Anderson is a lawyer. After many years of service in local government, he should have been well aware that, like all such processes, meetings of a local authority are governed by rules. The Council's Standing Orders required that the Lord Provost, or his representative, be in the Chair. After I had departed therefore, and particularly after all of the opposition members had also walked out, the meeting simply became a Labour Group meeting. John Anderson, however, was unconvinced by these procedural niceties and ruled that the meeting should proceed in the terms of the Standing Orders but a new Chairman should be appointed.

From the floor of the house, Councillor McAveety proposed that Councillor Gordon be appointed as the Chairman. He was seconded by Councillor Gordon himself, to which other Labour members shouted 'agreed'. This was in itself irregular, as Standing Orders require that such a motion should be put to a vote.

Councillor Gordon then took the Chair and asked that the house deal with the business before them. At this point, Susan Baird asked if the meeting could proceed when the mace was not in the Chamber. Charlie Gordon spoke again with John Anderson, who advised that the role of the mace was 'only ceremonial' and that the meeting could proceed. Bill Harley, another of the Labour councillors clearly discomfited by the whole proceeding then asked if the meeting could legitimately proceed in light of the recent Court of Session decision. Again, Councillor Gordon declared the meeting to be legitimate.

The motion that the Council's Standing Orders should be changed to allow the removal of the Lord Provost was then put forward by the Leader, Frank McAveety. This was formally seconded by the Group Secretary, Des McNulty.

In a properly constituted Council meeting the Chief Executive would take the vote, indicating first how it would be taken, whether by a show of hands or a roll call, but this didn't happen on this occasion. Again contrary to normal procedure the division bell was not rung. Charlie Gordon simply asked the members to raise their hands if they were in favour and then he asked those who were against to raise their hands. The minute of this most irregular meeting does not record how many were in agreement with the motion, simply that it was passed. Councillor McAveety then moved that the house should adjourn.

Immediately after their departure from the Council Chambers, councillors McAveety and Gordon held a press conference, at which they said that the meeting had proceeded on advice from the Chief Executive. In response to a press enquiry I simply confirmed the fact that 'when the Lord Provost leaves the Chair, the meeting stands adjourned'. The Conservative, Bill Aitken, described events as 'Kafka-esque', while the SNP's Kenneth Gibson commented that the Labour Group 'could not run a whelk stall'.

The way I closed the Council meeting had an undeniable drama about it, which the press inevitably seized upon. However, the attempt to railroad through an ill-considered change in Standing Orders was in itself a contravention of the Standing Orders that governed the decision-making process of the Council in the public interest. My opponents regarded my behaviour as anarchic, but it was in fact they who were attempting to introduce a sort of selective anarchy into the running of the Council. Their attitude was 'We'll obey the rules when it suits us'. Call me old-fashioned, but I hold to the ancient tenet 'Rules is rules'.

Next day the *Daily Record*'s headline was 'Mayhem as Lally storms off with the mace', an inaccurate but attention-grabbing description of the proceedings. Elsewhere, the word 'farce' was used more than once. The *Herald* predicted that I would almost certainly face further discipline from the Labour Party, and the *Scotsman* a few days later expressed the view that I would 'be forced out of office within the next fortnight'.

The 'Alternative Pocket Encyclopaedia' column in the *Scotsman* provided a satirical view which I appreciated. It explored attempts to remove a Councillor Pat Laldy for unreasonably attempting to do his job: 'Attempts were made to legally challenge Mr Laldy's gainful employment by his close personal enemy Councillor Frank McArticle28'. The column went on to describe a number of tactics which had been employed towards this end: 'The one closest to success – pulling funny faces at him in the Council Chamber.' The piece made some telling points. Councillor McArticle28 was quoted as saying ' "It makes the Council look like a total farce. I mean, if he's going to give the voters some decent public service, what's he doing in the Labour Party?" McArticle28 and his colleagues are currently studying the Council's Standing Orders to make sure that every opportunity to oust the Provost is made a complete hash of.'

Immediately after the specially convened, and very rapidly concluded, meeting I wrote to the Chief Executive, John Anderson. I outlined what had happened at the meeting and quoted verbatim my reasoning for concluding it. I added, 'I have to advise you that any decisions made after my departure are not valid.'

In response to what the Leadership of the Council was describing as my 'huff' I was invited to meet with the Assistant Whip, Councillor Roberton, who was acting as Chief Whip in the absence, through illness, of Bailie Marshall. The meeting was postponed until 9 March, because the earlier date which had been set coincided with one of my important duties as Lord Provost, the presentation of the Lord Provost's Art Prize.

The investigation procedures of the Labour Party stated that 'the Whip should ask another member, not someone who has an involvement in the complaint to be present'. So I was surprised to see that Councillor Roberton was accompanied by Councillor Gordon, since the letter inviting me to the hearing made it quite clear that Councillor Gordon did have a direct involvement in the complaint. He had also been involved in the events which took place after I ruled the Council meeting invalid.

The Whip's report at the conclusion of this ill-constituted disciplinary hearing betrayed either a misapprehension of what had taken place at the Council meeting or a misunderstanding of the rules. Councillor Roberton judged that I was in breach of Rules 8(b) and 8(c). As Rule 8(b) relates to members asking questions at Council meetings it is not relevant. Rule 8(c) relates to members speaking or voting in opposition to the decisions of the Labour Group. Since the Council had not reached any agenda items before I had adjourned the meeting, that too was inapplicable.

As the Labour Party's procedures were under judicial review at the Court of Session, I felt that matters should be left to the courts to decide.

My lawyer's earlier suggestion that the Council should defer any action until after the Court of Session's ruling had been ignored. In acting as I did I was sticking to the principle that Peter McCann had outlined of letting the courts settle the issue. But even this was deemed to be a misdemeanour. Councillor Roberton's report went on to state: 'By preferring the advice of his own solicitor against that of the Chief Executive, the Lord Provost effectively ruled on a matter in his own interest. By refusing to consult the Group leadership and refusing to take procedural motions from them during the Council meeting, he endeavoured to frustrate the Group decision.'

But the National Code of Local Government Conduct stipulates that elected members should be 'familiar with the rules of personal conduct which the law and standing orders require'; and that if there was any doubt on these matters members should 'seek advice from your Council's appropriate senior officer or from your own legal advisor'. So I had acted precisely according to the code of conduct that guides the actions of all councillors.

With the considerable experience he had had of being a former Lord Provost of Glasgow and Chairman of the Glasgow Corporation's Parliamentary Bills and Standing Orders Committee, Peter McCann was in a far better position to advise on appropriate conduct than most solicitors. As Lord Provost I was custodian of the Constitution. It was my duty to act fairly and equitably between all members of the Council without fear or favour, which is exactly what I had done. Had the matter been brought to the Council in a proper manner, I would have been obliged to support the decisions of the Labour Group. But in any case my conduct at the Council meeting on 3 March was not in breach of any Labour Party rules and observed the National Code of Local Government Conduct.

At the Labour Group meeting which considered Councillor Roberton's report, I made my views known and refuted his mistaken presumptions over Group rules 8(b) and 8(c). I challenged the way in which his report was brought to the meeting, as this was not in keeping with the Group's own Standing Orders. To my great satisfaction the Group Chairman, Jean McFadden, had to concede that I was right and put off the matter until the next Labour Group meeting on 18 March.

I was now reluctantly obliged to pursue two legal adjudications. My case against the Labour Party was on-going, and now I initiated a review of the Council proceedings with regard to the ruling Labour Group's attempts to manipulate the Council's Standing Orders with the sole purpose of ousting me from office.

On 11 March, the *Daily Mail*'s headline read, 'Farce of the Labour Sleaze Crusade' and the *Scotsman*'s, 'Labour Admits Sleaze Inquiry Faces Collapse'. The party had admitted that its cases against Bob Gould, Gordon Macdiarmid and Jim Mutter did not stand up to legal scrutiny, and these three councillors were reinstated. This was a correct decision in the cases of councillors Macdiarmid and Mutter, but had the strict terms of Clause 2A.8 of the Party's constitution been applied I doubt that Councillor Gould would have found himself back as a 'fully functioning' councillor.

On 18 March, the Court of Session granted an interim interdict barring the Council from ousting me. Lord Johnston pronounced that my decision to adjourn the meeting of 3 March had been taken in good faith and suggested that the subsequent proceedings were of questionable validity. Yet in spite of this decision, the Labour Group determined that what they still called my 'breach of discipline' at the Council meeting on 3 March was sufficient grounds to dismiss me. They even set the process of choosing my successor in motion once again.

Peter McCann described this arrogance against the court decision as 'appalling', but Jean McFadden, who as a lawyer herself might have known better, commented that 'there are other mechanisms for dealing with this matter which don't involve going to the courts'. Just as she had previously suggested that pretending I was dead might be an appropriate method of removing me from office, now she was intimating that once again some devious mechanism could be found to achieve her goal.

CHAPTER TWENTY-SIX

While I defended my reputation and the role of Lord Provost, I was unable to put the time and effort I would have liked into my work on behalf of the city. Two successive disappointments over initiatives I had supported served to show that the time councillors spent pursuing the Scottish Labour Party's questionable agenda was harming the interests of the city.

It was announced that the Scottish Parliament would start its life in Edinburgh. Glasgow had previously offered the potentially superb former Strathclyde Regional Council offices and debating chamber as an interim home for the parliament. Pending the creation of the new building, which was being designed by the Barcelona architect Enric Miralles, the new MSPs would have to be accommodated somewhere.

The scale and quality of Strathclyde's offices would have given every MSP excellent accommodation, their own offices and plentiful space for their support staff. With good road, rail and air transport links this seemed the ideal solution. Instead, Donald Dewar was brow-beaten by the Edinburgh establishment into accepting the Church of Scotland's General Assembly building as a debating chamber, which is undoubtedly very fine, and the grossly inadequate former Lothian Regional Council offices, which were to be vacated by Edinburgh officials.

By comparison with the Glasgow option, the much smaller Edinburgh offices were cramped and unsatisfactory, with the added disadvantage that the distance between them and the debating chamber was actually quite substantial. On those rare occasions when it rained in Scotland the new Members of the Scottish Parliament stood a very good chance of getting wet. But the decision had been made and I was in no position to argue against it.

The other, much more substantial disappointment was the refusal of the Heritage Lottery Fund to support the proposed Scottish National Gallery of Art and Design. The reason was quite clear: Lady Airlie, the

Chairman of the National Gallery's trustees, had spiked the bid, sending a private letter to the Chairman of the Heritage Lottery Fund undermining the project.

Some time previously I had advised Donald Dewar that as Lady Airlie was so much at odds with the views of her fellow trustees he should sack her. Unfortunately, although he had been supportive of the notion of one of the National Galleries being located in Glasgow, his refusal to acknowledge Lady Airlie's implacable opposition to the idea ultimately led to the loss of the project.

Rather than ditch Lady Airlie, Donald Dewar had appointed a number of highly regarded trustees to review the matter. The previous Chairman of trustees, Angus Grossart, and senior trustee Lord MacFarlane of Bearsden had held a realistic view of the importance of the gallery to Glasgow and Scotland.

When one of the Charles Rennie Mackintosh rooms which Glasgow held in its collection was restored for the 1996 Mackintosh exhibition it attracted over 200,000 people when it was shown in Glasgow and was a huge success in New York, Chicago and Los Angeles. Had Glasgow been able to reinstate all of the rooms which it held in store this would have provided a 'home grown' centrepiece of world importance for the new gallery.

Donald Dewar's decisions had thus deprived the future Members of the Scottish Parliament of a temporary home which, for quality of accommodation, comfort and access would have been unrivalled. The Scottish people were similarly denied a gallery which would have attracted many more tourists to this little country – Scotland could undoubtedly do with the money they would bring and the new jobs they would support. Instead, the MSPs found themselves in a hotch-potch of buildings in Edinburgh and the gallery, for which there are still very powerful arguments, suffered a major setback.

One pleasant respite from my own concerns and the pasting that Glasgow was getting at the hands of a Secretary of State who seemed to have forgotten his roots, was a superb press profile in the *Herald*, thoroughly deserved, of Glasgow's talented and hard-working Lady Provost, Peggy Lally. Peggy was working hard preparing the second major Lady Provost's Fashion Show, which would raise money for two causes very close to her heart, Marie Curie Cancer Care and Alzheimer's Scotland – Action on Dementia. Again, the excellent Mr Neish at Marks & Spencer had agreed to stage the show in the City Chambers, where a thousand paying guests would see M&S's spring and summer collections paraded for their delight.

Sadly Peggy had considerable experience of the importance of the charities the event would support. Two of her uncles had died of cancer and she was determined that other victims and carers should benefit from her fund-raising endeavours. And now, as the *Herald* piece by Marian Pallister recorded, Peggy had to endure the anguish of the slow decline of her mother and her aunt through Alzheimer's. She talked of the stress of caring and guilt of eventually admitting that the burden was too great and specialist care in a home was the only solution.

Peggy was, in a sense, speaking for both of us when she commented that she valued her civic role for the opportunity it gave her to serve the city and work for charity: 'You don't take this job to wear a chain around your neck. You take it to go out there and work ... There is more to life than living just for yourself. Society has to learn that you have to live with other people. I get stressed out and agitated and feel I can't take any more, but when you go out there into the public and you get the response from the people, that's what it's all about. They support me as much as I support them.'

Peggy was talking perfect sense, but others used the press to continue their assaults upon me. Michael Kelly, whose persistent line had been in support of his friend Mrs McFadden and the Scottish Labour Party, seemed increasingly to adopt the role of a party spokesman rather than that of an objective journalist. Although in the *Scotsman* he had supported many initiatives for which I had been partly if not wholly responsible, he still consistently adopted a negative attitude towards me. The deliberations of the Court of Session were of little relevance, according to Mr Kelly's thinking: 'Politically, Pat Lally is a dead duck. He doesn't speak for the Council. He certainly could not deliver any commitments he might be asked to make on behalf of his Council.'

Michael Kelly was clearly unaware of my continuing work on behalf of the disadvantaged in Glasgow or the many civic responsibilities I had undertaken as Lord Provost. I had determined early on not to shrink from this task or become morosely preoccupied with my own problems. Peggy and I continued to have full diaries and to work often from very early in the morning until very late at night, attending innumerable functions on behalf of the city.

Among my duties as Lord Provost I had noticed a recurring theme: the number of police functions I was invited to attend seemed unusually high. While it was never stated, I'm sure that John Orr, the Chief Constable of Strathclyde, was demonstrating his faith in me in a characteristically forthright way. Throughout my conflict with the Labour Party and the months of distorted and misleading information in the press, he continued to be hugely supportive. In fact, I would go so far as to say I was ostentatiously supported by the Chief Constable. I was by John Orr's side at innumerable police functions and he was always generous in his recognition of my presence and the comments he made about Peggy and myself. I think the implicit message was clear. If the Chief Constable had felt that my probity was in any way in question, he would not have come within a mile of me. I will never forget John Orr's admirable integrity and strength of character, nor his support of me and Peggy during this most difficult period in our lives.

A more surprising source of support was the journalist John Macleod, who was the brother of Angus Macleod, the spokesman of the General Secretary of the Scottish Labour Party. It was unexpected but pleasing to read a *Herald* piece by him describing the Labour Group's actions against me as 'an attempted coup, on official Party orders, against a fairly elected Lord Provost, leading a democratically elected City Council, on grounds that are not specified and in an unfolding farrago that is making lawyers happy and judges famous and the great city the laughing stock of Europe'.

In the last days of March, there were reports in the press that the Labour Party was about to abandon its bid to expel me from the Lord Provostship. But although the *Herald* commented on the imminent collapse of the Party's 'high profile disciplinary crack-down', this merely reflected the Party's fear that they might be thwarted by the courts, not an acknowledgement that they were wrong. The article reported 'a senior Labour source' as blaming Scots Law for having brought them to this sorry pass. But as 'the Labour Group in Glasgow was still determined to remove Pat Lally from office', and I had not received any word from the Party, any celebration on my part would have been premature.

The event which had led to this dramatic Labour climb-down was the National Executive Committee's decision not to contest the judicial review on my suspension. Having effectively lifted my suspension, the NEC also agreed at the same time to lift temporarily all of the suspensions which had been imposed upon my fellow councillors. However, although the *Daily Telegraph* described this situation as 'an embarrassing about-turn', they also reported that 'Party sources' had 'made it clear that alternative forms of disciplinary action would be explored'. The *Scotsman*, which had before consistently supported Jack McConnell and his regime, now observed in a profile of McConnell that he was finding 'his words coming back to haunt him'. Those words, which the *Scotsman* quoted, were: 'New Labour will clean up politics and is committed to tackling sleaze in order to restore public confidence in all those in public life including MPs, ministers, councillors and other public officials.' There was some irony in the fact that the Scottish Labour Party's General Secretary, a man whose organisation had spent the previous year issuing non-attributable briefings and off-the-record commentary, was now the victim of critics and sources who preferred to remain unnamed. One of these sources described the whole sorry process as 'a complete fuck-up', although the *Scotsman* coyly substituted four asterisks for the 'f' word. The article presumably quoting the same source continued: 'There is a view that all of this is Jack's fault, and the fault of Keir Hardie House (Labour's Scottish Headquarters) and that the result is that everybody runs around blaming everybody else.' Another 'well-placed source' commented 'Jack spends too much time briefing the press and not getting on with the job of organising the Party. He also leaks like a sieve.' Even comments from his supposed friends weren't particularly helpful in expressing their view that 'most of his problems have come from London, where officials do not realise even the basic differences between England and Scotland'. This new line of blaming the English was absurd. I felt it conveyed just a hint of desperation.

On the same day as the *Scotsman*'s profile of Jack McConnell, Tony Blair was forced to defend his Party's somewhat flawed position in the House of Commons. In response to a question from a Tory MP, the Prime Minister acknowledged that the Party was taking action against me and that, as was my right, I was now pursuing the matter in the courts.

'Well done, Prime Minister!' I thought. But it was a pity that the Party that Mr Blair led had approved a constitution which seemed designed to prevent members ever having the opportunity to seek such redress in the courts. In England, alas, the Party seems able to do this successfully. But thankfully the law of Scotland does not allow such abuse. Human rights are, it seems, alive and well and living in Scotland!

Perhaps the leader of the Party will now consider amending the Party Constitution and extending Scottish rights to Party members in England and Wales. On the other hand, Donald Dewar might feel that there is no justification for Scots having rights which don't exist south of the border and seek to bring us into line. This would be par for the course.

In spite of the sharp turn of events against them McConnell and his acolytes were still failing to get the message that was coming from both the courts and an increasingly enlightened press. The *Scotsman* reported that 'senior Scottish officials' would be using the dossier of evidence from their inquiry as the basis for a 'retrial'.

In another curious – but perhaps predictable – twist, with the Tories on the offensive their Scottish Chairman, Raymond Robertson, wrote to the General Secretary of the Labour Party, Tom Sawyer, contending that Donald Dewar should be disciplined for breaching the Party's Rule 2.A8, the same rule that had been applied to achieve my temporary suspension from the Glasgow Labour Group. Mr Robertson argued that in his relentless pursuit of me Donald Dewar had contravened Rule 2.A8 by engaging in 'a sustained course of conduct prejudicial, or in any act grossly detrimental, to the Party'.

In early April, the Glasgow Labour Group Executive reinstated the Depute Lord Provost Alex Mosson as Chairman of the Environment Committee, and Councillor Mutter as Chairman of the Parks and Recreation Committee. After a year of sustained attacks, we were now witnessing a gradual climb-down on the part of the Party and the Group. They were certainly not going to give in all at once, but the cumulative message was becoming clear. The Scottish Labour Party's campaign against me and several of my colleagues had been so severely flawed that – with the prospect of further court action looming – they did not want to suffer continuing embarrassment. Yet a complete climb-down would have created quite the wrong headlines, so they were taking their time.

The *Evening Times* continued to follow the increasingly questionable McConnell line on matters. In mid-April, it reported that Council Leader Frank McAveety had introduced a new code of conduct to 'sleaze-rocked Glasgow City Council'. In fact, Frank's committee, which had included representatives of all the political parties and a number of outsiders from business and academia, had come up with a set of rules that any honourable councillor with the least common sense should have been observing anyway.

This simplistic new code was endorsed by Donald Dewar, who had, according to the *Evening Times*, 'hinted that he is set to get tough with all councillors who step out of line'. Considering all that had gone before, he might have been wise to apply the same strictures to Party officials.

The end of April offered a welcome escape from the Scottish Labour Party's shenanigans. My younger son Derek was married to Claire Fitzpatrick in a delightful, low-key wedding. Our two families got together for a ceremony at the Church of Christ the King in Simshill. Afterwards we gathered with Derek and Claire's friends and many of my close Party friends for a delightful reception, which, in accordance with Glasgow custom, concluded with a 'right old knees-up' (at least by all of those who could manage to get their knees up!).

Preparations were well underway for the judicial review of – to use the legal phraseology – the 'Pretended Decision of Glasgow City Council' concerning the Council's Standing Orders. The task Peter McCann and I had set ourselves was to counter the Council's attempt to amend Standing Orders in order to expel me from the office of Lord Provost. As the members of the ruling Labour Group on the Council were all compromised by the proceedings that had occurred after I had left the Council meeting on 3 March, Peter decided to interview members of the opposition. The court would examine the propriety of the proceedings themselves; the actual order of events; the appropriateness of the Chief Executive's advice to the leadership of the Labour Group; the assumption of control of the meeting by Councillor Gordon and the resolutions which arose as a result. Much of my case rested on the fact that, as Lord Provost, I had properly decreed matters concluded before the resolutions were considered.

About a week before our visit to the Court of Session, Peter McCann suffered a stroke. His illness was severe and, initially at least, his doctors feared for his life, but he is an extraordinarily resilient character. Despite childhood polio and his resultant disability, Peter has achieved high standing, both in law and in the city of Glasgow. I am quite sure that it was the same determination not to give up the fight that saw him sitting up in bed within a few days of his stroke and giving instruction to his associates with regard to my court appearance. So it was, buoyed up with the fighting confidence of this extraordinary man, that I was to appear before Lord Eassie on 27 May in order to continue my own good fight – for my reputation.

CHAPTER TWENTY-SEVEN

Our visit to the Court of Session was another long and tiring day. The counsel representing Glasgow City Council, Neil Davidson QC, was determined to pursue the two accusations which had been raised in my meeting with the Acting Chief Whip, Councillor Roberton. The contention was that in acting as I did at the Council meeting on 3 March, I had preferred the advice of my own solicitor over that of the Chief Executive and that in adjourning the meeting as I did, I had ruled on a matter in my own interests.

On the appropriateness or otherwise of preferring the advice of my own solicitor, I was able to demonstrate that the National Code of Conduct, which councillors are required to follow, advised consultation with either the Chief Executive or with a councillor's own solicitor. I explained that in this instance I had, in fact, consulted both, discussing with John Anderson in advance my proposal to adjourn the meeting and the terms on which I proposed the adjournment. John Anderson complained that I consulted him only 'fifteen seconds' before the meeting, but I refuted this absolutely. My consultation with him had in fact taken place a full eight minutes before the meeting. Mr Anderson had been opposed to my suggested course of action. But Peter McCann argued that it was wholly appropriate within the terms of the Standing Orders, which demanded that, as Lord Provost and Chair of the Council, I should decide on 'all matters of order, competence and relevance'.

In seeking to show that I was ruling in my own interests, Neil Davidson drew attention to the fact that as Lord Provost I received an allowance of £18,000 per annum from the Council. This, he argued, rather than my reputation was motivating my actions.

In building their argument, lawyers can ask seemingly absurd and simple questions. When Mr Davidson asked me what would be the effect of my early removal from the position of Lord Provost by a vote of the Council, the only answer I could give was that I would no longer be Lord Provost. When he subsequently referred to my actions on 3 March as a 'ploy', I asked him what he meant by 'ploy'. A 'tactic, stratagem, trick', he replied. I then retorted that contrary to his implication, my decision was a 'ruling'. 'A ruling?' he asked, querulously. 'A ruling!' I replied.

Mr Davidson went on to inquire whether the disorder among my Labour Party colleagues had precipitated my adjournment of proceedings. Was the disorder in the Council Chamber that day any greater than what one might see on television, occurring more or less daily, in the House of Commons? I was quite unequivocal: 'Well, I hope we wouldn't sink to those depths!'

During Mr Davidson's long cross-examination, I made it quite clear that my ruling was thoroughly competent within the terms of my remit as Lord Provost. I had not ruled in my own interests, or in response to any disorder, but on the basis of the unsatisfactory nature of the Standing Orders.

When Councillors Young and Gibson gave their evidence, they made it quite clear that on 3 March my actions had been thoroughly in order and not motivated by narrow self-interest. John Young stated that he had known me for thirty-three years and that he was convinced that upholding my good character and reputation was of far greater importance to me than any financial considerations.

Councillor Gibson, Leader of the Council's official, SNP opposition, confirmed that he and his colleagues on 3 March had acted in defence not of me personally but of the position of Lord Provost. He said that he didn't believe that the meeting which took place after my departure from the Council Chamber was a valid Council meeting or even a valid meeting of the Labour Group. He also expressed his view that John Anderson, the Chief Executive, had ruled in the interests of the Labour Group, rather than in his proper non-political capacity. When pressed by Mr Davidson over whether he was suggesting that John Anderson had not acted in a politically independent manner and reminded that this was a serious accusation, Councillor Gibson confirmed that, having been asked his opinion, he had given it honestly.

Mr Davidson asked Kenny Gibson if I had 'a clear and significant personal interest in the issue'. He replied, 'Obviously, if there's a motion on the table to remove the Lord Provost and one is the Lord Provost, then one could say that one does have an interest.' His view differed somewhat from my own, but was, nevertheless, amusing.

The proceedings of 27 May were, like so much that had gone before, a protracted scratching-around among the minutiae of the Council's

Standing Orders and the Local Authority Code of Conduct. At the end of the day Lord Eassie told the court that as the judicial review had originally been timetabled for only one day, the case would have to continue 'to a diet yet to be fixed'. Three weeks later, we learned that the case would not resume until 18 February 1999. The implication was clear. As my Provostship would have only a few weeks to run after this date, there seemed little point in the Council pursuing the matter. But in what the *Evening Times* described as a 'Last-Ditch Bid to Oust Lally', the Council appealed to Lord President Rodger of Earlsferry to bring the date of the hearing forward. I doubted that the Lord President would act at the bidding of Glasgow's Labour administration, and I turned out to be right. It was confirmed that the review would be resumed at the date determined by the Court.

On 29 June, I attended the funeral of an old friend. Sir Alexander Stone was one of Glasgow's best-known and most highly respected lawyers. He was also a man of extraordinary goodwill and generosity. For many years, numerous charities in the city had benefited from his provision of legal services at reduced cost or no charge at all. He was also a substantial benefactor of many good causes. Peggy and I had particular reason for sadness, because Alexander Stone and his wife Betty were personal friends who had been extremely supportive, even over the last year when Sir Alexander was extremely ill himself.

It was a sad irony that news he would have rejoiced at was made known to me on the very day of his funeral. Peter McCann, hiding his delight and excitement under a very thin veneer of legal professionalism, insisted on giving me the news in person. The Labour Party had abandoned its defence of the case in its entirety. A great weight was lifted from my shoulders. My months of anguish and frustration, and the suffering which had been imposed upon Peggy and my sons, were at an end.

The front cover of next morning's *Herald* showed me laughing uproariously at the written confirmation that the Party would not be defending its own case against me. They had, at long last, acknowledged that their chance of proving their case in law was somewhere between very little and none at all. This review, which had been set for the Court of Session in the first week of July, would simply have further embarrassed the Scottish Labour Party and exposed their internecine machinations to public scrutiny.

The *Herald*'s lengthy article was an inclusive feature, which I had decided to give John MacCalman, their excellent political correspondent. As he reported, the Party's withdrawal was the conclusion of their bungled attempt to discredit me and remove me from office. I was hugely relieved and delighted that my ordeal was at an end, but also angry that the Labour Party had ignored and abused its own procedures.

My side of the case had never been discussed at the National Executive, something which had been confirmed by no less a person than Ken Livingstone MP. The Party's seeming preference for a campaign of press insinuation and misinformation over any proper, accountable, legal process had caused great damage to my reputation, which their capitulation would do little to redress. Although I had spent a lifetime working very hard for the people of my native city, inevitably the belief that 'there's no smoke without fire' would cause many to continue to question my probity.

But the damage I had suffered angered me less than the effect the whole business had had on my wife, my family and indeed on the city of Glasgow. In the *Evening Times* I described my adversaries as 'scoundrels' and 'political pygmies'. It was, in the circumstances, remarkably temperate language.

I was interviewed by Euan McColm in the *Daily Record* to which he had moved after his time at the *Scotsman*. He described me as 'wearing a matching face and tie'. The reference was to the depiction of dozens of 'Mr Happy' faces on my tie – an appropriate departure from my usual polka dots – which I wore in celebration of the day.

McColm speculated that the particular 'pygmies' to whom I had referred were Councillors Gould and McFadden. I refused to be drawn, but suggested that he might also look beyond the precincts of Glasgow City Chambers into the workings of the Scottish Labour Party if he really wanted to find pygmies. I was also delighted to confirm that my view throughout the whole tortuous fourteen-month affair had been that 'Honesty, integrity and justice would prevail – and so it has!'

The *Mirror*, *Express* and *Daily Mail* all attested once again to the appropriateness of my nickname 'Lazarus'. The *Mail* reported that Keir Hardie House was 'a hive of activity' with the leading lights of the Scottish Party attempting to explain how things, for them at least, had gone so badly wrong. I read in the *Mail* with sadness but without much surprise, that our esteemed Scottish Secretary, Donald Dewar, had no intention of apologising. Of the many characters who had been involved, it was Donald Dewar who disappointed me the most. I could quite understand the unacceptable behaviour of some others, but he had always struck me as a better man than that.

I had first been aware of Donald Dewar many years before, when he and his friends Jimmy Gordon and J. Dickson Mabon assumed prominence in Glasgow University's Labour Club. Jimmy Gordon went on to great things in business, particularly in his association with Radio Clyde, and Dickson Mabon of course became a Member of Parliament. Within Labour circles, they were strong right-wingers, and supporters of Hugh Gaitskell. Donald went on to win a seat in Aberdeen, which he lost at a subsequent election. He then became influential as a Reporter to the Children's Panel in Glasgow, and was involved with the introduction of important legislation which changed the way the courts dealt with young people.

His subsequent by-election in Garscadden, in a brutal fight against the Nationalist Keith Bovey, was a well-remembered triumph. As the Shadow Secretary of State for Scotland, he did a first-class job in opposing much that the Tories were doing against the interests of the Scottish people. After Labour came into power he was a front-runner for the post of Secretary of State. The night before his election to that office, I recall a chat with him when I informed him just how much I hoped he would succeed.

When Labour won power and Donald became Secretary of State, I was delighted for a number of reasons, not least because he was a Glasgow Member of Parliament. I hoped that just as his Tory predecessors Malcolm Rifkind and Iain Lang had looked after their East Coast interests, so he would be a special supporter of initiatives in Glasgow. I wrote to him, wishing him well on his appointment, and expressing my sincere view that he would do a great job as Secretary of State.

Drafted speedily and implemented effectively through the parliamentary machine, the legislation on the introduction of the Scottish Parliament was a first class effort, but Donald Dewar's actions in many other respects were a great disappointment. Like a number of other Labour politicians, he seemed more concerned to display his boldness than to consider the appropriate ethical position to adopt.

On more than one occasion, he demanded that heads should roll before due legal process had been observed. He called for the resignation of the former Chief Constable of Grampian when he should have been aware that as Secretary of State he was the last court of appeal. In North Lanarkshire, he was demanding heads in advance of the findings of any inquiry. Both instances would have been embarrassing for any lawyer, never mind the Secretary of State.

Throughout the Scottish Labour Party's attacks on me and my colleagues in Glasgow City he seemed content to sit on the sidelines when his role as the senior representative of the Government in Scotland demanded much closer involvement. A number of his close friends, who also happened to be friends of mine, spoke to him about the situation. The response sadly was no action.

He was, it seemed, among the many who believed that the Party would benefit from a show of strength. In adopting this attitude towards its internal affairs the Labour Party strayed from the path of social justice. And without social justice within the Party, it was impossible for people to expect social justice from the Party.

Exactly what lay behind the Scottish Labour Party's actions in Glasgow may never be known. There were numerous players. Some relentlessly pursued the chosen goal, others who may have disagreed simply went along with it.

Over the fifteen months between the *Evening Times*' original scoop and the Labour Party's final decision not to pursue matters further, going to the press had become something of a habit for the top figures in the Scottish Labour Party. Jack McConnell, the General Secretary, was the man who declared at the outset that he would be 'ruthless', but it was the hapless Angus Macleod, the youthful and inexperienced press officer, who maintained constant contact with all the key correspondents, issuing what the *Herald* was to describe as 'a series of venomous, off-the-record press briefings by Labour Party officials during which evidence and even possible sentences were trailed'. One of these off-the-record briefings had gone as far as to suggest there would be hangings in George Square. Presumably these were to be metaphorical hangings, just as, on a subsequent occasion, the City Council's Executive, under the temporary leadership of Jean McFadden, was to propose and even promote my metaphorical death. That due process should have been so blatantly undermined is appalling.

Over the protracted period of the Labour Party's attacks on my integrity, I gathered around 500 press cuttings from newspapers all over the United Kingdom, regurgitating the scurrilous bile that by all accounts Labour Party headquarters in Glasgow had pumped out. From the outset it had been apparent that the press was receiving its information on good authority from a high level within the Scottish Party. In September 1997 the *Herald* reported that Labour Party leaders nationally 'were furious over the leak to a London-based newspaper'. Later the same month the *Scotsman* referred to 'a series of high-profile leaks' and the *Daily Mail* reported 'the latest leaks from the inquiry'. According to the *Herald* on 23 September the 'leaks' had prompted 'a media feeding frenzy'. On the same day the *Edinburgh Evening News* quoted 'one insider' as saying 'mud sticks'. The following day the *Daily Telegraph* quoted details 'not included in Labour's report to the NEC but "confirmed by a Labour source".'

The process of informing the press through unattributable briefings continued and the 'information' being disseminated was frequently questionable and, on occasion, downright offensive. On 25 September 1997, according to the *Mirror*, a senior Labour source had revealed that 'the people to be expelled are up to their necks in sleaze, while those being suspended are up to their waists'. The *Express* on the same day referred to what seemed an overt threat, again attributed to 'senior Labour sources' that 'Councillors who defy the leadership and back Lally will "have to consider their future carefully".'

A possible motive for this succession of leaks appeared in the *Herald*, which quoted 'a senior spokesman' as saying 'whenever we heard about Glasgow we decided to make a virtue out of it and use it as a general warning'. The *Evening Times* confirmed that 'the detail of Labour's leaks to the media throughout the whole shameful sleaze investigation suggests the party has already made up its mind'.

Ultimately of course the press began to question the leaks, unattributable briefings and information from 'sources'. The *Observer*'s comment in January 1998 with regard to the party's accusation that I had conducted my defence 'through the media' was particularly telling: 'given the official party's fondness for leaks, this strikes some observers as rich.' In early February the *Scotsman* referred to the charges against me as a 'tissue of fabrication, gossip, backbiting and hearsay'. The same article referred to the accusation, arising from what it referred to as the 'blame culture', that Jack McConnell was the 'author of Glasgow's latest disgrace'. It also alluded to the 'parody of justice' produced by 'Labour's quasi-judicial procedure'. The *Herald* too, reflecting on the process by which information had been fed to the press, concluded that the charges against me made 'a nonsense of the energetic and visibly venomous briefing campaign which was conducted against him by one or two Labour officials'. In the end the press found new sources willing to speak out against the Party machine, including one quoted in the *Scotsman* at the end of March 1998 which concluded that 'Jack spends too much time briefing the press and not on getting on with his job of organizing the party. He also leaks like a sieve.'

At an early stage I supplied copies of these cuttings to Eileen Murfin. I also complained about the damage all this coverage was doing to the City of Glasgow, to my reputation, to the reputation of my colleagues, not to mention the suffering it was imposing on our families. I tried to point out that it couldn't be doing the Labour Party much good, either.

It was all to no avail. The wheels of injustice had been set in motion and nothing, it seemed, could stop them.

No explanation has ever been offered by the Labour Party as to why only thirty-seven members of the seventy-six-member Labour Group on Glasgow City Council were interviewed at the outset. This was despite the fact that, in the first instance, all of the members of the Group were notified that they would be interviewed. Lesley Quinn's letter of 28 May 1997 to Des McNulty and copied to all Group members stated: 'Each member of the Labour Group will be written to individually, advising of dates for meeting with the panel.'

The Labour Party never disclosed who decided who was to be interviewed, why these particular individuals were selected, what criteria were applied in their selection, and indeed why a list of those interviewed was never issued. The nine members of the Labour Group who were reported to the National Executive Committee were never advised of who had made allegations against them or given proper detail of what those allegations were.

Why members of Jean McFadden's faction on the City Council were never investigated remains unexplained. When her opponents were suspended from the Group, she was installed as interim Leader by the Labour Party in London, doubtless on the advice of the officers of the Scottish Labour Party and whoever else. Shortly afterwards, however, when she competed for the office of Group Leader, due process was observed and she was rejected by the Group.

Anyone who had worked with me over the years would have been well aware that I was always very careful to ensure that the rules of the Party were followed, I readily admit – and it was a serious error – that I had not given much thought to the implications of those rules. The Party had constructed rules which enabled the NCC to find members guilty of allegations without giving any reasons and which were apparently intended to prevent members from challenging those findings in court. Eric Wilson, Secretary to the National Constitutional Committee, the Labour Party's highest court, stated this to be the case: 'It has always been the position of the NEC that no reason or explanation is given regarding their decisions.' All that might be very well in England, but the Scottish courts are governed by the Scottish judicial system, which requires quite different standards.

No Party should have such rules and no Party should be allowed to have such rules. I have always believed that the Labour Party came into being to fight for social justice, and to protect the rights of the individual. I have always believed that its aim was to create a society with freedom and justice for all. Unless you protect the rights of individuals within the Party, you cannot defend this aim.

Like most Party members, I was not aware that the rules functioned in this way. Even after forty-eight years as a member of the Labour Party, I, obviously rather naively, believed that the purpose of the rules was to expand the rights of members, not to take them away. If justice is to be done within the Party, those people operating the disciplinary procedures, particularly at the highest level, must properly fulfil their responsibilities. Despite the assurances which I had been given, no matter how hard I tried to ensure I got a fair hearing from the National Executive Committee, the vast majority of its members were simply not prepared to consider my evidence.

To Mr McConnell, it must all have seemed desperately unfair. But alas, unlike the officers of the Labour Party and, indeed, the National Executive Committee, the Scottish courts just did not agree with him. By the middle of 1998, his Sleazefinder's uniform was a thing of shreds and tatters: all the allegations, claims of impropriety, venomous attacks in the press and promises of vicious retribution were revealed as things of no substance.

It could well be argued that the astonishing way in which the Labour Party conducted its inquiry into allegations of sleaze within Glasgow City Council demands further investigation. An inquiry into the inquiry would be thoroughly justified, but then in a sense that's already been done – through the Scottish courts. Lord Abernethy had ruled in my favour, and it was only when Lord Eassie seemed likely to follow suit that the Party finally recognised the writing on the wall. So it was that in the summer of 1998, the Lord Provost of Glasgow, scalp and reputation intact, emerged from under the Labour Party's cloud and recommenced his work on behalf of the people and the great city of Glasgow with renewed vigour.

CHAPTER TWENTY-EIGHT

In the weeks that followed the Labour Party's capitulation, there was a lot to be done. One decision I would have to make was whether I was going to stand at the Council elections in 1999. The Castlemilk branch had nominated me and made it clear that they wanted me to stand, but the Party had determined that all candidates would be subject to an interview process. I had received the approval of the Glasgow City Labour Party and was extremely confident that the representatives of the Scottish Executive would also find me eminently qualified, but it was all going to take some weeks.

A matter of some personal concern was the legal cost of my actions against both the Labour Party and the City Council. I have never been a wealthy man, so it was important that I recoup the substantial costs incurred in taking the Party and, latterly, the Council, to court. I felt fully justified in taking this course of action particularly because I had made it quite clear before embarking on both cases that I would far prefer an amicable, out-of-court resolution.

While the Labour Party had withdrawn from proceedings on legal advice, thereby admitting it was in the wrong, the Council had yet to decide whether it would pursue the case over the Standing Orders, which was scheduled for the Court of Session in February 1999. With the Party case so thoroughly discredited, the Council's case was looking more flimsy than ever. At this stage their legal bill was relatively modest. If they continued, it would inevitably be a great deal more, so I was confident that the leadership would see reason. With this in mind, I agreed that the Chief Executive should try to achieve an early resolution and close this final aspect of matters.

Freed from the burden of fighting for my career and reputation, I was once more in a position to battle for the city. Writing in the *Express* in early July, I reviewed the conclusion of the Labour Party's actions and lamented the way they had prevented us from putting our best energies into furthering the interests of Glasgow. Reflecting on how Glasgow had progressed over the previous decade, I emphasised that it was the major cultural events which had provided the momentum to move the city forward. These catalysts for change, markers along Glasgow's road to progress, had attracted world attention. With the Garden Festival in 1988, its title as Cultural Capital of Europe in 1990, the year-long Festival of Visual Arts in 1996 and now the forthcoming year as UK City of Architecture and Design 1999, the city had always been working towards a major event. Not only did this help to enhance Glasgow's infrastructure and public image, but it attracted major companies and organisations into the city, bringing tangible economic benefits in the form of new jobs and increased commercial activity. With this in mind, I advocated a major event for 2003. By this time, when we would be over the hiatus and euphoria of the Millennium, the city would undoubtedly need a further boost.

As always, in advocating such cultural events I was careful to make sure that the underlying reasons for staging such celebrations were clear. There are always those who regard such expenditure as frivolous and fail to appreciate its importance. Over the years I have frequently had to argue with individuals who felt that the very limited money which the Council was spending on cultural activity should be channelled directly into housing. Technically, this would have been illegal, but in any case I am absolutely convinced – and the figures argue the case very strongly – that without the Garden Festival or the Year of Culture Glasgow's economic situation would be much the worse.

Without long-term resources repairing leaking roofs and draughty windows is a temporary and to some extent cosmetic improvement. Creating jobs and giving people the wherewithal to look after their own roofs and windows are a much better long-term solution. That has always been Glasgow's policy, and it has proved singularly successful. I concluded my *Express* article by arguing that Glasgow should set out to achieve ambitious new targets for the new millennium.

In mid-July the Court of Session ruled that the Labour Party had to pay the costs of our court action. Some weeks later – ironically just shortly before the Lord Provost's annual visit to the Edinburgh Military Tattoo – the Council finally agreed that it would not continue the Court of Session case. It also agreed to pay costs.

The Depute Lord Provost Alex Mosson and I agreed with Frank McAveety that the new, post-election, Council was at liberty to review its Standing Orders and to introduce provisions for removing the Lord Provost during his or her term of office, if such action were justified.

Meanwhile, Peter McCann and I were reviewing the possibility of pursuing the Labour Party for financial redress, given the considerable damage which had been caused to my reputation and the anguish that the matter had brought upon myself and my family over the whole protracted affair.

In mid-November the new General Secretary of the Scottish Labour Party, Alex Rowley, announced that my name, along with the other Glasgow Council candidates, would be recommended for approval to the Labour Party's Local Government Committee. Mr Rowley was demonstrating a degree of enlightenment which had been sadly lacking in his predecessor. In the meantime, Jack McConnell was planning his campaign for the Motherwell and Wishaw seat in the Scottish Parliament. For a while he considered both standing for the Parliament and serving as a high-paid parliamentary lobbyist, but in the face of hostile press coverage he dropped the idea.

A big frustration towards the end of 1998 was Glasgow City Council's churlish attitude to the commission of Peter Howson to produce a portrait of me for the Lord Provost's Gallery in the Chambers. For over a century the Council had commissioned portraits of outgoing Provosts. Securing the services of Peter Howson for only £10,000 had been a major coup – his normal fee was £18,000. Favoured by a number of international collectors including the pop stars Madonna and David Bowie, he is undoubtedly one of the best known of the excellent group of painters known as the 'New Glasgow Boys'. Now the Council had decided to break the agreement with him. This decision not to channel a relatively modest figure from the Contemporary Art Fund, which I had established in 1990, towards securing the Howson portrait seemed thoroughly petty. While I had to accept the situation in the short term, it was certainly something I was determined not to let go.

The festive season of 1998 was thoroughly relaxing and enjoyable. Glasgow's annual Shine On celebrations were marked with an impressive community parade and street entertainment on Victorian themes, much of it performed by children from local schools. I was happy to be able to celebrate my final Hogmanay as Lord Provost without any of the previous year's burdens, and all those who thronged George Square seemed to share my mood of elation if not for quite the same reasons.

The advent of Glasgow's reign as UK City of Architecture and Design was celebrated by a number of events, including the illumination of prominent structures. In the early months of the year Deyan Sudjic's strategy for the festival was very much exhibition-led. It would not be until the summer, with the planned opening of the Lighthouse, the Centre for Architecture, Design and the City, the exhibition element of Homes for the Future and the community-led projects which would see the creation of five 'Millennium Spaces', that 1999 would really start to make an impact on the wider Glasgow public.

On 22 January we held the Lord Provost's Burns Supper. With 830 guests we reckoned it was the largest such event in the world. Our speakers included Stuart Cosgrove, the boss of Channel 4 in Scotland, and my old friend, the famous trade-unionist turned journalist, Jimmy Reid. Neither could resist the odd affectionate reference to my recent travails. But it was Dorothy Grace Elder who made the best quip. Referring to the recent anniversary of the sinking of the *Titanic*, she commented that if I had been on board, the ship would have hit the iceberg but would still have made New York – under tow!

A few days later I had the great pleasure of presenting the annual Lord Provost's Awards. Among the recipients was Bill Neish, the highly regarded general manager of the Argyle Street Marks & Spencer store. Bill had supported Peggy's initiative of the Lady Provost's Fashion Show from the outset. This year he was retiring, but he told us that once again Marks & Spencer would gladly show its popular summer ranges at this major charity event. Also receiving awards were the excellent Chief Constable of Strathclyde, John Orr, who had given such unwavering support when I was under attack from the Labour Party, and Julian Spalding, the City's former Director of Museums. In the reorganisation of the City Council, Julian had applied for, but sadly failed to secure the much expanded post of Director of Cultural and Leisure Services. In my view, he had been an outstanding officer and his departure was a great loss to the City.

But the award which gave me the greatest pleasure was the presentation of the Glasgow Loving Cup to Princess Anne. The Princess Royal, whom I greatly admire, was a frequent visitor to the city and has given enormous support to a number of charities which are active in Glasgow. In her acceptance speech she emphasised that her relationship with Glasgow was mutually beneficial. She had been inspired by Glasgow's efforts to help its disadvantaged communities and had exported these initiatives to other parts of the United Kingdom.

The Lord Provost's Awards was the last major event in my period of office. The Labour Party's agreement to my candidacy in Castlemilk was a remarkable turnaround. Honour was satisfied and I decided to announce my departure from civic politics. I was going out at the top after three decades of service to the city. Although I hadn't achieved everything I would have wished, I had enjoyed a great deal of success in my years as a senior politician, as the press coverage of my decision made clear.

The imminent Scottish Parliament would substantially change the political landscape: inevitably, there would be a period of considerable uncertainty over the division of responsibilities between the local authorities and the new Parliament. This was another reason for my retirement. Furthermore, my intention to pursue the Labour Party for recompense and to publish my memoirs would be difficult to reconcile with my position as a serving councillor.

The last three months of my Provostship were eventful, but a great deal less fraught than much of my term. A *Herald* profile of Peggy described her as the 'Jane to Mr Lally's Tarzan'. Less flattering was the piece's assumption that I was seventy-four when in fact I was still weeks off my seventy-third birthday. Peggy was once again busy organising the Lady Provost's Fashion Show, which would take place in mid-April, raising many thousands of pounds.

On this occasion, the Fashion Show would run for two nights, being hosted by Nick Nairn and Carole Smillie on the first and Viv Lumsden and Alan Douglas on the second. The fact that over three successive years Peggy's major charitable endeavour had raised over £75,000 was a remarkable testimony to her hard work, enthusiasm and determination. I was mightily proud to walk out on to the catwalk with her that last night to the tumultuous applause of the crowd.

On the morning of Saturday 10 April 1999, in the august setting of Edinburgh's St Mary's Episcopalian Cathedral, I was invested by the Grand Priory and Bailiwick of Scotland into the Military and Hospitaller Order of St Lazarus of Jerusalem. So unlikely did the invitation seem that several of my colleagues advised me to check carefully before attending the event. For years my name had been connected with that of St Lazarus, so many were the comebacks that I had made. So to find myself, along with Peggy, invested into the charitable order which bore his name was an extraordinary culmination that seemed almost too fitting to be coincidence.

On 23 April 1999 I chaired my last Council meeting and, indeed, the last meeting before the elections to both the Council and the new Scottish Parliament. Although the meeting had an end-of-term mood about it, it was conducted with all the usual rigour.

When I came to make my concluding comments, I was sorry to note that Jean McFadden had already left the Chamber. I had no wish to crow, but simply to take my leave in a manner that was without acrimony or bitterness. All the same, it was probably just as well, as I couldn't resist mentioning her famous jibe about the Lord Provostship being a 'knife and fork job'. Now, I said, I had the waistline to prove that having my knife and fork at the ready to serve my city was no idle promise. There were few occasions during my term as Lord Provost when I had been able to dine at home. Indeed, there were very few days, evenings or weekends when I hadn't been 'chained up'.

I thanked all of those colleagues who had supported me during my period of service for the City. I singled out the new Chief Executive, Jim Andrews, Glasgow's many excellent officers and the Lord Provost's staff for special thanks. But above all I acknowledged the huge debt of gratitude I owed to Peggy and my sons Derek and Robert, who had been my constant supporters. It was certainly a cliché, but I bowed out with these words from Frank Sinatra's great retirement number: 'I faced it all, and I stood tall, and did it my way!'

My Council colleagues, however, were determined that mine should not be the last word. Frank McAveety, the Leader of the Council and a candidate for the Scottish Parliament, spoke on behalf of the Labour Group. He was warm in his praise and, doubtlessly sincere, but couldn't resist expressing his hope that he would be treated kindly in my autobiography. Kenny Gibson, another prospective member of the Scottish Parliament, spoke for the official opposition and Christopher Mason for the Liberal Democrats.

My long-time fellow councillor and adversary John Young, another prospective member of the Scottish Parliament, had the final word. He paid fulsome tribute to Peggy, who he declared had been a superb Lady Provost. He complimented me on my personal kindness to him, and praised my sense of humour. I was, he declared, an individual who had aroused passions and who would, in his view, go down as one of Glasgow's great Lord Provosts. The nickname 'Lazarus' was no longer appropriate, he suggested, despite my innumerable comebacks. Instead, he advocated a new name which would reflect the considerable work I had done over the years for my native city. I have to confess, it brought a wee tear to the eye. Rather than 'Lazarus', he opined, I should be known in future as 'Mr Glasgow'.

Postscript

A number of those who feature in this book have gone on to better, or at least different, things. Some have left the stage, and others are doing much as before. The following little list is given in alphabetical order to avoid any implication of hierarchy:

Bill Aitken: Leading Glasgow Tory councillor and frequent political adversary, vociferous in support of me during my tribulations – elected as a Member of the Scottish Parliament on the Tory top-up list for Glasgow.

Susan Baird: Witness in my defence and a long-time friend – re-elected as Councillor for Braidfauld and to a senior role in progressing socio-economic development in the city.

Donald Dewar: The senior representative of the Labour Party in Scotland who, despite the advice of numerous friends, refused to acknowledge that there was anything improper in the process of press leaks and Labour Party show trials which brought so much damage to his native city of Glasgow. Now First Minister in the Scottish Parliament.

Tommy Dingwall: The man who continuously tapped his briefcase, declaring 'it's all in here', and who escaped censure after headbutting one of his colleagues. Re-elected to serve for the Maryhill ward.

Kenny Gibson: The Leader of Glasgow's official opposition. A Scottish Nationalist who gave evidence in my support. Elected as a Member of the Scottish Parliament on the Scottish Nationalist top-up list for Glasgow.

Charlie Gordon: The Depute Leader of the Council who assumed the role of Chairman of the Labour Group meeting which took place after my departure from the Council Chambers on 3 March 1998. Now Leader of Glasgow City Council.

Bob Gould: The former Leader of Glasgow City Council whose fatuous remarks about 'votes for trips' proved immensely damaging to the City of Glasgow. Turned 'Queen's Evidence' and escaped censure. Re-elected as Councillor for Pollokshaws.

Frank McAveety: Elected Leader of Glasgow City Council after the departure of Bob Gould and the short-lived interim leadership of Jean McFadden. Elected to the Scottish Parliament and appointed Depute Minister for Local Government.

Jack McConnell: The General Secretary of Scottish New Labour, the man determined to be ruthless. Directly responsible for a sustained campaign of 'off-the-record' press leaks and for overseeing the case against the accused Glasgow councillors. Also responsible for pressuring the Glasgow leadership and councillors in his endeavour to secure my expulsion from the post of Lord Provost. After negative press coverage of his plans to combine lobbying and being an MSP he narrowly won through in the controversial selection process for Motherwell and Wishaw, and was elected to the Scottish Parliament. Appointed by Donald Dewar as Minister for Finance. We must be thankful for small mercies – at least he is not Minister for Information or Justice!

Jean McFadden: Long-time crony of Donald Dewar and good friend of the Scottish Labour Party. Reselected for the Scotstoun ward, although her opponent was defeated on the technical issue of having forgotten to pay his Party dues on time (on previous occasions a rapidly written cheque has sufficed). Re-elected for the Council and serving as Chairman of the Labour Group.

Des McNulty: The Secretary of the Glasgow Labour Group, conduit for information between the City Chambers and the Scottish Labour headquarters. Elected as a Member of the Scottish Parliament for Clydebank and Milngavie.

Alex Mosson: Re-elected to the Council and, despite a dirty tricks campaign against him, elected by a large majority to the position of Lord Provost.

Lesley Quinn: Jack McConnell's number two at Scottish Labour headquarters. Responsible for the preliminary interviews in the Scottish Labour Party's campaign against me. Appointed General Secretary of the Scottish Labour Party after the departure of Jack McConnell's successor, Alex Rowley.

Tom Sawyer: Former General Secretary of the Labour Party. Now a member of the Party's National Executive Committee.

John Young: Long-serving Glasgow City Councillor and Leader of the Glasgow Tory Group. Vociferous in my defence and a witness at the Court of Session hearing on 27 May. Elected as a Member of the Scottish Parliament on the Scotland West Tory top-up list.

And finally, that portrait:

After the City Council backed off from funding the balance of the cost of the portrait, I considered ways of covering Peter Howson's agreed fee. The National Galleries of Scotland indicated that they were willing to fund the balance, subject to conditions, which included displaying the portrait in Edinburgh for part of the year. Taking the portrait out of Glasgow in this way would have broken with tradition. This generous offer, though much appreciated, was declined. Other potential sources of funding were approached, but happily the new Leader of Glasgow City Council, Councillor Charles Gordon, decided that, as a gesture of reconciliation and goodwill, the new Council should fund the painting. In late June 1999 I received a call from Mark O'Neill, Julian Spalding's successor as Head of the Museums Service, indicating that the balance of funds had been agreed and that Peter Howson was to restart work on the portrait. The painting was unveiled on Friday 1 October 1999 to great acclaim.

Index